FDR and His Enemies

FDR and His Enemies

ALBERT FRIED

St. Martin's Press
New York

ISBN 0-312-22119-3

Library of Congress Cataloging-in-Publication Data

Fried, Albert.
  F. D. R. and his enemies / Albert Fried
    p. cm.
  Includes bibliographical references and index.
  ISBN 0-312-22119-3 (cloth)
  1. Roosevelt, Franklin D. (Franklin Delano), 1882-1945-
-Adversaries. 2. United States—Politics and
government—1933-1945. I. Title.
E807.F77 1999
973.917'092—DC21   98-56141
                                                     CIP

Book design by Acme Art, Inc.

First edition: September 1999
10 9 8 7 6 5 4 3 2 1

For Jack Widick
who was there,
in the thick of it

CONTENTS

ACKNOWLEDGEMENTS

It is a pleasure to thank those who have helped me at every step along the way, from the first tentative conception of the book to its completion years later:

To my friends Richard Elman, whose suggestions were invaluable and whose passing I still mourn; B. J. Widick, who freely shared with me his extensive knowledge of the 1930s—the knowledge of a participant and observer both; Peter Schwab, on whose keen understanding of American politics and other kindnesses I drew more often than he realizes; Ralph DellaCava, who may also have no idea of what I owe to the conversations we have had several times a week, year in and year out; Adam Shatz, Barbara and Sol Resnik, and Michael Wreszin, whose numerous favors and benefactions I shamelessly took for granted; and Jenine Lindner, who somehow managed to make a barely legible manuscript into a reasonably clear one.

To the students at SUNY Purchase, who graciously served as my sounding board in the numerous courses I gave on the 1930s. To the research libraries—Columbia University, the New York Public, the Library of Congress and, above all, the magnificent Franklin D. Roosevelt Library at Hyde Park—whose personnel and other riches I exploited to the utmost. To the authors whose scholarly works (see the bibliography) proved indispensable, given the paucity or unavailability of primary documentation on the political lives of every one of Roosevelt's enemies, in particular T. Harry Williams (Huey Long), Sheldon Marcus (Father Coughlin), A. Scott Berg (Charles Lindbergh), and Melvyn Dubofsky and Warren Van Tine (John L. Lewis). To my editors at St. Martin's Press— Karen Wolny, Alan Bradshaw, William Berry, and Amy Reading—each of whom were first-rate and helpful beyond the call of duty.

And especially to Edith Firoozi Fried, as ever unfailing in her encouragement, whose talent as critic and stylist has once again astonished me.

POLITICS AND POPULARITY

> Our bending author hath pursued the story,
> In little room confining mighty men,
> Mangling by starts the full course of their glory.
>
> *Henry V*

The 1929 Wall Street crash surprised America, but it hardly diminished the prevailing euphoria. For more than 30 years the country had enjoyed mounting prosperity, marred only by occasional downturns and by weaknesses in some industries and regions. If the bad news augured a decline, Americans could therefore reasonably assume, it would be a brief one at worst, followed by another sharp rise in living standards and the level of opportunities. By every rational criterion the persistence of the euphoria, or at least optimism, was justified.

The national mood had completely changed by the time Franklin D. Roosevelt became President on March 4, 1933. During those three years and four months America went through a double trauma: the realization that there was a deep crisis, not a mere shakeout of the markets or a temporary economic adjustment; and then the dawning truth that the crisis might endure indefinitely, that such upswings as did occur were now so many interruptions, at best brief and spasmodic, of the melancholy norm. A thick pall of gloom had settled over the land.

In some ways, the trauma which Americans were going through surpassed even the one experienced by the generation that fought the Civil War. That generation had long been preparing itself for the bloody showdown, as inexorable as a Greek tragedy. And after Fort Sumter it understood what it had to do. But Americans in the early, or Hoover, years of the Great Depression—those most hurt by it—scarcely knew what hit them. Having little idea of what produced the crisis, they were ignorant of how they should respond to it. The rampant confusion, the stupefaction, added greatly to the malaise.

Out of the humus of despair naturally sprung up a rich multitude of groups and individuals bearing radical or revolutionary answers. Never had America—which had always prided itself on its freedom from the rancorous and divisive political disputes so characteristic of the Old World—seen anything like such a rich crop of disparate factions and ideologies.

On the far left were the Communists, fast rising and increasingly militant, who looked to the Soviet Union, with its five year plans and full employment and bright vision of justice, as their model of the good society. Next on the political spectrum were the several grouplets claiming to be the authentic legatees of the Bolshevik Revolution and its Marxist-Leninist ideal: Trotskyists, Musteites, Lovestoneites. Then came the Socialists, led by the redoubtable Norman Thomas, whose ranks also were growing by leaps; they promised to bring about a democratic-socialist America, this in keeping with *their* legacy, embodied in their saintly hero of old, Eugene V. Debs. On the extreme right were the new fangled apostles of direct action: the Silver Shirts, the White Shirts, the Black Shirts (mostly Italian-Americans), and the equivalent of the Nazi Brown Shirts (mostly German-American), along with other sects too numerous to mention, all of them modeling themselves on the paramilitary outfits that Hitler and Mussolini employed to such excellent effect in their countries. True, none of these American Fascists amounted to much, and they and the men who led them are today historical curios. But they existed because, obviously, they were convinced that they had a fighting chance, that the American people would turn to them, everything else having failed, just as the Italian and German people turned to Mussolini and Hitler out of desperation, each of them having also been scoffed at and ridiculed when they began their astonishing crusades.

Towering above the rest of the insurgents in mass appeal were two men who adhered to no formal ideology apart from the amorphous populism they espoused, to wit, that America was enthralled to a naked plutocracy consisting mainly of urban and international bankers and their political retainers, and that only a massive and immediate redistribution of wealth and power could save the nation. One of them was Louisiana's boss nonpareil, Huey P. Long, whose opponents, the state's economic elites, had made the lethal mistake of underestimating his extraordinary talents as demagogue and political infighter. The other was Charles E. Coughlin, reigning priest at the Church of the Little Flower in Royal Oak, Michigan, and universally know as the "radio priest" because such a large audience across the country regularly tuned in to his Sunday jeremiads and gratefully contributed millions of dollars a year to his magnificent edifice of a church and his ministry of the air.

This profusion of "extremists," left and right and nondescript, constituted in toto not so much a worrisome threat to the established order as an unmistakable portent of what the future might hold should the trauma continue.

Not that the established order, troubled as it was, lacked defenders. The rich, it goes without saying, still comprised a very influential tribe. As is their wont in all times and places, they counseled patience and trust while the system, momentarily out of joint, righted itself. But as a small minority of the electorate, the rich alone could not have held the line for conservatism. This task fell to the huge middle class, huge despite the ongoing travails. It is worth remembering that about three-quarters of Americans still had jobs even after unemployment reached its highest level, and a considerable percentage of them—accurate statistics are impossible to come by—were relatively well off indeed.[*] No more than the rich did the broad middle class have an appetite for experiments whose costs they would have to suffer but from which they presumably stood to benefit little.

Nonetheless, more and more of them were switching allegiance, voting Democratic for the first time. They too now felt insecure: they could not know who among them might next lose their jobs, who might suddenly find themselves in the ranks of the dreaded proletariat.

The major political parties reflected the attitudes of the silent majority. Ideologically, Republican and Democratic hierarchs were indistinguishable from each other; indeed, rarely had they been closer. Alfred E. Smith, the Democrats' 1928 presidential candidate and thus their titular head, believed as fervently as Herbert C. Hoover, the man who had crushingly defeated him, that government intervention beyond the barest emergency measures would be worse that the disease it purported to cure, this even though Smith was himself a son of New York City's impoverished ethnic ghettoes, having risen step by step through the Tammany Hall apparatus to become governor for an amazing four terms. As far as both parties were concerned, the radical upsurge in America was nothing more than an excrescence of an otherwise healthy organism and as such would soon disappear. And if the armed forces of society from time to time had to teach unruly mobs a lesson in civic obedience, so be it.

Franklin D. Roosevelt was generally acceptable to conservatives, though many Democratic conservatives would have preferred Smith as President; of course, nearly all Republican conservatives would have preferred that Hoover stayed in office. Roosevelt carried Smith's imprimatur despite their recent rivalry. Smith had helped make possible his political comeback following his two-year struggle with polio and been instru-

---

[*] Prices of course were very low; labor was very cheap. Those who had money were indeed privileged.

mental in getting him, against his own better judgment, to run for governor of New York. What is more, during the presidential campaign Roosevelt often criticized Hoover from the *right*, calling Hoover to account for profligate spending and reckless disregard of a sound budget. And no one could accuse Roosevelt of having the slightest interest in, or for that matter knowledge of, anything approximating radical ideas and movements. In every important respect, he was safe.[1]

He differed from conservatives, however, in assuming, as did the radicals, that the crisis would not simply go away and that the federal government, more exactly the President, must act as boldly as the parlous situation required, state and local governments and private agencies being themselves destitute. He had hinted of his views during the campaign, and even earlier, and he made his intentions luminously clear in his ringing inaugural speech, which had such a marvelously tonic effect on the country.[2]

But, unlike the radicals, he never really concerned himself with underlying causes. The very notion of underlying causes he regarded as speculative and theoretical. For Roosevelt the crisis could be likened to the presence of a foreign army on American soil. How and why it got there might be interesting, but secondary. The task was to recognize the danger it posed. So it was that he summoned America literally to do battle, just as Wilson and Lincoln and Washington had summoned it in previous crises. So as commander-in-chief he used the most unorthodox tactics to bring the war to the enemy with a view to forcing its unconditional surrender.[3] We are referring to the whole vast armamentarium of New Deal reforms, temporary and permanent, over which he presided with such fanfare and show of energy—reforms, it must be emphasized, calculated to bring about not a new order of things but a restoration of the peace and quiet of normal times. Audacious means for traditional ends; this was Roosevelt's formula for subduing the crisis.

Above all, he acted as he did in the conviction that he was keeping faith with the moral ideals of his early political career, when he valiantly fought the twin iniquities of Tammany Hall and the special interests and enthusiastically enlisted in Woodrow Wilson's New Freedom crusade. Wilson in return appointed him Assistant Secretary of the Navy, a position he held for seven years with sufficient distinction to run as Vice President in 1920, thus gaining invaluable notoriety.

Those moral ideals of his progressive years kept faith in turn with the genteel mugwumpery of his youth and adolescence. Roosevelt grew up in a universe defined by noblesse oblige, where limits on the exercise of power and desire for advantage were expected to be honorably observed, where the social classes, upper and lower and middling, were expected to owe duties to each other, and where, accordingly, the business of everyday life was expected to proceed harmoniously, uneventfully, securely. Whether this idyll ever existed outside the privileged confines of the eupatridae into which he was born and had his being is beside the point. It was the premise on which he, like his cousin Theodore Roosevelt and his wife, Eleanor, was reared and which was burned into his dutiful soul.[4] For him, it followed that the problem of America, the reason for the current malaise, lay in the failure or unwillingness of powerful men to carry out their part of the implied bargain—to discipline those among them consumed by greed or indifferent to the welfare of others, especially the weak and dispossessed. Not only were they morally obtuse, they were imprudent; they put their own futures in jeopardy as well. The New Deal can be seen as Roosevelt's attempt to save the members of his own class from the consequences of their folly and avarice. That they did not appreciate the favor was consistent with his view of them.

He had no doubt that Americans would patriotically do what he asked of them, that they would remain as steadfast, calm, temperate, forbearing, and courageous as their fathers were when they too defended hearth and home. That is why his inaugural's celebrated phrase, "We have nothing to fear but fear itself," logically so meaningless, empirically so fallacious, caught so precisely the spirit of his leadership; it was the signature of his presidency. To each American he in effect said with unmatched persuasiveness: Return with me to the better angels of our nature, to our hallowed sense of shared obligations and friendly feelings toward one another, citizens all of the chosen community that America still is—return with me to that America, disregard the preachers of despair and the minions of evil, and the war of redemption cannot be lost.

Roosevelt's optimism, which never flagged, thus transcended the ordinary canons of evidence and rules of probability. It was optimism based as much on wish fulfillment, the prayerful hope that fortune will come to the aid of virtue—it always had in America—as on sound planning and firm leadership.

Roosevelt had every right to take credit for the happy outcome, but whether he and the New Deal were in truth responsible for it is doubtful. That the New Deal put money into people's pockets, did therefore save lives and property, and did help to stimulate the economy, at least for a while, is undeniable. Roosevelt owed his tremendous 1936 victory largely to the business revival of his first term. Yet it has been plausibly argued that the economy was bound to revive in any case, given the normal course of the business cycle, and might have revived more buoyantly and durably without the New Deal.[5] As for the permanent reforms in social security, labor relations, farm policy, manufacturing, banking, stocks, utilities, housing, transportation, communications, and so on and on, laudable as these were, their full benefits were generally not realized until the Depression had ended. And the Depression, it should be added, ended only after World War II got under way in Europe and America itself began arming in earnest. Unemployment during the New Deal years never fell below levels which today would be considered intolerable. The condition of millions of small farmers, farm tenants and laborers, and sharecroppers was almost as bad at the close of the 1930s as at the opening. And then there was the very sharp downturn, in effect another depression, that struck in the summer of 1937. Shocked and incredulous, Roosevelt again blamed the "economic royalists," and more angrily than ever, for betraying America just when it seemed that trust and confidence and unity had been restored. But the charges were ringing hollow now, and much of the blame for the latest downturn unavoidably stuck to him. Whether he would have suffered a corresponding loss of popularity is impossible to know—though to judge from the opposition Congress now gave him, especially after the disastrous 1938 election, this was starting to happen—because the other great crisis, the encroaching war, came to his rescue in the nick of time.

Why Roosevelt's enemies did not share his optimism, his idealized conception of America, is therefore perfectly comprehensible. They argued, on unassailable grounds, that the New Deal was bound to fail, that it was hardly more than a set of palliatives on the one hand or wrongheaded, destructive experiments on the other. Before long, in their opinion, America must rebel against it and its author in disillusionment and rage and look to an alternative, presumably theirs, for a way out of the impasse. Roosevelt would then wear Hoover's mark of Cain.

Those among his enemies who knew or had worked with him were particularly emboldened to take him on. One has the impression that, having penetrated the myth of grandeur and destiny which enveloped him, they were the more keenly disappointed by the man himself. He seemed to lack an overmastering presence, the ability to bend circumstances to his will by the sheer force of character, intellect, vision. They gauged Roosevelt's leadership qualities—his indecisiveness, his temporizing, the sense of disorder he allowed, or cultivated, in his administration, along with his duplicitousness and stealth and calculation—by their own and of course found him sorely wanting. Al Smith, who knew him longest, had refused to believe that the charismatic President and world figure was anyone but the rather harmless subaltern of years past. To all of them Roosevelt came across as weak and inadequate.

But here, on the personal plane, his enemies probably committed their most egregious blunder. The fact is, he permitted none of them, not even Smith, to get anywhere near his real self. The impression they received was usually the impression he wished to convey, the impression, more exactly, he thought they deserved to have. None was his friend except for the moment and as a matter of convenience, and he owed them nothing beyond the manifest quid pro quo. If he therefore encouraged them in their misconception of him—no one was a more deft provocateur than he—it was because he regarded them as potential or actual adversaries and rivals. Getting them to wrongly estimate him was no small part of his political finesse.[6]

In the final analysis, however, the exercise of that finesse would have been for naught, and so would his grand speaking voice, pleasing countenance, genial open personality, and whatever else endeared him to so many Americans,[7] had his enemies been proved correct in their prognosis of America under the New Deal and, later, in the shadow of war. All of his virtues would have been used against him, and he would have been pictured as a grinning charlatan and dissembler, a sinister magician who had duped the innocent.[8]

The irreducible truth is that Roosevelt knew America to its depths, and his enemies and critics and the leaders of radical movements and sects did not. He knew that Americans by and large were content with allaying the crisis, taming it, reducing its baleful effects; they did not expect it to end, at least not in the foreseeable future. Relief from the blows which the early Depression years had rained down on them mercilessly (before they realized what was happening to them), a modicum of security against yet worsening conditions, against the threat of pauperdom and homelessness, the prospect indeed of some improvement of their children's lives if not theirs—these were what Americans willingly settled for and what the New Deal, with all its shortcomings (from whatever point of view), did provide. At bottom, it enabled them to cope with their travails and gave them a basis for hope. Roosevelt's enemies failed because most Americans refused to listen to darkly prophetic men who sought to impose heavy, unceasing demands on them. His policy of leaving Americans alone within the limits of his modest reforms, making them understand, though, that a beneficent government was there to assist them in their extremity and mobilize their energies if necessary—that policy, under the circumstances a non-policy, suited them fine. And so it was that Roosevelt's ebullience and hortatory idealism thrilled them while his critics' animadversions left them cold.[9]

Roles were reversed when foreign affairs came to occupy center stage. Now it was Roosevelt who sought to initiate radical new policy and his critics who sought to preserve the traditional policy unimpaired.

As international tensions deepened, ideological rather than pragmatic considerations increasingly dominated Roosevelt's thinking — pragmatism (his enemies would say opportunism) having been his hallmark and the New Deal's. There is no doubt that he loathed Hitler and everything Hitler stood for from the instant Hitler took power, coincidentally a few weeks before he did. To loathing was added apprehension as the Führer made good his promise of German expansion and conquest. Meanwhile, joining Hitler in an anti-Comintern (Axis), bloc were Imperial Japan and Fascist Italy, themselves committed to a course of relentless expansion and conquest. Thus encouraged, pro-Fascist movements sprung up in the smaller countries of Central and Southern Europe and Iberia. In this collapsing environment Roosevelt tried to make America a force for peace, that is, for international law and order, but he could do nothing. American neutralist sentiment was too strong. The greater the troubles afflicting the world, it seemed, the more determined Americans were to avoid foreign entanglement at all costs, no matter how much they sympathized with the victims of aggression in Ethiopia, Spain, Austria, China, Czechoslovakia, Albania. Their sympathy only intensified their isolation.

To be sure, America's attitude changed after Hitler invaded Poland on September 1, 1939, and especially after he defeated France the following spring (which effectively established his hegemony over western and central Europe) and then launched savage air attacks on Britain two months later, the prelude, obviously, to invasion and conquest. Most Americans thus went along with Roosevelt's strategy of arming and otherwise assisting Britain; indeed, of arming and assisting any country that would fight Hitler, including the Soviet Union when, in June 1941, Hitler attacked it too.

But how far Americans would go along with Roosevelt remained the fundamental question. They certainly gave him no blank check. Most of the people who voted against him in 1940, some 45 percent of the electorate, did so, it can be safely inferred, because they opposed his interventionism. Roosevelt was engaged in a titanic struggle with his adversaries over how much freedom of action he should have in making America, as he phrased it, the world's "arsenal of democracy."

Ranged against him was a de facto coalition more astounding even than the one that fought his domestic program years earlier. The various groups forming it heartily detested each other, but what united them was their aversion to Roosevelt and his foreign policy. After all, if Stalin and Hitler could come to terms so could anyone. Socialists denounced Roosevelt as a warmonger. So, until Hitler broke his word with Stalin, did Communists. And so did the host of tiny sects, most of them on the extreme right. Father Coughlin was still holding forth, still preaching the gospel of discontent to millions of listeners, his culprit this time being a putative Jewish-Bolshevik cabal which, he claimed, ran the Roosevelt administration and much of American life; Coughlin and his band of faithful were now blatantly pro-Fascist and pro-Axis. (Gone from the scene was his populist yoke-mate of old, Huey P. Long, assassinated in 1935.)

Enlisting in the coalition were two new names, formidable as any in America. One was the much feared Brobdingnagian figure of a man, John L. Lewis, longtime autocrat of the United Mine Workers (UMW), when coal was the king of industry, and founder of, and the driving force behind, the large and militantly progressive Congress of Industrial Organizations (CIO). Until recently, Lewis was Roosevelt's ardent champion and ally. Now Lewis was asserting, as only he could, for he was as charismatic as anyone in public life, that Roosevelt had abandoned social reform and surrendered to the ruling classes so that by leading the country into war he might retain his dwindling popularity. More formidable yet was Charles A. Lindbergh, the famous aviator, America's premier hero, boyishly endearing as ever (he was still under 40), and now the uncompromising paladin of isolationism. Lindbergh, who had only contempt for political factions of any stripe, believed as a matter of personal conviction that Nazi Germany, for racial and ideological reasons both, was and should be the dominant power in Europe; it was the West's bulwark against Communism and the lesser peoples of Asia. Here then was a most improbable coalition, animated by a single task: to see to it that America allowed the war to run its course without interference.

Roosevelt's enemies, as we said, had a decisive advantage over him. A solid majority of Americans did willingly give him broad freedom of maneuver—and to just that extent rebuffed his enemies—but only within carefully defined parameters. Their hatred of Hitler and Musso-lini and the Japanese military chieftains notwithstanding, the majority in effect told Roosevelt: thus far and no further; generous military and economic help to nations fighting the Axis by all means, war never; the arsenal of democracy of course, the dispatch of American boys to battlefields abroad never. To defeat his foreign policy Roosevelt's enemies needed merely to hold fast to what remained of the isolationist tradition, and what remained of it was considerable.

In this, then, consisted the reversal of roles. Now Roosevelt's enemies of every persuasion, from revolutionary left to Fascist right, were denying the existence of a crisis, while he pulled out all the stops, using all of his eloquence and authority and cunning to persuade America that it faced a crisis as life-threatening as any in its history.

And again events completely justified him. His foreign enemies, the Axis leaders, proved in the end to be the fatal enemies of his domestic enemies, achieving on his behalf what he likely would not have achieved on his own. Pearl Harbor was his vindication.

I am interested in bringing out Roosevelt's relations with his outstanding critics—Smith, Coughlin, Long, Lewis, and Lindbergh— because it was they who dared to compete with him in the arena of public opinion, who had their own constituencies, who possessed personalities no less distinctive and colorful than his.

His quarrels with them fascinate us as case studies in the uses of political power, in the Machievellian arts if one pleases, and as clashes of principles and ideologies, the fate of America, ultimately the world, hanging in the balance.

They fascinate us as well because they provide another way of discussing the 1930s through all its remarkable phases, from Roosevelt's first election to the introduction, triumph and incapacitation of the New Deal, and culminating in the preparation and mobilization for war. Each of these phases, taken separately, is the thematic and chronological frame within which Roosevelt and his foes played out their stupendous conflicts. Taken together they are nothing less than a comprehensive history of the era that ushered in the modern world.

In 1970, four years before he died, the excerpts he published from his wartime journals reminded the world of the Lindbergh it had bracketed out of its consciousness, the Lindbergh who had sided with Nazi Germany and had found himself at the center of the most enormous controversy of modern times. Reading those pages we see how wrong he was, especially in his assessment of Franklin D. Roosevelt, his *bête noire* of those unhappy years. Lindbergh again enables us to discover where

Roosevelt's greatness lay: in having first sensed Hitler's malign danger, then conveying it to the American people with all the eloquence and leadership skills he could muster, and finally mobilizing them to resist and overcome it.

ONE

WINNING THE PRIZE

AL SMITH

On New Year's Day 1911 Franklin D. Roosevelt arrived in Albany to attend the inauguration of the new governor, fellow Democrat John A. Dix, and take his seat in the state senate to which he recently had been elected.[1]

He was lucky to have won that election. His district, which was made up mostly of farms and villages—and his Hyde Park ancestral home— had gone Democratic only once since the Civil War, and then only for two years. The local Democratic bosses had agreed to put him up because he was such an engaging young man—actually not so young as he looked: he was 28 and had been practicing law without noticeable success in New York City—and possessed such a famous name, the enormously popular ex-President being his distant cousin. Nor was it Franklin Roosevelt's abilities on the stump and personal charm that got him elected. It was the deepening schism within Republican ranks throughout the state and nation between the old guard, or "standpatters," and the insurgents, or progressives, with cousin Theodore lending his enormous prestige to the latter. That was why the 1910 election proved so bountiful for state Democrats, winning as they did not only the governor's chair but both houses of the legislature, something they had not done in 18 years. They had a lot of catching up to do when they convened in Albany.

Now the state Democratic Party was run by New York City's ageless machine, Tammany Hall, byword and symbol across America for corrupt politics, the target, closer to home, of reformers and mugwumps and men of ambition of every stripe. Over the decades opposition to Tammany had nourished many careers (and would do so for decades to come). Its "grand sachem," its boss of bosses, as everyone knew, was Charles Francis Murphy, the most astute and highly regarded chief the "Wigwam" ever had in its long, checkered career. Murphy moved cautiously and unobtrusively behind the scenes, performing with great skill his task of keeping the organization intact—reconciling its numerous, often warring, factions, acquiring jobs and emoluments for its faithful, keeping its army of foes at bay, and appeasing public opinion. His ability to carry out that task could not be faulted, least of all by his adversaries. Tammany controlled the city and state governments and, given the drift of events, might have a good deal to say about who the next President of the United States would be. The organization was riding high and Boss Murphy was at the top of his bent.[2]

Franklin D. Roosevelt was one of the Democratic insurgents. That is, he counted himself among Tammany's critics or enemies. Ideologically, he stood closer to the progressive wing of the other party than to the dominant wing of his own. He also felt that government at every level must discipline the special interests, economic and political, and that the people must participate more actively in overseeing the affairs of state and choosing their leaders—not only electing them but nominating and if necessary recalling them as well. These and like reforms, central to the progressive agenda everywhere in America, were of course anathema to Tammany. And even if Roosevelt had lacked those convictions he still would have been an insurgent, publicly at least, for the obvious reason that his solidly Republican district would have required him to be one.

Several other Democrats from similar upstate districts shared his aversion for Tammany, and together they constituted a sufficiently large group to deny the party establishment a working majority in one or both of the houses (provided, that is, Murphy reached no accommodation with his Republican counterparts). This much, at any rate, was certain: Democratic nay sayers like Franklin D. Roosevelt were seeking an issue on which to take a stand against the bugbear of their constituencies.

The issue in fact arose almost at once. The legislature had to elect a United States Senator (the Seventeenth Amendment having not yet passed). That he would be a Democrat went without saying; both houses combined gave the party a substantial majority (114 to 86). It was an election Murphy and the machine eagerly anticipated. The office of United States Senator was rich in patronage: judges, court clerks, marshals, post office appointees, custom officials, and so on and on. After much deliberation Tammany decided on William "Blue-eyed Billy" Sheehan, whose primary or exclusive claim to distinction was the amount of money he contributed to Democratic Party coffers and the fact that he was less unacceptable than the representatives of the other factions. But he was totally unacceptable to the insurgents, whose leader and main spokesman happened to be Senator Roosevelt. Why Roosevelt came to hold this position his many biographers have failed to make clear. Presumably his name and social status and kinship with the legendary ex-President had much to do with it. No doubt he wished to demonstrate virtues of his own: he was handsome and personable, high-spirited and tirelessly energetic. He also proved to be a clever tactician, for it was he who orchestrated the maneuvers which thwarted Tammany's plans. The press, always happy to beard the tiger, gave the affair extensive coverage and singled out Roosevelt for special praise, comparing him to Theodore, who had also started out in the New York legislature as a party rebel nearly 30 years ago.[3]

Murphy and company found little to praise of course. They beheld in their midst a dandified aristocrat, scion of an old Hudson Valley patroon family, a graduate of the best schools, namely Groton and Harvard, upper class in locution and manner—he would habitually throw back his head when he talked and look down through pince-nez glasses—in short, an English squire among the Irish peasantry. "Awfully arrogant fellow that Roosevelt," said one of them, Lower East Side boss Timothy F. "Big Tim" Sullivan, summing up the impression conveyed by this dabbler in politics, this amateur who had drifted into their bailiwick and would soon return to a more comfortable abode.[4]

On the face of it such an impression was justified. Until he entered the legislature Roosevelt had never stepped outside the bounds of exclusivity in which he had been born and raised; he had even married another Roosevelt. Cousin Theodore, by the time *he* was 29, had cut a broad swath through life, had already revealed indomitable will and ambition: he had been a maverick in the state assembly, a rancher on the North Dakota frontier, a candidate for New York City mayor in a famous and long-remembered campaign, a police commissioner, the author of several volumes of American history and biography. Compared to Theodore Roosevelt, Franklin seemed a flash in the pan, a fluke, a nonentity.

So he may have been, but in the teeth of every wile and stratagem the organization could devise the ranks of his men held fast. The stalemate persisted week in and week out, forcing Tammany to seek a compromise with Roosevelt and the insurgents before the legislative session ended. Whatever the outcome, whoever replaced Blue-eyed Billy Sheehan, it was clear to the outside world that Roosevelt had won the battle.[5] There might have been more to him than the pols saw—or more that he permitted them to see.[6]

Conducting the negotiations with Roosevelt was one of Boss Murphy's most trusted lieutenants, the assembly majority leader, Alfred Emmanuel Smith. Of Smith it could be said that he, like Roosevelt, was an "ideal type," that he no less faithfully than the Brahmin from Hyde Park embodied the universe in which he moved and had his being. That universe was Manhattan's Lower East Side, or that portion of it—facing the river in the shadow of the newly built Brooklyn Bridge (whose christening in 1883 he witnessed as a lad of 10)—which remained Irish well into the twentieth century, the rest of the area having fallen to Jews and Italians and other immigrants.[*] He was a good boy who attended

---

[*] Until recently Smith's biographers, like his contemporaries, assumed he was purebred Irish; it would not have occurred to them to suppose otherwise. Thanks to Frances Perkins's research, published after her death by Matthew and Hannah Josephson (*Al Smith, Hero of the Cities* [Boston: Houghton Mifflin, 1969], 9-15), we now know that in fact only one of his grandparents was Irish, the others having been Italian, German, and English. But the ethnic mix, which gave him a rather nondescript face set off by a prominent nose, mattered little in the making of his character. What mattered, totally so, was his environment—Irish Catholic and Tammany Hall through and through.

parochial schools, went to church regularly, rarely got into trouble, and from the age of 13, when his father died, worked long hours in one job after another to help support his mother and sister. In keeping with neighborhood tradition he spent whatever time he could spare at the local Democratic club and in back of the saloon that Tom Foley, the huge, moon-faced boss of the Fourth Ward, owned on Water Street. While politics came as easily to countless other young men in the community as it did to Smith, his oratorical talents—his voice, he claimed, "could be heard a block away in spite of the rattle of the horse cars and the general racket of city noises"—and his winning personality inevitably brought him to Foley's attention. He put in time as a process server (tracking down qualified men to sit on juries) and then, in 1902, was nominated and of course elected to the assembly from his district.[7]

Even before meeting Smith, Roosevelt must have known he was no mere Tammany hack, that he was quite unlike his legislative confreres—those who would show up occasionally for a vote and draw their $1,500 annual salary, no small sum in those days, aside from other benefactions. Smith was from the start a conscientious member of the assembly. He sedulously learned the issues, especially those dealing with social problems and the condition of the working class, sat in the committees to which he was assigned, read the bills thoroughly, and debated on the floor with increasing skill and authority. Colleagues on both sides of the aisle came to appreciate his first-rate mind, able to call up and marshal an army of statistics, his lively wit, and above all his trustworthiness and integrity. He was one of the most effective legislators, an anomaly among Democrats, and just the sort of politician Murphy was seeking out to furbish Tammany's image. Hence his rise in the assembly.[8]

If Roosevelt was impressed there is no sign of it. Roosevelt might have acknowledged the distinction between Smith and the lesser Tammanyites, but it would have been to his mind a distinction without a difference. He pretty much saw Smith as Smith saw him: through dark distorting lenses. In viewing each other stereotypically they were blinded to the real person and his capacities.[9]

Tammany did finally produce a candidate who was acceptable to the insurgents and whom the legislature promptly approved as Senator. There is some indication that Murphy may have had the last laugh after all—that he really had opposed Sheehan but could not openly do so for fear of offending an important segment of the party. The blame for choosing someone else could therefore be ascribed to Roosevelt and his followers.[10] Be that as it may, the public considered the incident a defeat for Tammany and credited Roosevelt with having caused it. The news of his accomplishments traveled well beyond the precincts of his grateful district.[11]

He quickly garnered the rewards. In 1912 he handily won a second term even though a protracted illness kept him from campaigning. A year later he joined the new Wilson administration in Washington as Assistant Secretary of the Navy, a post which, by further coincidence, his cousin Theodore had also once occupied. So far as the regular Democrats were concerned it was good riddance to this nuisance. A persistent one, it might be added: he ran as a Wilsonian, or progressive, Democratic against the machine in the 1914 primary for United States Senator. This time his insurgency failed him, and he received a sound drubbing, an object lesson in how Murphy dealt with recusants.[12] So Roosevelt stayed with the Navy Department for the next six years, utilizing his position to political advantage. True to family tradition, he was a staunch advocate of preparedness and all-out war even before it came. His enlarged responsibilities took him to every part of the country, enabling him to get acquainted with its leading politicians, to a number of whom he was already a name to reckon with.

But his broad-based appeal meant little in itself in the absence of a viable home base. He was thus forced to confront the paradox of his success. He had risen this far on the strength of his opposition to the Tammany machine. To continue opposing Tammany would delight its foes, who were legion to be sure, but at the sacrifice of his career. He would be another mugwump carping and scolding on the sidelines, waiting for something to turn up.

He accordingly made a shift in his political strategy. More accurately, the shift urged itself on him, his choice—Canossa or retirement from politics—being for a man of his ambition no choice at all.

The change of direction was occasioned by Tammany's amazing show of resilience and tenacity. For a time it appeared as if the mighty Wigwam might collapse in a heap. Following sensational scandals of police corruption, drawn-out trials, and the executions of four gangsters and the police captain on whose behalf they had murdered a gambler, New York City and State reform governments were swept into power on a tide of public indignation. That was in 1913 and 1914. The demise of the infamy seemed at hand. In 1917, however, Tammany recaptured New York City and a year later, to universal surprise, the New York State governorship. What was more, the new governor was that true and avowed child of the organization, Alfred E. Smith.[13]

Doubly astonishing to the Roosevelts of America was Smith's performance in office. He was a model of probity, and so were his appointees, a surprisingly high number of whom were men and women—emphasis on women—of distinction in their own right. Despite a Republican legislature Smith gave a virtuoso account of himself, getting an assortment of social reforms passed and, especially to his credit, standing up for civil liberties during those dark hours of the red scare, when it was unpopular to do so. Smith may have had little sympathy for radicalism, but he was too familiar with radicals—the Lower East Side probably having produced more of them than any community in the land—to be taken in by the prevailing fear, the hysterical alarums and excursions. This quintessential Tammanyite, then, was proving to be a first-rate governor, cast in the mold of such progressive governors as Wisconsin's Robert La Follette and New Jersey's Woodrow Wilson.[14]

Roosevelt therefore had fewer compunctions in coming to terms with the chieftains of the New York Democracy. And they for their part showed a certain magnanimity in letting him back in. They demanded nothing of him beyond his acquiescence in the fact that a phase of history had run its course, that the spirit of insurgency had yielded to the spirit of "normalcy" (this well before Warren G. Harding coined the word). Roosevelt's former adversaries could afford to be generous toward him. Because he was fairly harmless now they readily accepted him as the party's vice presidential candidate at the San Francisco national convention of 1920, Smith himself delivering one of the seconding speeches.[15]

What could be better than having him run for an office of no conse-
quence on a doomed ticket? It must have given the hard-boiled men of
Tammany quite a laugh. And if by a miracle the ticket should win he
would be safely immured in Washington.

Roosevelt's willingness to make the run arose from the same impulse
which dictated reconciliation with Boss Murphy and company. For his
was a two-pronged strategy. Securing the home base—propitiating
Tammany—was one. Cultivating anti-Tammany politicos was the
other. He had been cultivating them as Assistant Secretary of the Navy,
and he cultivated them more strenuously while campaigning for the vice
presidency. Friendships previously acquired throughout the country
were reinforced and new ones acquired. It was hard not to like the tall,
handsome, eupeptic young man (only 38), so well spoken and earnest,
bearer of the illustrious name (Theodore having died in 1919), who
delivered an average of seven speeches a day. Of course he appeared to
love every second of the grueling campaign. The tremendous defeat of
the whole ticket—it was the Republican Party's greatest landslide—
personally hurt him not a whit.

He scrupulously kept up those friendships even after polio struck
him down in the summer of 1921, leaving him, after a long, painful
recovery, unable to use his legs except with the help of very heavy metal
braces, and then only minimally. The files in his library are packed with
letters he wrote to well-wishers across America, most of them politicians
he had met since going to Washington. They were artfully composed
letters, revealing as they did the knowledgeable interest he took in their
affairs. It was an heroic endeavor on his part, his way of combating the
fatigue, debilitation, and depression that enveloped him, and refuting
the widely held assumption—held certainly by the members of his
innermost family—that his public life was over and done with.

The one person who never shared that assumption was his intimate
advisor and retainer and amanuensis, the gnomish, sickly, irascible
Louis McHenry Howe. Howe had abandoned his own successful career
as a political reporter in 1912 to serve Roosevelt heart and soul,
becoming the jealously indefatigable guardian of Roosevelt's hopes. He
made it his business to compile extensive dossiers on everyone who ever
crossed Roosevelt's path and see to it that Roosevelt kept constantly in

touch with all of them. Howe had from the start set his sights on the presidency.[16]

Roosevelt meanwhile concluded that Al Smith was going to be decisively important for his future, that, indeed, without Smith he probably had no future. Roosevelt could scarcely have foreseen the profundity of his insight; the full implications of it would become clear to him as the decade unfolded. He was convinced even before his incapacitation that Smith happened to be the best politician in New York State—best by any standard of valuation—and that Smith's chances for moving upward and onward far exceeded those of any other Democrat. Early on Roosevelt hitched his star to the man he had once dismissed out of hand.

In fact, Roosevelt needed no special acumen. He read the same election returns everyone else did. Though Smith in 1920 went under along with the rest of the Democrats he ran miles ahead of the national ticket, his popularity obviously undiminished. That the party would nominate him for governor again was certain should he seek it. He went through the customary charade of seeming reluctant, of having to be asked or cajoled or implored by the respected citizens of the state. And at the head of those respected citizens stood Roosevelt, whose expertly timed open letter to Smith gave Smith his pretext, in the form of another open letter, for agreeing to serve the welfare of the party and the state.[17] Smith by then had grown so fond of this charming and genial grandee and his admirable wife that he offered him the United States senatorial nomination, Boss Murphy concurring. (A nice ironic touch here: it was the very office Murphy et al. had denied him eight years earlier.) This time Roosevelt was too unwell to consider running for anything. Smith at any rate handily won the 1922 election and promptly resumed where he had left off, as the champion of moderate reform and the enemy of the "privilege seekers and the reactionaries," to quote from Roosevelt's letter.

Roosevelt's long-range strategy came into play at this point—the point at which Smith emerged as a presidential possibility. The governor of New York was automatically such a possibility: the Empire State accounted for 10 percent of the country's population and a like ratio of its electoral vote. But Smith's prospects were hedged in with qualifications that would have daunted a lesser man. There he was, a Tammany Hall Catholic of recent immigrant forebears and a vociferous opponent of Prohibition, a "wet," in short. In the calmest of times these would have been fatal disabilities as far as the southern and western regions of the Democratic Party were concerned. These regions had been the heartland of the progressive movement of old; Woodrow Wilson twice owed his election to them. Now they were the heartland also of the Ku Klux Klan, which boasted millions of members, and were instrumental in the establishment by Congress of a quota system, a *numerus clausus,* as the basis for practically eliminating further immigration from eastern and southern Europe—these being the areas from which Al Smith's mainly Catholic and Jewish constituencies originally came. One can imagine how those Democrats who had to answer to the nativism and religious bigotry in their communities received the news of his intention to run for President.[18]

And nothing in one's imagination compared to what actually transpired at New York City's Madison Square Garden, scene of the 1924 Democratic convention, the galleries of which were filled with leather-lunged and abusive Tammany hirelings. That the party did not decompose then and there was something of a miracle. The enmity between the two camps, essentially pro- and anti-Smith, was evident from the fact that the convention turned down by a hair's-breadth a resolution condemning the KKK and that it took 102 ballots, an all-time high, before finally naming a candidate, as it turned out neither Smith nor the choice of the southern and western bloc, ex-Secretary of the Treasury (and President Wilson's son-in-law) William Gibbs McAdoo, but a lackluster and uninspiring alternative, John W. Davis.[19]

That convention was Roosevelt's coming out as it were, his first important political assay since the 1920 campaign. The delegates who saw and heard him deliver his electrifying "Happy Warrior" speech for Smith, a speech they could not help admiring whatever their persuasion, must have been struck by how much more mature and filled out he looked than when they last saw him. Because he carried so much authority with the anti-Smith forces, had so many friends among them, exuded such good cheer and good sense, he as much as any person there brought about the necessary compromise and so kept the party intact, minimally that. He deserved the congratulations that both sides lavished on him.[20]

Smith should have been thankful that the nomination went to someone else. The Democrats suffered a crushing rebuff in the 1924 election. No one could have beaten Calvin Coolidge, whose quiet espousal of business enterprise was just what most Americans favored. This quite apart from the millions of votes for Senator Robert La Follette, the Progressive Party candidate, an indeterminate number of which would have gone to the Democrats. Smith believed that he at least would have given Coolidge a close race. He could entertain that belief because he was convincingly re-elected governor despite the Republican landslide; it was another tribute to his popularity. The triumph was followed in 1926 by yet another, his fourth. The next time around the presidential nomination obviously would be his for the asking.

With some pride Smith could point to his record. Single-handedly he had wrought a small revolution. Under his beneficent leadership low-rent housing, a 48-hour work week for women and children, and anti-injunction laws were enacted, municipalities acquired the right to own utilities and traction systems, the better to install public power facilities one day, extensive conservation, park, and recreation programs went into effect (overseen by his faithful and completely autocratic lieutenant, Robert Moses), and the administration, hitherto a sprawl of feudal baronies, was thoroughly reorganized and made to resemble a cabinet answerable to the chief executive. Smith was without doubt the best governor New York had ever had and arguably the best in the United States. It was hardly vain of him to assume that he would be a first-rate president, even though he was, in Mencken's words, "as provincial as a Kansas farmer. He is not only not interested in the great problems that heave and lather the country; he has never heard of them."[21]

Smith's Democratic Party adversaries did not exactly agree with his estimation of himself, but they were no longer in a position to stand in his way. In fact, they were pleased that he was offering himself up for the slaughter that was sure to come. Fed by uninterrupted prosperity, a national euphoria was abroad in the land, a Republican euphoria based on the conviction that wealth was every American's birthright. And in Secretary of Commerce Herbert Hoover the Republicans had the avatar of their ideals, the worthiest of replacements for Coolidge, who had chosen not to run again. If, then, Smith wished to sacrifice himself, so much the better, since his inexorable defeat, coupled with his departure from the governor's office, would effectively disqualify him as a future presidential candidate. There would be no repetition, in short, of the 1924 Madison Square Garden fiasco.

Because Smith faced so little opposition he had correspondingly less need of Roosevelt's active assistance. In 1926 he had again asked Roosevelt to run for the United States Senate and Roosevelt had again said no, citing again reasons of health. The reason, though, lay elsewhere: he had no desire to spend the rest of his days on the shelf, in semi-retirement.[22] (The Democrat who was nominated and elected that year, longtime state senator and Tammany loyalist Robert F. Wagner, was to become during the next 24 years the chief legislative architect of Roosevelt's New Deal and one of the great Senators in American history.) Not that there was any discernible hostility or tension between Smith and Roosevelt. Smith knew he could count on Roosevelt's unswerving support, and they remained on the best of personal terms.

There was tension, however, between Roosevelt and Smith's closest advisers, his privy council, and it was growing. Over the years, Roosevelt and his wife Eleanor and his alter ego Louis M. Howe—these comprising *his* privy council—felt increasingly estranged from Smith's associates, but they uttered not a syllable of public complaint. They were acutely aware of how dependent Roosevelt was on Smith's good will and therefore how useful to Smith he had to go on being even if it hurt. Roosevelt allowed himself to be put forward as a front, a countervailing image of upper-class white Anglo-Saxon Protestant rectitude. And precisely because he seemed to ask for so little in exchange for his service Smith and his confidants found it hard to take Roosevelt seriously. They regarded him as an amiable and likable man, void of substance, fit to be hardly more than what he was, a front or image. One detects a certain contempt in the cavalier and sometimes dismissive way they treated him. The Happy Warrior speech, for instance, they in effect wrote for him after mercilessly gutting his version. When, on another occasion, he tried to secure a patronage job for Howe in one of the state park agencies whose commission Roosevelt chaired—a tiny reciprocation for the help Roosevelt (and Howe) had given Smith—Commissioner Moses issued a sharp and insulting refusal.[23] Roosevelt complained angrily to Smith but Smith sided with Moses. Roosevelt swallowed the insult and the rebuff and kept true to the strategy he had marked out: to support Smith while sedulously cultivating Democrats on the other side of the divide.

In gearing up for the presidential campaign ahead Smith brought in several new associates who were politically indistinguishable from conservative Republicans. Chief among these was the financier John J. Raskob, like Smith a religious Catholic and a militant anti-Prohibitionist, whose working life had been devoted to serving the Du Pont family as financial specialist. (It was Raskob who in the early 1920s had persuaded the Du Ponts to buy General Motors stock when it was a highly speculative issue.) Though a true-blue Republican over the years, Raskob had taken a shine to Smith when they met in 1926. With the help of the Du Ponts and other rich families Raskob decided to play the role of Smith's patron and sponsor. It pleased Smith enormously that such a man would now serve *him,* product of the Fulton Fish Market and Tom Foley's saloon. As Smith's campaign director, Raskob set up campaign headquarters, rather tastelessly some thought, in the General Motors building on Fifth Avenue. One thing was settled at all events: Smith would not lack the resources to bring his message to the American people.[24]

Roosevelt looked upon this whole development with quiet chagrin. A moderate wet himself, or at least a committed anti-dry, Roosevelt thought the Prohibition question had to be handled gingerly—in such a way as to prevent it from antagonizing the millions of fervently dry

Democrats who had other, more important questions on their minds and were, all things being equal, the most fervent of anti-Republicans. The Raskob influence, he feared, threatened to worsen an already poor situation and condemn the Democrats to permanent minority status, a possibility that bore directly on Roosevelt's own future. The fundamental question was what would become of the party. Was it to be a party that followed Republican principles on every issue save one? As far back as September 1926 Roosevelt had warned Smith: "Some of your friends are without your knowledge and consent giving aggressive publicity in the South and West, where such publicity is at this time harmful."[25]

Still, Roosevelt was able to turn to his own account his support of Smith, critical as he was—in private—of the direction Smith was going. Smith asked him to give the nominating speech at the 1928 convention, in Houston, Texas, as he had in 1924, hoping by this gesture to keenly remind the audience that the Happy Warrior (by now Smith's official title) was about to do battle, and, as he had done so often before, confound the naysayers. Roosevelt prepared for this address as carefully as he had the one four years earlier, less to impress the delegates wilting in the dank heat than to be heard by the uncounted millions who were listening to the proceedings on radio. Radio was already having a noticeable effect on popular taste, and Roosevelt was hardly alone in realizing that a politician who knew how to use the medium, who possessed the right personality and voice and delivery, would enjoy a definite advantage. He may have also realized that he was precisely such a politician. His nominating speech, flawlessly delivered, did have the effect he intended: in its plain and direct language, in its freedom from oratorical flourishes and hackneyed phrases, it successfully appealed to both the radio listeners and the convention delegates, with many of whom he was by now on very cordial terms.[26]

His Houston performance was a decisive moment in his life. It helped convince the New York State Democratic leaders, including members of Smith's entourage, that he should run for governor. How this came to pass is itself an interesting story.

They wanted Roosevelt mostly because in their judgment he could best unify the party—he was acceptable to Tammany and non-Tammany (or anti-Tammany) upstate factions—and so beat back a particularly able and respected Republican challenger, state Attorney General Albert Ottinger. Now Smith personally did not necessarily share that judgment. He believed that his coattails would carry into office just about any gubernatorial candidate. He was not averse to Roosevelt running; he simply thought his Democratic colleagues should leave the squire alone if that was what he preferred. Indeed, it was exactly what Roosevelt preferred, and he could not have been clearer and more categorical in making it known to everyone.[27] While the state Democratic convention was going on in Rochester he happened to be bathing in his Warm Springs, Georgia, rehabilitation center, the one he was building for fellow polio sufferers. Why he was staying away was an open secret. He was certain that any gubernatorial candidate would ride Smith's coattails to defeat. Losing would injure his plans, irreparably perhaps. Howe, whose whole life was consecrated to the single object of seeing Roosevelt become President, absolutely opposed the candidacy. Eleanor thought ill of it too. His strategy, they all agreed, was to wait until time and circumstances had ripened his chances.

But the party insisted, refusing to take his noes as final. Nor could Smith avoid the issue. The disarray among state Democrats was worse than expected, and its persistence might affect his campaign after all; it might even cost him the state. If that should occur he had no chance whatever, never mind the accompanying embarrassment. Smith's fate thus turned by a strange quirk on Roosevelt's decision.

One can understand, then, why Smith and Raskob went to such lengths in getting Roosevelt to change his mind. They pulled out every stop. While the convention hung fire in Rochester they managed, through Eleanor (who was in New York), to reach him by phone. He tried repeatedly to duck them, using a succession of ruses.[28] In vain; they kept getting through to him. He then offered one pretext after another: he needed more time to get well and therefore might not be able to carry out his duties as governor;[29] he had no immediate political ambitions and wished to devote such energy as he had to raise money for the Warm Springs Foundation; etc. They naturally had no trouble meeting every objection. Should his condition necessitate trips to Warm Springs, they assured him, he would have a perfect surrogate in the lieutenant-governor they had found for him, the faithful and beloved financier and philanthropist Herbert H. Lehman. Besides which, they went on, a governor's active period of work (in those days) was usually only the length of the legislative session, from early January to April at the latest, giving him ample time to rest and recuperate. As for the Warm Springs Foundation, Raskob promised to contribute whatever amount Roosevelt specified to launch it on its course. Roosevelt still refused to yield. Smith then played his final card. He made it a question of party loyalty, the obvious implication being that if Roosevelt failed his Democratic brethren now he could count on nothing from them in the future. Thus was Roosevelt made to acquiesce; thus against his will was he handed the nomination.[30]

In the bitter pain and humiliation of his defeat Al Smith might have comprehended why the country as a whole, still so bigoted and close-minded, overwhelmingly rejected him, why even some of the Deep South states went Republican for the first time since Reconstruction. What defied comprehension, however, was the fact that New York State voters, having elected him four times, should have chosen Hoover. That slap in the face explained his solemn vow the morning after. "I do not expect ever to run for public office again. I've given a quarter century of my life to it. I will never lose my interest in public affairs, that's a sure thing; but as far as running for public office is concerned—that's finished."[31] Even the lowliest ward heeler of the old neighborhood knew what to do when he was no longer wanted.

If Smith found any glimmer of satisfaction amid the ruins it was Roosevelt's surprising victory, exiguous though it was (by 24,500 votes out of over 4 million), Roosevelt having run as Smith's heir and legatee. Smith could also assume that it was he, after all, who had made Roosevelt what he was. With some justification Smith looked upon Roosevelt as his protégé.

How much credit he gave Roosevelt for winning the election is a matter of speculation, for in this as in most things he maintained an iron-lipped reticence. That Roosevelt possessed talents—charm, speaking ability, a capacity to make and keep a vast range of friends—Smith could not have denied. But that Roosevelt could be a leader of the state government and Democratic Party, be Smith's double in other words— this he refused to acknowledge. He had been in politics too long and had been too successful at it to expect wholesale transformations in people. Was the Franklin Roosevelt who was about to occupy *his* chair different from the featherweight he had known since 1911? Smith could hardly bring himself to think so.

Smith, it could be said, was the victim of his own self-proclaimed virtue. He was too worldly-wise to see transformations where they did occur, beneath the facile appearances. He was too set in the habits which had served him perhaps too well to question his long-held views about men. Smith, let it be added, was not alone in failing to see Roosevelt as Roosevelt really was. Many were taken in by his amiability, genteel manners, and show of adolescent enthusiasm, the marks of a featherweight. On this superficial level Roosevelt had indeed not changed at all over the years. But Smith's acute intelligence should have told him that only a first-class politician, a leader of great promise, could have pulled off such an astonishing victory. Not only did Roosevelt handle the issues brilliantly, tacking and veering with rare skill between Smith's urban and ethnic and anti-Prohibition constituency on the one hand and the mainly dry, rural and small-town Protestant electorate on the other.[32] He also put together a team of political advisers and speech writers who served him exceptionally well. From beginning to end he remained the master of his campaign. And throughout he conveyed to his associates and the audiences on the hustings his invincible optimism and sense of assurance. In 1928 the phrase "Happy Warrior" better applied to him than to Al Smith.

Smith soon reaped the folly of his misperceptions. He suggested to Roosevelt, discreetly of course, that Robert Moses should stay on as secretary of state and that another and still closer helpmate, Belle Moscowitz, become the governor-elect's personal secretary.[33] The suggestion was unwise, to say the least. Politically, the secretary of state was important: he distributed patronage and cared for other party matters and therefore had to be entirely loyal to the governor. No one fit the requirement less than Moses, a strong-willed, arrogant, ruthlessly ambitious man who gave his fealty to Smith and only Smith, and whom, as we noted, Roosevelt had ample cause to despise. Neither was there any love lost between Roosevelt and the redoubtable Mrs. Moscowitz. Her influence on Smith in getting progressive laws enacted, her devotion to Smith—these were legendary, as was *her* arrogance and willfulness. As Roosevelt's secretary she obviously would have served Smith's interests, whatever they might be, and Roosevelt would have been reduced to the status of a surrogate, a simulacrum, and, in the end, a laughingstock.[34] He accordingly let Smith know that he and he alone would be captain of the ship and, for better or for worse, would choose his own mates.

But if Smith felt hurt—he claimed that he wanted only to help his protégé—he gave no sign of it, gentleman that he was, and the two men parted company after the inauguration on New Year's Day.

They remained on amicable terms so long as the status quo prevailed. It was clear from the outset of his gubernatorial career that Roosevelt would seek to implement and expand on what Smith had done rather than initiate anything startlingly new. Roosevelt concentrated on his executive duties with a view of increasing his statewide popularity and building up Democratic strength in Republican counties, especially the most rural among them. This Smith had not done. As governor Smith had successfully played what might be called the Tammany game. Tammany traditionally rewarded New York City's Republicans, a minuscule group, because they usually cooperated with the organization. So Smith arranged deals with local Republican bosses in the state and never or rarely encouraged Democratic opposition in their bailiwicks. Roosevelt quietly departed from that policy.[35]

Meanwhile, however, Smith was still titular head of the national party, and his man, John J. Raskob, was still its chairman. And even though the chairman was supposed to be neutral, Raskob was dedicated to Smith's welfare, and he had the financial muscle to subordinate the party's apparatus to his will. But by the end of 1930 the status quo had undergone a seismic change. Roosevelt had just been re-elected governor by the largest plurality any candidate for the office had received, 725,000, winning in the process most of the upstate counties, itself an unprecedented feat for a Democrat. America took instantaneous notice, for something tremendous was rising on the political horizon.

The Democrats could now actually look forward to winning the presidency. The economic downturn, which had caught the public by surprise, was becoming a chronic condition, mocking every day the reassurances that came from the White House, the corporate boardrooms, and academia. The Depression had turned American politics around, giving Democrats a taste of victory at every level of government. Roosevelt's own re-election triumph was directly attributable to it. Even if he lacked ambition he would have been a prime contender for the Democratic presidential nomination. And he did not lack ambition.

In the early months of 1931 he set loose on America the personal machine which had operated so effectively for him in New York. Prominent Democrats throughout the country received a battery of letters, telegrams, calls, and visits from his superb field commander, James A. Farley, a seasoned politico. Drawing on the friendships he had accumulated over the past 20 years, especially in the South and West, Roosevelt began to secure commitments of support. The ground that he and Louis Howe had been plowing so carefully was about to yield up its harvest.

Smith regarded Roosevelt's possible nomination with incredulity and rage. It was as though he held Roosevelt responsible for not being the person Smith had taken him to be; as though Roosevelt's spectacular rise was itself a betrayal, an act of perfidy, a colossal deception.[36] Whether he expected Roosevelt to step aside in his favor is debatable. What cannot be debated is the ferocity of his opposition to Roosevelt's hopes.

Smith and Raskob knew that they had to stop Roosevelt in his tracks lest his lead become insuperable. So, in March 1931, Raskob set a trap. Raskob almost persuaded the rest of the Democratic National Committee to recommend that the party and its presidential candidate, whoever he might be, come out in favor of repealing Prohibition. The recommendation, had it gone through, would have badly hurt Roosevelt's chances because it would have placed him squarely on one side of an irreconcilably divisive issue. Smith was already on that side of it and had nothing to lose. Roosevelt and the party's liberal wing were also concerned that the emphasis on Prohibition would swamp the other and infinitely more important issues, those centered on the collapsed economy. Precisely such an emphasis would have pleased Smith, Raskob, and the conservatives since they had no quarrel with Hoover's policies and did not believe that anything was fundamentally wrong with the economy.[37] While Roosevelt opposed Prohibition too he did not think it was worth losing an election, or a nomination, over. So he made a fight of it in the Democratic National Committee and easily prevailed over Raskob.[38]

Later that year Smith openly broke with Roosevelt. Smith's obvious intention was to demonstrate to the country just how ineffectual this upstart was. Frank Freidel describes the quarrel as "quixotic," and so it was, but only in hindsight. While it was in progress both men took it very seriously, and with good reason.

Roosevelt was backing a $19 million bond issue, to be presented to the state's voters in November 1931, to enable the government to buy poorly utilized, submarginal farmland, then restore it and turn it into forests and parks. The bill had few enemies; both parties and both houses of the legislature backed it. But Smith suddenly denounced it in his press releases and speeches as an extravaganza and a giveaway (which to some extent it was). Now no one was less quixotic than Smith, and no one understood state affairs better than he. From firsthand experience he knew that New Yorkers habitually rejected bond issues, not one of them having come even close to winning approval since 1920. In flinging down his challenge Smith imagined he had trapped Roosevelt: should Roosevelt fight to a finish he would suffer a humiliating defeat; should he retreat he would seem weak and cowardly. Smith, in other words, could not have anticipated that Roosevelt would make a fight to the finish and win. Yet that was what happened. Roosevelt brought in every weapon he could muster—farm and conservation groups, Republicans and Tammany politicians alike—and, shattering precedent, easily carried the day. It was yet another triumph for him, yet another humiliation for Smith.[39]

Smith's increasingly strident negations played excellently into Roosevelt's hands. So much so that a cynic might say they were secretly in collusion, with Smith acting the heavy the better to improve Roosevelt's prospects. That is, had Smith retired from politics after his 1928 debacle, as he promised, Roosevelt might have failed in his purpose or attained it with the greatest difficulty.

The brute fact was that southern and western Democrats feared Smith as much as ever, and they constituted Roosevelt's base of support. Given the notorious deliquescence of American politics, the solidity of that support depended largely on the extent to which his adherents saw him as the only or most acceptable alternative to Smith.[40] When on February 8, 1932, Smith announced his availability for the nomination—"if the Democratic Convention should decide it wants me to lead, I will make the fight," was how he put it—Roosevelt's stock climbed another cubit or two. It was with some sense of alarm that the South and West viewed this latest example of arrogance by the big-city juggernauts of the Northeast, all of them Irish Catholic and dripping wet. Smith proved unexpectedly strong in several of the primaries, beating Roosevelt in Massachusetts, Rhode Island, and Connecticut and making deep inroads in New Jersey and Pennsylvania. The big city love for Smith disappointed Roosevelt, but it served to consolidate his hold on the rest of the party. For front-runners in presidential campaigns the basic desideratum is the reliability of their officers and troops under fire—that is, after the first convention roll call. The threat suddenly emanating from the Smith camp was Roosevelt's best assurance of that reliability.

Roosevelt profited too from the widening ideological differences between the two men. They had started from pretty much the same positions but were, under the press of events, moving in opposite directions. Smith always thought Roosevelt was something of a dreamy-eyed visionary, an overgrown boy scout, a condition made possible, in Smith's opinion, by Roosevelt's privileged life, his innocence, his inability to grasp the reality of human nature and affliction. Smith in his own eyes typified the proud conservatism of the self-made man who has risen up American style from lower-class anonymity, and he expected others similarly deprived to achieve no less.[41] He considered it iniquitous in the extreme to lump all the poor together and attempt by government fiat to raise or reduce them all equally.[42] Roosevelt for his part felt that Smith had succumbed to the blandishments of material success, that the distance between Smith and his heritage, and for that matter his accomplishments in office, could be measured by the company he now kept and the splendidly handsome life he led. The differences which may have been festering for years beneath the surface of their comradely relations needed only a specific occasion to reveal themselves to the world.

The occasion was the April 13, 1932, Jefferson Day dinner in Washington, at which Smith was the featured speaker. A few days earlier, in a radio talk to the nation, Roosevelt had called for government assistance to workers and farmers, "the Forgotten Man at the bottom of the economic pyramid," as he phrased it, who lived in dread of losing the little they still had and joining the ranks of the homeless and unemployed.[43] It was a harmless enough talk, vague and general, with a suitable show of concern. Roosevelt's inexcusable error, in Smith's judgment, was to have raised the question of economic suffering at a time of mounting discontent and even violence both in the countryside and city. The papers were reporting more and more protests led by radicals, Communists chief among them, ending usually in confrontations with the authorities. Smith by inference accused Roosevelt of sanctioning if not encouraging these lawless elements, of seeking like them to set class against class, the poor against the rich, and doing so for blatantly opportunistic reasons. To Smith the poor and the unemployed redeemed themselves by their own effort, not by buying the nonsense that America had "forgotten" them and therefore owed them something. He minced few words in his speech to the party. "This is no time for demagogues," he asserted. "I will take off my coat and vest and fight to the end against any candidate who persists in any demagogic appeal to lead the masses of the working people of this country to destroy themselves by setting class against class." Smith did not think unemployment would end "before the people who . . . employ them [the workers] ordinarily are restored to conditions of normal prosperity."[44] This was precisely Hoover's argument.

Once again, Smith had done Roosevelt a huge favor. His animadversions established more firmly in the public mind than would otherwise have been possible Roosevelt's compassion for the plain folk of America. Smith appeared by contrast to be more interested in defending the system than its victims. And by accusing Roosevelt of demagoguery he was tacitly acknowledging that the issue of the "forgotten man" was too powerful to contain, the only question being who would exploit it and for what ends. If Roosevelt wanted to give the impression that he was and would be no Herbert Hoover he had Smith above all to thank for enabling him to do so.

Smith granted Roosevelt a last consummatory favor at the convention itself in Chicago. Because Roosevelt fell just short of the number necessary for the nomination—two-thirds of the delegates[*]—there was an outside chance he might be stopped. His very advantage accounted for his vulnerability, and he might go the way of so many front-runners who had "peaked" too soon. To defeat him, however, the other candidates had to agree on a single candidate, presumably someone drawn from outside their own ranks. Since Smith was the runner-up, with 201¾ delegates, the impetus for such an agreement had to come from him. But he refused to provide it, maintaining to the end that he had one aim only: to win the nomination. So it was that Roosevelt's strength remained constant in successive roll calls. But there was not much movement in his favor either—an ominous portent—until, at the conclusion of the third ballot, one of his competitors, House Speaker John Nance Garner of Texas, agreed to run with him. The deal easily put Roosevelt over the top. "The failure of the opposition," Mencken wrote, "was the failure of Al Smith. [I]t was far beyond the technique of the golf playing Al of today."[45]

Smith's enemies had returned to haunt him. It was the switch in the California vote from Garner to Roosevelt as the fourth roll call got under

---

[*] Three thousand, two hundred of them met to cast 1,154 votes; 770 was thus the winning number. Roosevelt could count on no more than 666¼ votes.

way that set off the stampede. And the head of the California delegation, William Gibbs McAdoo, whose dramatic announcement of the switch electrified the convention, had also been Smith's rival through 102 ballots eight years before. That piece of irony, that wound of retribution, did not go unremarked.[46]

But as ever Smith was the perfect sport, the most gentlemanly of Democrats, publicly at least.[*] He and Roosevelt made up and embraced, and he campaigned for his old comrade-in-arms where he would do the most good, in the big cities.[47]

Self-interest undoubtedly figured in Smith's support for Roosevelt. That he still believed he might one day be President after all seems ludicrous to us today. The possibility was not so ludicrous then, in the dark autumn days of 1932. He could not get it out of his head that Franklin D. Roosevelt was simply not up to the task of running America, that Roosevelt's rise was adventitious, the prelude to a gigantic pratfall, much like the one poor Herbert Hoover had just taken. The path might then be open to him, Smith, in 1936.

He may have been fantasizing about his future, but this prognosis of what lay in store for the new President was widely shared at the time, even by Roosevelt's well-wishers.[48] America was in the throes of an overwhelming pessimism, with no end in sight of the crisis that brought it on. The problems seemed insurmountable and sure to doom any President, especially a President, according to Smith's lights, who was guilty of wrongheaded policies, lacked leadership abilities, and possessed an obviously weak character. Smith may even have counted himself lucky that he was denied the nomination. Maybe his star had not declined for good.

FATHER COUGHLIN

Just as the campaign for the 1932 Democratic presidential nomination was getting under way, Governor Franklin D. Roosevelt received two

---

[*] But not at first. When it was clear Roosevelt had the nomination locked up Smith left the convention and went home in a dudgeon, thereby preventing the acclamation from being unanimous.

prominent visitors in his New York City office. One of them, Detroit Mayor Frank Murphy, was a compassionate liberal, the first Catholic mayor of a city that had experienced more than its share of religious bigotry (and was indeed still a Ku Klux Klan stronghold), who had recently been re-elected by a sizable plurality, giving further evidence of the growing importance of the Catholic electorate. Thanks largely to Murphy, Roosevelt enjoyed the solid backing of the Michigan Democratic Party. In years to come Roosevelt would repay his debt manyfold.[49]

The main reason for the visit was Murphy's companion, none other than the famous "radio priest," Father Charles E. Coughlin, whose parish lay in a Detroit suburb, Royal Oak. For some time Coughlin had wanted to meet New York's progressive governor and presidential aspirant, and offer him his support.[50] It was support Roosevelt sorely needed, his chief rival for the nomination being Al Smith, hero and martyr to American Catholics. And American Catholics, it was safe to assume, listened to no one more attentively week in and week out than to Father Coughlin. His value to Roosevelt might be inestimable.

Yet Roosevelt had mixed feelings about him. Roosevelt admired Coughlin's ability to use the radio, which was coming into its own as an instrument of mass persuasion. For not only did millions, Protestants as well as Catholics, tune into him every Sunday afternoon; they registered their enthusiasm for the message he was conveying to them by donating their small bills to his outfit, the Radio League of the Little Flower, named after his Royal Oak church, the Shrine of the Little Flower of Jesus (the "Little Flower of Jesus" having been a Carmelite nun, St. Therese of Lisieux, who died in 1879 and had recently been canonized for her "childlike faith, humility, littleness"). That church had been a wooden building set in a wasteland of anti-Catholicism when Coughlin delivered his first broadcast back in October 1926. Now it was a gigantic edifice, a cathedral really, capable of seating thousands, with a tower so high it would soon reach (in his words) "the Virgin Mary's bosom."[51] Roosevelt had to admire Coughlin's technical genius—his superb delivery, his beautifully modulated baritone voice, his rolling cadences, his delicate trills, his endless alliterations. Here was an artist of the airwaves.[52]

And Roosevelt might even have agreed with Coughlin when he preached social justice in the abstract, when he criticized capitalists in general for their greed and excessive power, when, for example, he would point out that "one thirty-third of one percent of our total population" owned "over fifty percent of the total wealth of the country," or when, with soaring eloquence, he alluded to the broken homes, the confiscated farms, the slavery of the machine, the banditry, the bread lines . . . the poverty amidst the plenty, the forty thousand millionaires and the fifty million destitute citizens. . . ."[53]

What gave Roosevelt pause was the specific target of Coughlin's animus, those he held most responsible for bringing America to her knees: the international bankers. Tom Watson and Ignatius Donnelly and the other fathers of Populism would have felt completely at home with Coughlin's jeremiads on the subject. They would have heartily endorsed his explanation for the suffering in the land, for the loss of home and farm mortgages, the collapse of small businesses, the disappearance of savings, the massive unemployment, the deepening despair. International bankers, in his view, by their control of the world's gold controlled America's money supply, lifeblood of the economy. In language that reminded many of his older listeners of the sainted William Jennings Bryan, Coughlin accused the bankers of lifting their "voices until their clamorous shout has gone mocking to heaven: 'Give us Barabbas—the Barabbas of gold begotten greed!' And today Christ's millions of brothers are treading their weary way from Pilate's Hall to the height of crimson Calvary. Their brows are embedded with thorns of worry. Behold them with bodies emaciated with the lash of poverty! Behold them as they stumble and fall and rise again until they carry the cross of gold upon which civilization shall be crucified."[54]

With this sort of rhetoric, and above all with the easy-money philosophy that underlay it, Roosevelt was completely out of sympathy, although, as we saw, he kept his own counsel. He allowed the southern and western wings of the Democratic Party, where easy-money advocates were deeply entrenched, to think that he shared their sentiments, or at least was not averse to them. On this issue, in fact, Roosevelt stood closer to Al Smith and John J. Raskob, and for that matter President Hoover, than he did to them.

Roosevelt may also have caught the anti-Semitic drift of Coughlin's assaults on the bankers. That Coughlin despised Jews years before he openly said so we know from the letters of his that are available to us. In the early 1930s he gave only intimations of anti-Semitism. He would often single out the Rothschilds and Warburgs for condemnation and link them to such well-known practitioners of evil as J. P. Morgan. "We have lived to see the day," he would assert "when modern Shylocks have gotten fat and wealthy, praised and deified, because they have perpetrated the ancient crime of usury under a modern racket of statesmanship"; in Shakespeare's medieval Venice, by way of contrast, their "Jewish gabardine was spat upon."[55] Coughlin, it will be noted, possessed the knack of dredging up the stereotypical Jew who best suited his purpose.[56]

Roosevelt had a fair idea of whom he would be dealing with. Along with every other American he was familiar with Coughlin's contretemps with the Columbia Broadcasting System a year or so before. It was an example of the kind of punishment the priest was capable of meting out to those who crossed him.

In the fall of 1930 CBS had signed Coughlin on, providing him with a coast-to-coast forum. As his audience rose—it was believed to number about 40 million listeners—so had the stridency of his attacks on bankers and other mischief makers of the left and right. Now some of his ideas he took from a member of the House of Representatives from Pennsylvania, Louis D. McFadden. A rabid anti-Semite, McFadden ascribed every social affliction to "the Jewish plan of a World State," which, he maintained, and been hatched in the Versailles Hall of Mirrors, scene of the 1919 peace treaty deliberations, and was being carried out by such institutions as the League of Nations, the Court of International Justice, the Bank of England, the House of Morgan, and, most sinister of all, the House of Rothschild. Coughlin was going to disclose the story of the Versailles conspiracy in his January 4, 1931, program, information about which McFadden had been feeding him partly by telephone. On January 3 Coughlin called McFadden and read him excerpts from the broadcast he was preparing. What Coughlin did not know was that the call somehow got transferred to the Hoover White House and that another man, never identified, was listening in. Around midnight that evening a CBS vice-president called Coughlin and said serious complaints were coming from high officials. Would Coughlin therefore delete the objectionable comments—the slashing attack on bankers and international agencies? Quickly thinking it over,

Coughlin promised that he would indeed speak on another subject. That satisfied CBS. Coughlin then called McFadden and learned that McFadden had not been his interlocutor. His conclusion: a phone tap! High officials indeed!

Coughlin was as good as his word. His talk dealt not with Versailles but with the virtues of free speech and the attempt of industry executives to muzzle him. He would never be muzzled, he said, even if he was taken off the air. The issue, in short, was made to order for him, and he exploited it brilliantly, rising in the process to unexampled heights of alliterative eloquence.[57]

That broadcast marked Father Coughlin's arrival as a public figure. It evoked a response never before seen. He received over a million letters and cards of support. Defeated and humbled, CBS said nothing when next Sunday Coughlin delivered the remarks that had caused the furor in the first place.[58] He was serving notice to future critics of what they could expect.

Yet, until the waning days of 1931 Coughlin had avoided taking political sides. His views of Hoover and the administration he kept to himself. But he became more partisan as partisanship itself grew in America, as the level of rancor and discontent increased. On February 14, 1932, he finally waded into the President by name for serving the banking fraternity and the rich at the expense of the people. He blamed Hoover's policies for denying the people access to money precisely when their lives depended on it, thereby making the President, whether he realized it or not, the servitor of those who would enslave America.[59] Coughlin's politicization endeared him still further to his burgeoning public. To be a two-fisted fighter, to in effect remove his turned collar, this evidently was what his listeners wanted him to be—the volume of mail and contributions was the test—and he obliged them.

Such was the man who accompanied Mayor Murphy to Roosevelt's office in New York. Roosevelt may have been impressed by Coughlin, who even in public cut an attractive figure: he was ruggedly handsome and athletically built and earthy in conversation and taste, a man of action as well as words. But Roosevelt was as usual in command of the situation, encouraging Coughlin to believe they saw eye to eye on the large questions of justice and the predacity of certain capitalists, without, however, going into the particulars, not on this occasion at any rate.

So impressed was Coughlin that he volunteered then and there to help Roosevelt any way he could, even in the absence of specific commitments. It was what Roosevelt wanted to hear.

The plan went ahead as scheduled. Toward President Hoover Coughlin was the soul of contumely. Toward Governor Roosevelt he was the soul of deference. He appeared at the 1932 Chicago convention to plump for Roosevelt and help draft the party platform. To Coughlin's huge satisfaction Roosevelt stopped in Detroit during the fall campaign and delivered an important speech aimed obviously at Coughlin and his wing of the Catholic Church and the discontented throughout the region. Roosevelt cited *Quadreggisimo Anno,* Pope Pius XI's reaffirmation two years earlier of *Rerum Novarum,* the church's classic statement on social justice under industrial capitalism, calling it "just as radical as I am," "one of the greatest documents of modern times." Sounding every bit like the priest, Roosevelt assailed the privileged few in America who battened on the misery and want of the masses.[60] Coughlin could hardly be blamed for assuming that he and the President-to-be were kindred spirits animated by the same ideals. He pondered the fact— he would soon state it publicly—that he was closer to this aristocratic High Church Protestant than he was to his fellow prelates of lower-class Irish extraction.

HUEY LONG

Like most Americans who read the newspapers, Franklin D. Roosevelt first paid serious attention to the name of Huey Pierce Long in the early spring of 1929. For that was when Long, the recently elected governor of Louisiana, seemed on the verge of being thrown out of office.

Roosevelt had been hearing about this fiery petrel for years but had scarcely noticed him, a minor politician in a minor state. Now Long was regularly in the headlines, the object of more than passing curiosity.

He had, after all, brought off quite a feat. The lower house of the Louisiana legislature by a wide majority had adopted articles of impeachment against him, and it was generally assumed that the state senate, following a perfunctory trial, would easily find him guilty, ending his stormy career then and there.[61] But in a startling turnabout Long somehow got the required number of senators to swear in writing that they would never vote to convict him, no matter what evidence was produced. So, the trial was never held.[62] Roosevelt, artist that he was, must have appreciated Long's dexterity in snatching personal triumph from the chasm of defeat. Here was a man to be watched and perhaps cultivated, for Louisiana too figured in Roosevelt's scheme of things.

It would be no exaggeration to say that even before Huey Long caught the world's interest Louisiana had never encountered anyone quite like him. He was already sui generis.[63]

From the moment he entered politics in 1918 he generated controversy, the more of it the better so far as he was concerned. His strategy was elegant in its audacity. He would attack the most powerful and best-connected politician in a given community on the theory that about as many people opposed as supported the politician, with the rest sitting on the fence. Long therefore began with a sizable body of adherents; his next task was to win over the fence sitters, enough at any rate to give him a plurality of the votes. Such a strategy, it goes without saying, could only be accomplished by a certain kind of person, by someone who possessed the requisite skills, love of combat, downright cynicism, and courage in the face of incalculable hostility, a good deal of it physical. Long was that kind of person.

It was as though great elemental forces had prepared him for the role he chose to play. He was a prodigious stump speaker. No one was quicker on his feet, or wittier, or able to call upon such a repertory of homespun stories, epithets, and put-downs, which he invariably tailored to his audience and the specific target of his derision. His memory was a gigantic storehouse of information, in which nothing was misplaced or lost. In other words, he bore an uncanny resemblance to New York's Al Smith. Both of them were naturals, born to their vocation, and they owed everything they were or came to be to their own native genius, planted in the rich soil of American politics.

From the outset of his political career Long was a demagogue in the classic sense of the term. He knew how to appeal to the common folk, the rural and small-town poor who overwhelmingly predominated in Louisiana. He knew how to address their daily concerns, to articulate their mingled rage and frustration, for they had experienced nothing but defeat, disillusionment, and betrayal, and expected little from politicians. The term "demagogue" also suggests someone who is driven less by his regard for the people than by his regard for himself, and he thus has no compunction against deceiving or abandoning them when it serves his convenience to do so. In Long's case, the suggestion did not apply, at least not yet, to judge from the esteem in which his constituency, the poor, continued to hold him.

Not that he ever attempted to disguise his ambition. He was always campaigning either for himself or for his allies, sowing enemies in the process like dragon's teeth. Those enemies were the special economic interests, chief among them Rockefeller's Standard Oil Company, the utilities, the banks, and the large planters, they and their political cohorts and sycophants—all in all, a familiar host, pilloried by insurgents well before Long appeared on the scene. Louisiana had its share of Populists and Progressives and even Socialists, particularly in the northern parishes. Long was born and grew up in one of those parishes, his father having been an unsuccessful farmer-entrepreneur. Long used the lesser positions which he won—first as a railroad and then as a public service commissioner—to turn the state upside down. The press was full of his escapades, his fights, his occasional arrests, and mostly the verbal shafts he let loose upon his adversaries. He was an effective gadfly, but could he reach high office? His adversaries did not think so, and they welcomed his decision to run for governor in the 1924 primary, convinced as they were that he would make an ass of himself. But he did amazingly well, coming in third, close behind the two establishment candidates. During the next four years he campaigned even more strenuously, assaulted the special interests even more vehemently. Louisianans loved every minute of it, and in 1928 handed him the prize he sought by the largest vote in the state's history.

Even so, the coalition of political bosses who ran Louisiana were confident they could handle him. Previous troublemakers, some even more radical-sounding than he, had been brought into tow and properly rewarded for it. What else in their view could Long want now that he was chief magistrate? He too could look forward to riches and a happy retirement as head of a large Shreveport law firm. And he was only 35 years old!

To everyone's astonishment he set about carrying out his promises. He was, in office, more aggressively insurgent than before.[64] During his first year as governor he got the legislature to distribute free textbooks to school children, build roads in small towns and rural areas, and bring natural gas by pipeline to New Orleans (this over the frantic objection of the local politicos). To help pay the cost of these programs a tax was imposed on the state's oil producers. To ensure that it was faithfully administered he staffed the regulatory bodies with his own followers. In the meantime, he demonstrated another talent: a tremendous capacity for leadership, especially in the thick of battle, when decisiveness and quick thinking and cool judgment count most. In those moments he was a fury, a whirligig of activity. Though he infrequently slept, he was always fresh, always coming up with new and daring ideas. And always he managed to bring the public, *his* public, into the deliberation. He had his own communications network, a system of delivering broadsides (short, pithy statements akin to stump speeches), by the hundreds of thousands across the state that same day. He worked with Napoleonic verve and speed and efficiency. He was more than a match for all his adversaries combined.[65]

Yet they might have been reluctant to challenge him to a fight *a outrance* had he been less intent on creating a political machine completely independent of them and entirely obedient to his will. Nor could they doubt that time was on his side, that the masses were with him, that, in a word, unless they ousted him immediately he would oust them eventually. That was why his adversaries strove so resolutely to bring him down in the spring of 1929. They really had no choice.[66]

His victory did indeed sound their death knell—those among them who persisted in opposing him. To those who wished to join him he extended a welcoming hand. His standing with the masses was higher than ever. Even in the Catholic parishes and in New Orleans, where he had been weakest, his favored candidates for elective office usually won and the candidates he fought usually lost. At the same time, his machine was devouring most of the appointive offices, giving him not only a vast army of loyalists but a steady flow of money (office holders and companies doing business with the state having to kick back a percentage of their earnings), the lubricant that kept the machine in sound running order. But even as he went from one victory to another Long never allowed himself to forget that his organization existed in the first place because it effectively delivered the goods to the plain people of Louisiana and saved them from the familiar predators.

In calling himself "the Kingfish"—after the character in the immensely popular *Amos 'n' Andy* radio show about Negro roust-abouts—Long was announcing a simple fact. He was the boss of Louisiana, and to all appearances invincible while he remained in office.

Unable by law to succeed himself, Long became United States Senator in 1930, easily defeating the incumbent (whom he had helped elect), two years before his gubernatorial term ended. He had a problem, however. The lieutenant-governor, Paul Cyr, once his crony, had become his blood enemy, a leader in the impeachment move against him. So fierce was the ill will they felt toward each other that Long dared not leave the state, even for a moment, lest Cyr, in his absence, legally assume the governor's power. The whole affair was very amusing, another case of Huey's high jinks, and never more so than when Cyr declared, on the day Long was to take his Senate seat, that he, Cyr, was henceforth the governor and swore himself in (prompting many Louisianans to swear themselves in as well). Nothing came of the joke beyond Cyr's sudden demise.* Long then handpicked his own man (O. K. Allen, a nonentity) to succeed Cyr and safely journeyed to Washington early in March 1932. Not since Robert M. La Follette the elder entered the Senate in 1906 after setting Wisconsin afire did so much notoriety and fascination surround a newly elected occupant of that august body. And, like La Follette, he did not disappoint his public.[67]

Long paid serious attention to Franklin D. Roosevelt for the first time in 1931, soon after Roosevelt's smashing victory made him a presidential candidate. What Long saw from a distance hardly impressed him, however: a typical eastern Democratic stick-in-the-mud, a conservative in the tradition, broadly speaking, of such New Yorkers as Grover Cleveland, Alton Parker, and John W. Davis. It was when Roosevelt and Al Smith publicly fell out, when Roosevelt gave his "forgotten man" speech, with its egalitarian overtones, its vague intimation of class conflict—that Long decided to join most of the Democratic South and West in backing Roosevelt for the nomination, the least undesirable of the available candidates. Otherwise, Roosevelt meant nothing to him.

Roosevelt and his political advisers, Jim Farley and Louis M. Howe, were pleased to have Long in their corner. Every convention vote counted, and Long controlled six of them. But in this as in everything Long was also a problem. The Roosevelt people had to take him as he was or not at all.

For one thing, there was the question of the Louisiana delegation. Long's enemies, hoping to cut a deal with any of the presidential candidates who could offer them one, sent a rival group to the Chicago convention. They maintained that Long had rigged the delegate election. On the face of it, however, his delegation appeared to be the

---

* Under Louisiana law the president pro tem of the state senate became lieutenant-governor when the lieutenant-governor left office. According to Long, Cyr vacated the office in the act of swearing himself in. The president pro tem, one of Long's henchmen, promptly took possession of it, and Cyr suddenly found himself without a job.

more representative one, containing as it did both U.S. Senators, the governor, the mayor of New Orleans, all of Louisiana's Congressmen, and many members of the state legislature. But which delegation would be seated depended ultimately on who ran the credentials committee, and it was universally acknowledged that the Roosevelt forces were in command of it. To liven the proceeding up a bit, and mock the interlopers, Long brought along to Chicago yet a third delegation, "the Unterrified Democrats," as they styled themselves, all unknowns, who pledged to fight for the inclusion of the gin fizz (a New Orleans Prohibition drink) in the party platform. Long's clowning was often gross; it was never without a purpose: he made sure he would have plenty of reserve toughs on hand.[68]

At the convention, Long, true to his reputation, played the *enfant terrible*. He was at the center of the shouting and pushing, sometimes with fisticuffs, and generally the horsing around, that went on in the section reserved for the Louisiana contingent. His antics, the presence especially of "the Unterrified Democrats," did not exactly sit well with the Roosevelt people, who feared that he would turn the convention into a joke, a national theater of which he was star performer.[69]

But at the propitious moment Long showed the convention his other persona. The clowning and levity ceased when he spoke for the seating of his delegation. He presented a straightforward, factual, well-reasoned argument that, said Roosevelt's floor manager, Jim Farley, "some thought was the best of the debate" and may have contributed to the strong committee vote in his delegation's behalf.[70]

On another matter he inadvertently brought Roosevelt plenty of trouble. Because a Democratic presidential convention rule required that a nominee get two-thirds of the votes, a determined, disciplined minority had often defeated a candidate who otherwise carried most of the delegates with him. Roosevelt believed Al Smith's followers might constitute such a minority. So he and his lieutenants toyed with the idea, which had been around for decades, of getting the convention to change the rule to a simple majority. They had to tread very carefully, however. Roosevelt did not want to leave the impression that he would discard a venerable tradition because it inconvenienced him. He might back an effort to abolish or modify the rule if it could be done circumspectly, without offending friends and allies. He preferred to keep the issue in the background.

He failed to reckon with Huey Long. The story, as Farley and others tell it, went as follows. Just before the convention got under way Farley called a secret meeting of 65 pro-Roosevelt politicians, among them Long, to hear their views on whether the two-thirds rule should be brought to the floor, for it was already common knowledge that Roosevelt could not win on the first ballot. There is no record of the discussion. There is only a description of what happened when Long, shedding his jacket, argued for straight-out abolition. It was, writes Farley, a "stem-winding, rousing stomp speech that took his listeners by storm." He "went over with [such] a terrific bang," Farley thought he had enough votes on the floor to institute the change.[71] Within hours the convention and the press had learned of what transpired in the room, and a tempest of opposition rose up, with Al Smith in the lead, claiming that Roosevelt was trying to change the rules in the middle of the game, proving again how untrustworthy he was.

Roosevelt moved quickly to prevent further damage. He stated in person his intention to leave the two-thirds rule alone. "I decline to permit either myself or any friends to be open to the accusation of poor sportsmanship or to the use of methods which could be called, even falsely, those of a steamroller." He could not have been speaking of his friend Huey Long, though.[72]

Long was on the telephone to Roosevelt when the convention began with advice on how to "clinch" the nomination. This was the first time they had spoken to each other. Long, or "the Kingfish," as he introduced himself, did most of the talking. He advised Roosevelt to announce that if elected President he would at once pay Great War soldiers their bonuses, this being the demand of the thousands of veterans, the "bonus army," then encamped in Washington, D.C. Roosevelt said he could not do that because he, like President Hoover, opposed the bonus as recklessly inflationary. Inflation, the cheapening of the value of the dollar, was exactly what Long sought, this apart from the desirability of giving pocket money to millions of Americans, many of them destitute and jobless. "Well," Long said before hanging up, "you are a gone goose."[73]

Still, he remained one of Roosevelt's staunchest allies, performing yeoman labor for him in the convention—labor that more than redeemed the excesses he committed over the two-thirds rule. He was instrumental in seeing to it that two neighboring delegations, those from Mississippi and Arkansas, stayed in the Roosevelt camp after the first two ballots. A defection or two might have cost Roosevelt either or both delegations. And if they abandoned him others of the Deep South might have followed suit, such being the fragility of the Roosevelt coalition. Its ability to keep intact through the next ballot enabled his men to arrange the deal with John Nance Garner that carried the convention on the fourth ballot. Perhaps Roosevelt owed less to Long than Long claimed— full responsibility for the nomination—but he owed him something, in fact a great deal. Long put it down in his mighty ledger book of obligations outstanding.[74]

Long insisted on campaigning throughout the country from the rear of his own train, authorized and paid for by the Democratic National Committee. Farley refused to allow it, concealing from Long the real reason for doing so, which was that Long would have taken much of the play away from Roosevelt, who was also scheduled to campaign by train, and made himself the center of attention. Long flew into a rage when told. "I hate to tell you, Jim, but you're gonna get licked. . . . Hoover is going back into the White House, and that's all there is to it. I tried to save you, but if you don't want to be saved, it's all right with me."[75]

Part of Roosevelt's quandary was that he could not afford to alienate Long. Some place had to be found for him. Ideally, he should have been sent to work the southern and western states. But he was kept away from them, and the reason why is itself a vintage Huey Long tale.

As noted, he had wasted little time before making his impress on the Senate floor. His maiden speech of March 18, 1932, was a slashing attack on the "reactionaries" in both the Democratic and Republican parties who, in his words, "do not want the question of the concentration of wealth to be considered, who do not want the question of the gift tax to be considered, who do not want the question of higher taxes on the higher incomes to be considered."[76] Everyone in the chamber knew that he meant the Democratic Senate leaders, all of them fellow Southerners, the most respected and oldest members of the upper house in fact, men accustomed to deference, especially from young *arrivistes*. Long's reputation had preceded him, but they were surprised by the depth of his contumaciousness, or, as they preferred to interpret it, his disrespect for the hallowed institution in which they sat.

His conflict with the Senate "reactionaries" turned into open warfare a month later during the Senate debate over a new revenue bill, Long having proposed that the government confiscate incomes of more than a million dollars a year and inheritances of more than five million dollars. His amendment and accompanying remarks received a fair amount of publicity. He might be laughed off the stage: it was hard for most people to reconcile his clownishness, his radicalism, and his lust for power. But it was all too apparent that Americans were becoming more and more restless, the Depression having entered its third year and getting worse, that the revolutionary left, Communists and Socialists both, were growing in numbers and seeking to catch the burgeoning discontent. America, it could be said, was Louisiana writ large, and no one understood this more clearly than Huey Long.

Senate Majority Leader Joseph Robinson, Democrat of Arkansas, mainstay of the "reactionaries," the very embodiment of Senate decorum,[77] attempted a dangerous thing: he engaged Long in open combat. Not only did Robinson condemn Long's amendment as pure demagoguery, an appeal to class war, he had some fun at the expense of "the great actor from Louisiana." Robinson said he never resented Long's remarks because he realized that Long "must do something extraordinary, make some unusual display of himself, in order to have that publicity and notoriety which is his due." He, Robinson, had not the slightest objection "to being the target of an attack by such a handsome and spectacular figure." And so on and on went the contemptuous ribbing, with Long joining in the general laughter.[78]

A few days later the *Chicago Tribune* ran a cartoon showing Robinson with an American flag (at an angle which omitted the stars) protecting America from Long, seen cowering behind his red flag. The caption read, "Huey Long, new Senate radical." The cartoon gave Long his opportunity in a retaliatory speech delivered before a packed house. Why, he asked, were the stars on the American flag missing? Because, he said, each of them stood for a special interest which Robinson's Little Rock law firm represented, and he proceeded to name each of those interests, many of them tied to, or serving as the agent of, corporations headquartered in New York and other northern cities. Here, Long continued, was incontestable proof of his point, which was that Robinson and the rest of the Democratic high priests were in league with President Hoover and powerful corporate interests. It reminded Long of the salesman he once knew back home who used to sell two brands of patent medicine: "high pop-a-lorum" and "low pop-a-hirum." That, he concluded, "is the only difference that can be found in what is coming out now from the leadership of the Democratic side here under the distinguished Senator from Arkansas, akin in head, akin in kind, alike in purpose and intent and results—the same as Hoover has proposed and does propose. . . . The only difference is the name."[79]

Long soon after gave Robinson the scare of his life. In the broiling summer of 1932 Long spent a week campaigning in Arkansas for Mrs. Hattie Caraway, widow of a popular U.S. Senator who had died the year before. The governor had appointed her on the understanding that she would give way to one of the professional politicians when election time arrived. She was Long's devoted Senate follower, and at his urging decided to run in the primary against two of Arkansas' best-known Democrats. Her rebelliousness was universally believed to be an exercise in futility. Long obviously believed differently because in those seven days before the election he traveled 2,100 miles to deliver 39 speeches before some 200,000 people, a feat which only he could have pulled off. The results were amazing. Hattie Caraway not only ran first, itself an incredible upset, she won by a landslide. To be accurate, Long won by a landslide. The beast was inside the gates of Arkansas, and the question was, which state would be next, which political machine overthrown.[80]

We can see, then, why Roosevelt had to keep his distance from Long during the presidential race; that is, keep Long far away from the southern oligarchs and their territories. As President, Roosevelt would have to depend on those oligarchs, those committee chairmen, like them or not, for his legislation. It was their sensitivities Jim Farley had in mind when he had Long campaign only in carefully designated areas of the country—the northern cities, for example. Long, amused by the fuss, did as he was asked, but in his own fashion of course. He put on a show wherever he went, attracting large crowds, speaking the language of the urban masses almost as persuasively as he spoke the language of the rural masses. He thus alerted the Roosevelt team to the danger ahead. "We never again underestimated him," Farley wrote.[81]

So, it can be assumed, Roosevelt was prepared when Long showed up at Hyde Park to join the Roosevelt family and their friends for lunch. It was their first face-to-face meeting. For the occasion Long wore a loud pongee suit, orchid-colored shirt, and pink tie. Roosevelt's mother, Sara Delano Roosevelt, reportedly whispered loud enough for everyone to hear, "Who is that *awful* man sitting on my son's right?"—having, she might have added, such a friendly, animated conversation with him. If Long heard Mrs. Roosevelt—presumably he did—it did not appear to faze him; he had heard worse said about him, though probably never from such a distinguished person.[82] And we may further surmise that Long wanted to elicit precisely such a response from the nobility, to seem outlandish, a comic figure, a country rube, a walking stereotype—all the things he definitely was not. That he usually dressed as conservatively as anyone in his position normally did is amply borne out by photographs of him taken then and earlier. None of those photographs, in fact, resemble the "awful man" with his strange attire who visited Hyde Park. Why did he do it? To confuse his adversaries, actual or potential, by establishing a false impression? To demonstrate his authenticity, the pride he felt in his region and class? To draw people out, induce them to lower their guard, encourage them to reveal more of themselves, the better to surprise and overwhelm them at the right instant, when the other Huey Long suddenly sprang out of the closet? Whatever the possible answers, this much can be asserted: he came in disguise in order to take Roosevelt's measure; he was a master of dissimulation.

Long was also reported to have said afterwards: "I like him. He's not a strong man, but he means well. But by God, I feel sorry for him. He's got even more sons-of-bitches in his family than I got in mine."[83] He might very well have said this, or something close to it. Though who he could have meant by "sons-of-bitches" is unclear. No one in Roosevelt's family was known to oppose Roosevelt. Everyone in Long's own family except his wife and kids publicly opposed *him* at one time or another. As we noted, Roosevelt often struck people, including those who knew him well, as a rather shallow man, affable and cheery and lacking definition, who might not be up to the awesome responsibilities facing him. Roosevelt, in sum, was at least as clever as Long—cleverer even in his ability to manipulate his persona and see through Long's.

In one important respect Roosevelt had the clear advantage. His political career, including his tenure in office, gave scant insight into what kind of national leader he would be. Long, no matter how cunningly he tried to conceal his true self, how disarming his behavior, how clownish, was the same man who had single-handedly made a revolution in Louisiana and was running the state with an iron hand. *That* was the immense fact against which, willy-nilly, *he* was measured. *That* defined his persona.

So, in the end, Long may have erred doubly in his encounter with Franklin D. Roosevelt a few weeks before the election—by overvaluing his power to dissemble and undervaluing Roosevelt's.

THE FIRST NEW DEAL

FATHER COUGHLIN

Adulation would not be too strong a word to describe Coughlin's feelings toward Roosevelt in the extraordinary first year of the New Deal. Reading Coughlin's sermons and his letters to the White House one has the impression that he ascribed miraculous powers to Roosevelt, that he saw in Roosevelt's presence at such a critical instant in American history, and indeed the world's, the guiding hand of Providence.[1] Coughlin's saying, "Roosevelt or ruin," rang like a church bell across America. Everything Roosevelt did, beginning with his inaugural speech,[2] seemed to thrill Coughlin, calling forth his most fulsome compliments. Touched by the godhead, Roosevelt could do no wrong; he was perfection itself.

The adulation did not necessarily compass every New Deal law or every member of the administration. Distressing to Coughlin were several of the men who served Roosevelt, chief among them such prominent Jewish bankers and financiers as Henry Morgenthau Jr. (in the Treasury Department no less), James P. Warburg, and Bernard M. Baruch. Coughlin wondered out loud if one set of money-changers—Roosevelt's own celebrated metaphor—had been cast out of the temple only to make room for another. Coughlin sharply criticized the government policy of destroying farm commodities in order to raise their prices.

Nor did he care for such budget-cutting measures as reducing the salaries of federal employees (the Economy Act), and he wanted the administration to go much further than it did to promote inflation through monetary reforms (about which more later).

But always he carefully exonerated Roosevelt himself from blame. The money-changers infected the whole political system after all, and Roosevelt, he felt, had no choice but to work in and through one of its bastions, the Democratic Party. What accounted for Roosevelt's greatness in Coughlin's adoring eyes was the extent of his break with precedent, his ability to set a process of change in motion which was bound to carry a momentum of its own. And Roosevelt in his estimation showed a good deal of courage in appointing such an unusually large number of Catholics to high places. This was another break with precedent, redeeming some of the wrongs committed in the 1928 election.[3]

Roosevelt could not avoid feeling uneasy over Coughlin's strangely excessive enthusiasm. Coughlin bodied it forth, cloyingly, in his weekly broadcasts and deluged the White House with his notes, letters, telegrams, calls, all congratulating the "Boss" for a job splendidly done, or urging the "Boss" to push this or that law, policy, favor, appointment, and so on. He was going on the assumption that a deep intimacy, a unique rapport, a special relationship, existed between himself and the President. And he took Roosevelt's unwillingness to say anything to the contrary as approval, hence as authorization to persist in the fawning and flattery. One can argue that Coughlin was unconsciously setting up a situation calculated to bring on a crisis with his idol and that Roosevelt for his part was willing to let it happen. For Roosevelt understood that he was not and never could be the leader Coughlin esteemed so highly and embraced so passionately. Coughlin's adulation was reducing him to an object—someone deemed worthy of infinite praise, someone who was expected to conform to an absolute standard established for him by others. This reduction by exaltation was implied in every word from Coughlin to and about the "Boss."

We are reliably told that Roosevelt had never cared for Coughlin and had regarded him as a rabble-rouser of dangerous potential early on in their acquaintanceship. Nonetheless, Roosevelt had believed he could "tame" Coughlin, on the theory that wild colts often make the best horses.[4]

Now Roosevelt easily could have tamed Coughlin as long as Coughlin remained only a general irritant, a moralist who confined his denunciations to international bankers, or bankers as such, a group defended by scarcely anyone in those sullen years of the Depression. But Coughlin set about educating himself in monetary and fiscal matters and quickly arrived at concrete positions. His intellectual habits insured that those positions hardened into dogmas, or divinely sanctioned panaceas. His standards for judging Roosevelt's performance accordingly became more exacting and precise. Inevitably they meant conflict.

Coughlin's first panacea, which he adopted late in 1932, was the devaluation of the dollar, this to be achieved by jettisoning the gold standard and doubling the price of gold (from \$20.67 an ounce to \$41.34). Devaluation, Coughlin thought, would immediately throw more money into circulation, reduce debts, and lower the price of American exports. Roosevelt, partly to assuage the powerful and ever-expanding easy-money interests in and out of Congress, effectively came around to Coughlin's view. In his first year in office, acting under the sweeping mandates of the Emergency Banking Act, the Agricultural Adjustment Act, and the Gold Reserve Act, Roosevelt did take the United States off the gold standard, did buy millions of ounces of gold at inflated prices, thereby putting so much more money into circulation, and did lower the gold content of the dollar to an incredible \$59.06.[5] Coughlin congratulated Roosevelt on these measures, not least because, as noted, they lost him the support of so many conservatives.[6]

Neither Roosevelt's deeds nor Coughlin's dogmas brought the desired results, however. The cheapened dollar failed to appreciably increase new orders for American industrial and agricultural goods. The only relief for indebted farmers and small businessmen continued to come from direct federal subsidies and other forms of intervention in the market. The administration's hopes for a "commodity" or "reflated" dollar went aglimmering.

Coughlin's next panacea was the re-monetization of silver, that is, the use of it alongside of, or better yet, instead of, gold to undergird the dollar. Roosevelt balked at this hoary old Populist scheme, which he regarded as a shameless giveaway to the silver interests and speculators, with no compensating benefits to the rest of society. The strength of those interests was made clearer when, by overwhelming vote, Congress added a silver buying, or re-monetizing, feature to the Agricultural Adjustment Act of 1933. Roosevelt in the end could accept that feature because he also possessed the right to implement it as he saw fit. Since he needed the backing of Congressmen from the mountain states he found himself retreating steadily in the face of their demands. Coughlin was their strident and irrepressible voice. "The god of gold must be destroyed," he would say. "Our money must be nationalized! Our currency must be nationalized! Our silver must be restored!"[7] In December 1933 Roosevelt agreed to buy all the silver mined in the United States at a price one-third higher than the going world rate.

This seemed to make no difference either. Money was as scarce as ever; small farmers were being wiped out as relentlessly as ever; the debts were as monstrous as ever. Accordingly, in direct opposition to Roosevelt's wishes, the Dies-Thomas bill, vigorously urged on by Coughlin, made its way through Congress. It proposed that the government buy tremendous quantities of silver—between $1.6 billion and $4 billion worth a year (an astronomical sum then)—at 25 percent above the world price. Roosevelt could do nothing to stop the momentum of the bill.

As a last resort the administration tried a drastic expedient, and a potentially dangerous one. Every day between April 24 and April 27, 1934, the Treasury Department issued a list of those who held shares of silver and stood therefore to profit should the Dies-Thomas bill pass as written.[8] The biggest benefactions would of course go to the biggest holders: the speculators and mining companies. And among these the single most publicized name was that of "A[my] Collins, Royal Oak, Michigan," owner of a half million ounces. Royal Oak, as everyone knew, meant Father Coughlin, Amy Collins being the figurehead secretary-treasurer of the Radio League of the Little Flower (who, stretching the truth to its outer limits, said her chief had no control over the League's finances). Coughlin's interest in silver, widely heralded, called into question his motives, to say the least, and he was compelled to defend himself from an army of critics.[*]

He maintained that he was no speculator but someone whose philosophical commitment to silver led him to purchase and keep the metal, irrespective of price. He had nothing to apologize for, in other words. It was Secretary of the Treasury Morgenthau who, with his "Jewish cohorts," had everything to apologize for, he asserted. He referred to silver as "gentile," implying—he could not be more explicit without saying so—that gold was Jewish. Silver, by further implication, was the source of society's nourishment and growth, while gold, like the typical Jewish banker, was alien, inorganic, a lethal presence. Coughlin wanted to know if the Roosevelt administration was choosing the latter over the former. Not Roosevelt, to be sure, but his underlings. Were they part of the international banking conspiracy?[9]

He was by now beginning to have doubts about Roosevelt too. The adulation was losing its force. Coughlin was coming to feel like a lover who realizes he is being strung along. Some writers trace that feeling back to a well-advertised speech he gave in Roosevelt's defense in November 1933 at the New York Hippodrome on Sixth Avenue.[10] The administration greeted it with total silence, the "Boss" sending Coughlin not a single word of praise. Roosevelt may have hoped Coughlin would draw the appropriate conclusions from this show of indifference, this subtle reproof. What is clear is that by early 1934 Roosevelt, having incurred the enmity of the pro-gold and hard-money interests, having been severely stung by the conservative faction of the Democratic Party, wished to draw back; above all, he did not wish to be seen as an ally of Coughlin and Huey Long and the wild agrarians of the West. He was attempting to establish a more cautious and reserved and distant friendship with the priest, one based on a

---

[*] Publishing the list, it should be added, did Roosevelt little good. In the end he had to accept the main components of the Dies-Thomas bill, passed in June 1934 as the Silver Purchase Act. And "A. Collins" did make a killing.

commitment to broadly similar goals rather than to this or that program or course of action. But, having invested so much in Roosevelt, Coughlin could not settle for such a modest, low-key arrangement. Neither by temperament nor moral theology did he recognize a state somewhere between grace and perdition. He pictured the world in garishly contrasting colors, not in shades of gray.[11]

Shortly after the silver issue was resolved Roosevelt cast about for ways to neutralize Coughlin. He had the Justice Department look into the status of Coughlin's citizenship, Coughlin having been born and raised in Canada. Coughlin, he was told, could not be touched: his father had remained an American citizen while living in Canada all those years. Roosevelt wondered if Coughlin's radio stations could somehow be pressured. The answer was a flat no. Roosevelt asked whether the church hierarchy might be persuaded to silence the priest, a few of the American cardinals, Mundelein of Chicago in particular, being very sympathetic to Roosevelt and the New Deal. The answer again was no. The cardinals might, and sometimes did, condemn Coughlin, none more vehemently than Cardinal O'Connell of Boston.[12] But they had no power over him. Only his own bishop, Michael Gallagher, had that power, and Bishop Gallagher supported Coughlin to the hilt.

By now—the fall of 1934—Coughlin sensed that the White House was hostile territory, this despite the fact that its wily and elusive occupant was as cordial to him as ever. Absent from Coughlin's messages to the "Boss" was the familiarity and bonhomie that once characterized them.

Coughlin's obsession with "gentile silver" gave way to a new idea: the creation of a government-owned national bank to replace the Federal Reserve Bank, the instrument, in his view, of international and New York plutocrats. Coughlin, articulating an age-old agrarian dream, favored the establishment of a publicly run institution that would lend money directly to needy individuals at easy rates of interest, its object being to put capital at their disposal rather than enrich the "Shylocks," whose contribution to society might be compared to parasites which destroy their hosts. This people's bank, as Coughlin envisioned it, would be answerable only to Congress and to the directors, 48 of them, one from each state of the union.[13]

Though Roosevelt was bent on reforming the Federal Reserve Bank, cutting the umbilical cord that tied it to the big banks of New York, Boston, and Philadelphia (Coughlin's criticism being accurate on this score), he never considered administering a truly drastic remedy. In fact, the bill Roosevelt's assistants later drew up was calculated to prevent exactly that kind of remedy from going before Congress—the same Congress that voted for the Silver Purchase Act. It was the bankers who proved to be Roosevelt's best allies in the struggle. By attacking any further government controls over rates of interest, money supply, and open market procedures—these were to be embodied in the Banking Act of 1935—the bankers caused many Congressmen in both houses to side with Roosevelt, who might otherwise have taken up Coughlin's proposal when it came before them in the form of the Nye-Sweeney bill. As it was, the Nye-Sweeney bill lay buried under an avalanche of nays.[14] It was the last of his panaceas.

It had become obvious to Coughlin that specific measures provided no answers to the problems he was addressing. For one thing, those that were tried, the dollar devaluation and the silver purchases, for example, hardly worked as planned. And for another, they were offered out of sympathy for the administration, in the belief that they would help Roosevelt and the New Deal succeed; it was, after all, "Roosevelt or ruin." But now that Coughlin and the administration were increasingly at odds with each other, he adopted a fresh approach, a more comprehensive alternative, should the demand for it arise.

From Coughlin's standpoint it was just as well perhaps that he and Roosevelt were beginning to fall out. He had every reason to assume that Roosevelt might be a liability in the future. Roosevelt seemed to be floundering, overwhelmed by events. The labor troubles that broke out with such violence in the spring and summer of 1934 portended class war: the division of America into horrible extremes, the plutocrats and their blacklegs on one side, the Communists and their sympathizers on the other. And so Coughlin decided that he would have to step into the breach with a mass organization of his own, an organization which would serve as a shaping force in American politics, the equivalent—though one must not carry the analogy too far—of the vanguard movements of both left and right that had done so well in Europe and were starting to do well in this country too. The organization he had in mind, he announced on November 11, 1934, was "a group of citizens not only dissatisfied with the sham policies existing in America, but anxious for a cleansing of both political parties," citizens contemptuous of the "regimented poverty of Communism" and the "created poverty of Capitalism" both. Thus was born on that day the National Union for Social Justice (NUSJ).[15]

With the announcement came a 16-point summary of how the NUSJ would purge America clean. Of the 16 only 2 could be called concrete: that "public necessities," namely "banking, credit and currency, power, light, oil, natural gas, and all other natural resources," should be nationalized, and that the government had a "duty" to protect labor unions "against the vested interests of wealth and intellect." The remaining points were restatements of platitudes, drawn from papal encyclicals on social justice, such as the natural right of private property, "liberty of conscience," the responsibility of the state for the poor, the rich having "ample means of their own to care for themselves." Or they were so vague and amorphous one could interpret them as one chose: for example, that "every citizen willing to work and capable of working shall receive a just and living annual wage which will enable him to maintain and educate his family according to the standards of American decency," that taxes should be based more broadly on "the ownership of wealth and the capacity to pay," that government should be simplified, that in the event of war, "if there should be conscription of men, there shall be a conscription of wealth," and so on and on.

The lack of concretion was deliberate. Coughlin was attempting to catch all discontented Americans, but mainly those who owned or wished to own some property, those who, trapped by large and powerful interests, feared they would lose the little they still had and end up as mere proletarians, or worse. He was, in other words, going to build an organization mostly on middle- and lower-middle-class feelings of resentment and anger, feelings that transcended regional, ethnic, and religious differences.[16]

With the formation of the NUSJ Coughlin served notice on Roosevelt that he would henceforward speak for a more potent constituency than a radio audience, though how potent was too soon to say. The NUSJ structure was simplicity itself. The unit or chapter or cell could have no fewer than 25 or more than 250 members, each of whom swore "to follow the example of Jesus Christ who drove the money changers from the temple because they exploited the poor." It was to meet once a month, at which time its president, chosen by the members, would read a message from Coughlin and lead a discussion of the issues according to the 16-point formula. The units elected their own state supervisor who, however, answered to, and received orders from, one of the 12 regional heads appointed by Coughlin. The NUSJ, then, belonged to Coughlin body and spirit. He and he alone oversaw its finances and membership rolls, and, of course, its policies down to the merest detail. It was his creature, his voice, his weapon, and its simulacrum of democracy concealed that fact from no one.[17]

Meanwhile, he and Roosevelt kept up their polite and sometimes amicable exchanges. But they were eyeing each other warily now and mostly out of distrust, malice, and ill will.

HUEY LONG

Roosevelt's performance from the inaugural speech on astounded the country, particularly during the tense months of the special session of Congress which he called to pass his emergency legislation—the famous first 100 days of the New Deal. His performance above all astounded those political associates of his who could scarcely bring themselves to believe he was the Franklin Roosevelt they had known over the decades. Huey Long too must have been surprised by how expertly Roosevelt assumed the part of national Kingfish. In his ability to rally the masses, no one, Long had to acknowledge, could equal Roosevelt. And whatever lay in the back of Long's mind he was not about to challenge Roosevelt now, when America looked to Roosevelt as to a savior.

Long was a friendly critic of the New Deal, as were the other congressional radicals who found it too timid, too conservative, too solicitous of the very interests—the banks, the investment houses, the big corporations and planters, the upper class in general—that had in their view betrayed America and caused it so much suffering. Long was only one of numerous Senators from the farm and mountain states who felt that Roosevelt was appointing too many Wall Streeters to his cabinet and White House administrative positions, that he should instead seek to nationalize the large banks, replace gold and silver as the currency standard, making the dollar cheaper for debt-ridden producers, and propose a "soak-the-rich" tax for the sake of raising revenues and redistributing the wealth. This last had always been Long's pet idea, and in its behalf, as we noted, he had taken on the whole Democratic Senate leadership. He did so again in 1933, advancing the same bill to confiscate the nation's surplus private wealth. Again it was voted down, but now a score of Senators sided with him.[18] Labor, the unemployed, small farmers and businessmen, the poor—all beneficiaries of New Deal measures— had no more militant advocate than Huey Long.

His politics did not in itself trouble Roosevelt. It could even be argued that Roosevelt welcomed a certain amount of militancy on his left so that he could keep the right in line and appear all the more moderate. Senator Robinson and the rest of the conservatives who chaired the congressional committees abhorred some of the more liberal and innovative New Deal enactments—massive expenditures for unemployment relief, guarantees to workers of the right to organize unions and bargain collectively, creation of the Tennessee Valley Authority— but they also realized that the New Deal, for all its excesses, protected them from a much worse fate at the hands of the Huey Longs of America. Roosevelt of course realized what they realized, and it served his purposes to have the Huey Longs kicking up a fuss.

What troubled Roosevelt was this particular vessel of radicalism, the man himself. Roosevelt, who possessed a sixth, and for that matter a seventh, and even an eighth sense, recognized in Long a political rival, or at the least a force inside the Democratic Party and out that would be at once unpredictable and dangerous. Like Roosevelt, Long was taking to the airways to explain his positions on the issue of the day.

And while he was not as adept as Roosevelt or Coughlin in using radio as a political medium—no one was—he was very good indeed. For sheer entertainment he was unsurpassed: no one knew what he would do before the mike—sing, recite poetry, skewer an opponent, or simply deliver one of his fire-and-brimstone speeches. He had been reaching radio audiences in Louisiana as far back as 1926. He was no amateur, therefore, when he told the nation during those cataclysmic 100 days how he differed from the administration.[19] He was playing against Roosevelt's overwhelming popularity in order to enhance his own. Roosevelt, prescient sailor that he was, saw turbulent seas ahead, and he acted accordingly.

At first, Roosevelt treated Long as though Long were on probation, an unruly child who would have to be on his best behavior. For one thing, the available federal jobs—marshals, court clerks, postmasters, judges, et al.—were not going through Long's office, or were being held up unaccountably. For another, the administration was not dropping the investigation of Long's financial aides, those who collected and kept the tremendous sums of money on which his machine depended. That investigation had begun under Hoover, and it was headed by the same sleuth, Treasury agent Elmer Irey, who had successfully developed the case against Al Capone in 1931. Irey's method was to painstakingly detail the discrepancies between the amount of money the putative wrongdoer spent and the amount he reported on his tax returns. Irey had found such discrepancies in the returns of several of Long's sidekicks and had asked Hoover's Secretary of the Treasury, Ogden Mills, for permission to go ahead with the case. Mills had given it, and it thus became Roosevelt's. Long naturally assumed that Roosevelt, in payment for debts incurred, would order the whole matter dropped. But it was neither dropped nor pursued; it was left hanging. And, ominously for Long, a young, zealous federal attorney was assigned to New Orleans. Roosevelt's message—stay in line or else—was not exactly subtle.[20]

Such, then, was the backdrop of their celebrated encounter in the White House Oval Office just after the 100-day session ended. We have Jim Farley's word for what transpired, none of the others present—Long, Roosevelt, and Roosevelt's appointments secretary, Marvin McIntyre—having mentioned it, at least to our knowledge.

Without saying so, Long made it clear to Roosevelt that he was not going to capitulate, that he would continue criticizing the administration and its friends for selling out the people. His defiance was evident from his calculated show of disrespect. He had charged into the office, where Roosevelt was waiting for him, "in his usual breezy and jaunty manner," Farley writes, "nattily dressed in light summer clothes and . . . a sailor straw hat with a bright-colored band." Long contravened the established rules of behavior by keeping his hat on as he complained about the administration's unwillingness to grant him the customary rights of patronage. Farley was appalled, and the appointments secretary, watching in anger from a distance, was about to rush forward and remove the hat, when Long, in the nick of time, removed it himself. Roosevelt seemed not to mind a bit. He "leaned back in his chair, perfectly relaxed and composed. He had a broad smile on his face, which never changed for a moment. . . ." And with this cheery, unruffled aspect Roosevelt responded to Long's complaint. Only the best people, he said, would be appointed to federal offices in Louisiana; when they were, Long would certainly be consulted; and until then he could of course promise nothing. The rest of the conversation was Rooseveltian fluff to consume time.

When he left, Long told Farley, "What the hell is the use of coming down to see this fellow? I can't win any decision over him."[21] Many White House visitors were to feel or express the same sentiments.

A contest of wills is how Farley in his account interprets the episode. Farley, not exactly an unbiased observer-participant at the time, gives Roosevelt the "decision" hands down. "He was far and away the stronger man. In that test of strength which both of them recognized as such, meeting elbow to elbow and eye to eye, F.D.R. showed himself to be all backbone and brains. He had the situation in hand at all times, and his cool manner and well-chosen words and phrases had Huey fenced in completely."[22] Not for nothing was Farley once a New York state boxing commissioner.

The question Farley fails to take up is why Long entered the ring with Roosevelt at this point. Roosevelt obviously possessed formidable advantages. In addition to those already mentioned, he commanded a new army of bureaucrats that was marching into the states and administering the recently formed agencies for unemployment relief, industrial recovery, agricultural adjustment, and so on and on. And he was at the height of his popularity, the universally acclaimed hero of the hour, the leader who had restored America's self-confidence and was restoring its health. No one was more keenly aware of those advantages than Long. What Long did not know, or know yet, was whether Roosevelt would use them, and if he did, how. We can assume that Long behaved as he did, with contempt and bravado, bearding the lion in his den, in order to provoke an outburst of anger and threats. Instead, Roosevelt was all charm and smiles. The contest of wills, in other words, was fought without anyone landing a blow. Long wanted to mix it up with Roosevelt in order to get a more precise idea of who he was dealing with and how he could prepare his defenses in the future. But Roosevelt revealed nothing of his intentions.

When he did reveal them it was at a time of his choosing, namely in the months following the Oval Office encounter. And he revealed them, as was his wont, by accomplished facts, not words. Federal patronage in Louisiana was going not to the best-qualified people but to Long's enemies, the very people Long had vanquished in past struggles. Now, with Roosevelt's help, they had an invulnerable base from which to mobilize their divided legions against him. What was more, the federal prosecutor there, under direct orders from Roosevelt's man in the Treasury Department, Henry Morgenthau Jr. (soon to be elevated to Secretary), resumed the tax fraud investigation of Long's henchmen in hopes of eventually catching the Kingfish himself. Roosevelt's intentions were clear enough. What was taking place on the battlefields of Louisiana, the scene of so much carnage already, was more than a contest of wills.[23]

Now it was perfectly obvious to Roosevelt that Long could not be bested in his own fiefdom, certainly not by outsiders, however well liked they or their policies might be. On the issue of patronage, for example, Long operated from a position of great strength, all the federal jobs combined amounting to a fraction of the 25,000 or so jobs his machine handed out.[24] Few believed he could be implicated, and if implicated, convicted, of tax fraud; he was too clever. So long as the authorities did not know the whereabouts of his fabled "deduct," or cash, box, they were powerless to do anything to him. What, then, was Roosevelt's object? Quite simply, to goad or bait Long into doing something foolhardy: openly declaring war on the administration, acting the role of Thersites, ending up in the process a national embarrassment. He would be seen for what he really was, an unprincipled rowdy, a threat to the American commonwealth.

Long cursed his tormentor, saying to reporters toward the end of 1933 that the Roosevelt administration and all its works "can go to hell."[25] As for answering Roosevelt's provocation—that he would do in *his* good time and by means of *his* choosing.

The balance of advantages and disadvantages suddenly shifted in the winter of 1933-34. The correlation of forces between the two antagonists was changing; it was not what it had been only a few months before, when Roosevelt rode the crest of his golden hour.

The New Deal was slowing down, the victim of its successes. Employers, their confidence rising, were resisting the union drive, freely interpreting the provisions of the National Industrial Recovery Act to suit their interests. Workers in more and more shops were demanding that their right to bargain collectively be honored in the observance rather than the breach. Small farmers, farm tenants, and sharecroppers were complaining that the Agriculture Department was treating them unfairly, that if anything the Agricultural Adjustment Act was wiping them out. The jobless were taking to the streets in larger and larger numbers, insisting on their entitlements, not only to relief and handouts but to unemployment and old-age insurance. The spirit of discontent, it appeared, was being fed by the New Deal reforms themselves. They had inspired Americans with hope and self-respect, and the result was *heightened* insurgency, protest, and conflict. For a growing body of critics on the left and right Roosevelt too was fair game. It was a milieu more congenial to the likes of Father Coughlin and Huey Long.

Long had never doubted that the crisis enveloping America was too much for Roosevelt, that, like Hoover, Roosevelt lacked the equipment to combat it and must sooner or later be defeated by it. Long, who prided himself on his political acumen—his ability to intuit the public's mind before other politicians did and even before the public itself was conscious of what was agitating it—had no doubt that *he* could master the situation. The moment was ripening when he could bring out for all to notice the contrast between his leadership and the faltering President's. Attacked on his flanks, Roosevelt would at a minimum have to cease his adventures in Louisiana.

The literature on Long leads one to think that he sprung his Share Our Wealth plan on his henchmen in a Washington hotel room one night in February, 1934. Pencil in hand, he jotted the whole thing down on yellow foolscap pages and ordered his men to put it into operation forthwith. Here, we are told, was the incorrigible Kingfish at it again, frivolously launching a major endeavor as though it were an afterthought, a mere trifle. Nothing, of course, could be less plausible. That he wrote it in a single setting at 3 A.M. in the Mayflower Hotel is true. He usually operated that way, dashing off messages, statements, instructions, brevets, in the heat of war. He also might have invented the term "Share Our Wealth" then and there. The specific points and the structure itself might indeed have occurred to him in a fit of inspiration. But politics should not be confused with technique, ends with means. The broad concepts underlying the Share Our Wealth scheme were familiar to anyone who followed his career since the mid-1920s and listened to his speeches and debates since he came to the United States Senate. The novelty was his attempt to fashion an alternative to the New Deal—for that matter, to the whole social system—out of those well-nurtured concepts.[26]

By Share Our Wealth Long meant two things. In the first place it gave flesh to his radical agrarianism, hitherto a vague and abstract principle. The federal government, according to the formula now worked out, must guarantee the basic American "homestead"—must provide enough assistance, up to $5,000 annually, to enable each family to enjoy the necessities of life along with a home and other amenities, a car, a radio, appliances, and the like; and it must further guarantee each individual a college education (if qualified), a job, and an old-age pension, and each farmer optimum prices for whatever he produced (theoretically the basis of the Agricultural Adjustment Act). And, as he had often stated, the cost of these extraordinary measures, amounting to untold billions a year, would be borne by taxes on the rich, no inherited estate to exceed five million dollars, no annual income to exceed a million. In this way, power, like wealth, would no longer be concentrated among the privileged few but would be distributed to the masses. The Share Our Wealth motto, "Every Man a King" (Long's handiwork as well), would thus describe the American republic, but it would be a republic where, as one of the votaries put it, no one wears a crown.[27]

In the second place, the plan required an appropriate structure, a mode of organization. Otherwise it was an empty vision signifying nothing. Long accordingly called for the establishment of Share Our Wealth clubs or chapters, each consisting of a president and secretary and as many neighbors, friends, and relatives as could be induced to join it. He was fond of citing Scripture to justify the inducement. "The Lord says: 'For where two or three are gathered together in my name, there am I in the midst of them.'" Whether by "I" Long meant himself or the Lord is unclear; perhaps in his mind, and that of his devotees, they were one and the same. Members would pledge fealty to him and receive material for discussion, including the Share Our Wealth paper, *American Progress,* and a copy of his autobiography, *Every Man A King,* which detailed—in such dull and pedestrian language, with such lack of passion, as to make one wonder who the author was—the course of his fantastic odyssey through life.[28]

The clubs, if there were enough of them, would create a mighty force in the land, and he would be consulted and deferred to and above all feared. He never ceased to envisage the day when Roosevelt, properly chastened and humbled, would beg him to please stop by the Oval Office for a chat at his convenience.

Long officially announced the birth of the Share Our Wealth movement on February 23, 1934, in a nationally broadcast radio speech.

He always made excellent copy, and on this occasion the press and public had been notified that something important was in the offing. But those who expected, or counted on, a Longian display of fireworks, an acrimonious attack on Roosevelt and the New Deal, must have been disappointed, for what they heard was mostly a dry account of the Share Our Wealth idea and organization. The man now appealing to the American people for support was not the clownish apostle of negation but a responsible statesman bent on rescuing America, the present administration having failed, alas (this said more in sorrow than in anger), for want of courage, imagination, and leadership.[29]

Not even Long anticipated the response to his speech. From the next day on countless letters poured into his office from all over the country, most of them from the South and West, his own state in particular. In less than a month, according to T. Harry Williams, over 200,000 people had joined Share Our Wealth clubs, and the rate, astonishingly, showed no signs of decreasing. The emergence overnight of a movement gave proof again of Huey Long's power to seize and focus the attention of masses of people.[30]

What he intended to do with the movement was problematic, at least for the time being. Its very size and inclusiveness rendered it unwieldy for concerted action, the rapid turnover of members being a symptom of its weakness. But its existence inscribed in flaming letters Long's riposte to President Roosevelt.

Critics of course had a field day taking apart the Share Our Wealth scheme. They had no difficulty demonstrating its impracticability, its hasty and therefore sloppy arithmetic, its contradictions and inconsistencies. It was generally dismissed as hardly more than a demagogue's worthless nostrum, yet another trick by this purveyor of illusory hopes. Critics on the right condemned it as recklessly confiscatory, as communism in populist dress. Critics on the left, Communists among them, condemned it as irrelevant since it left untouched the real source of power, namely the ownership and control of the means of production.[31]

In a sense, Share Our Wealth transcended criticism or rational discourse. It was the expression, at once naive and cunningly clever, of a deep American myth—the myth of the completely independent, self-reliant man. Since the Revolution that myth had been a potent force—

there was perhaps none more potent in the life of the nation, and often, about once a generation, it gave rise to rebellion among the disaffected, the yeoman farmers, skilled craftsmen, petty entrepreneurs, professionals, and other such victims of the monopolies and special interests. Share Our Wealth was an audacious attempt to keep faith with that tradition of rebelliousness and the primal myth on which it rested.[32]

To take on Roosevelt in the coming struggle for national power Long had to be absolutely secure at home. So it was in 1933-34 that he made his machine into a remorseless juggernaut. It was a considerable achievement, and it stood as the final testament of his political genius.[33]

As usual, it was adversity that spurred him into action. In January 1934 his New Orleans opponents, the "Old Regulars," recaptured the city government. A few months later, one of his hated enemies, Jared Y. Sanders Jr., was elected to Congress. Emboldened by what they assumed was a groundswell of support for them, the anti-Long groups plotted to take over the state. Some among them plotted his assassination. This hardly surprised him. He lived in constant fear of his life and was always surrounded by bodyguards, supplemented when home by state troopers. Because the plot was very complicated, involving many and diverse players, it probably would have failed under any circumstances. As it as, he was posted on every move the conspirators made. Not only did they fail; they were routed and humiliated.

They also supplied him with a pretext for implementing his own plot, as it were. With electrifying speed he rammed through the supine Louisiana legislature a series of laws that invested him with near magisterial authority. Throughout the session he hovered about in the chambers like a shepherd tending his flock, not even bothering to maintain the illusion of due process: there were no hearings, no debates, no reading of the bills before the vote. It would be impossible here to summarize the laws that were passed. Broadly speaking, they fell under two heads. First, they enormously enlarged state power over local governments, those especially which Long was determined to subdue (such as New Orleans), and over the various and sundry regulatory commissions—utilities, taxes, licenses, and the like—which had still exercised a modicum of autonomy and therefore resistance. And second, new laws consolidated his hold on destitute Louisianans by providing them with increased benefits and social services and by doing away with the poll tax, a reform which at a stroke added tens of thousands of fresh adherents to his cause. And the one institution which had been particularly obstreperous in the past, the judiciary, also fell before his onslaught when he came to dominate the state's highest court, the court of appeals. His enemies were thus denied their last hope. Truly it could be said, according to the adage of the time, that the Kingfish had swallowed the pelican. (Louisiana is the Pelican State.)[34]

Long's Napoleonic finesse, or ruthlessness, was equal to every contingency. When bending the rules to fit his purposes did not suffice, he rewrote them. His resourcefulness knew no limits. Reading about him so many decades later one continues to be amazed at his prodigious feat.

Consider, for example, the Thomas F. Porter affair.[35] "If I owned a whorehouse," Long would say referring to this inveterate foe, "I wouldn't let him pimp for me." We have no record of what Porter thought of Long but it can be imagined. Porter, in September 1934, was running for judge of the state supreme court. The election was critically important to Long: a Porter victory meant that the court would by a bare majority be anti-Long, placing in jeopardy his whole legislative program. But Porter stood scarcely a chance. The incumbent, a faithful Long man, was too solidly entrenched in his southwest parishes. Two days before the election the incumbent betrayed Long by suddenly dying. Nor was this the worst of it. Under state law, the election automatically went to Porter. At the end of his tether, Long seriously explored the possibility of keeping the dead man's name on the ballot. This stratagem having proved unfeasible, he decided on another: a frontal assault. The district's Democratic executive committee met on the appointed day to officially certify Porter as its candidate, a routine matter. As the meeting got under way, Long, with the state's attorney general in tow, stormed into the room. The attorney general announced without explanation that the election was illegal. The committee, as though on cue, voted to hold it some three weeks later. (The chairman, who would have objected to this coup, had already been ousted.) Porter could hardly believe his eyes. Fraud and frame-up, he cried. Long's answer, accurate though irrelevant, was that Porter was "afraid to face the people." What followed was in keeping with the farcicality of the whole affair. Porter got a writ from a district judge giving him the nomination and enjoining the state from going ahead with the election. But the supreme court—the very court Porter was seeking to join—in a tie vote postponed the writ until a hearing could be held in late November, by which time of course the election would be over. So Porter had to "face the people" against an opponent handpicked by Long. Campaigning without a letup in every district village and hamlet, Long drove home the issue: an unfriendly supreme court would destroy what his program had done for the poor folks, and all his struggles would be for naught. His man, suffice it to say, beat Porter and he had his court.

Louisiana was not exactly the center of the political universe, but under Long's tutelage it had become world famous, already the subject of a growing literature. The question of definition arose, the question, that is, of where to locate the system Long had set up and where to locate Long himself on the ideological map. The informed public had a right, or rather an obligation, to discuss the question. It was, after all, an age of totalitarian systems and powerful leaders on the one hand and weak and foundering democracies on the other. Hitler, Mussolini, and Stalin had swept everything before them. Was Long cast in their mold? Or did he resemble the more benign dictators who had emerged in recent years—Salazar of Portugal, Vargas of Brazil, Dollfuss of Austria, Pilsudski of Poland, Horthy of Hungary, among others? Or was he, as Mississippi publisher Hodding Carter maintained, a "dictator sui generis"? There seemed to be no end of the definitions. Many simply labeled him an American fascist and left it at that. Hamilton Basso and Matthew Josephson called him America's version of Mussolini.[36] Roosevelt, without elaborating, regarded him as "one of the two most dangerous men in the country" (General Douglas MacArthur being the other) and went on to deplore America's apparent need for a "strong man a la Mussolini or Hitler." But then again it could be said that Huey Long did not have to go abroad to find his model. Perhaps he found it on native soil in the person of his great rival Franklin D. Roosevelt, who himself was frequently likened to Mussolini and Hitler.

Long was completely indifferent to definitions and labels. He emphatically denied that he was anything but an American democrat of Jeffersonian-Jacksonian lineage. Hitler's racism he held in contempt, and, as Williams points out, there was no discernible trace of anti-Semitism in him (several of his closest associates were Jews).[37] That he believed in white supremacy went without saying. In his attitude toward blacks he only typified the attitude of the white community at large. But, it should be mentioned, he never attempted to exploit racial, religious, or ethnic differences, all of them rooted in Louisiana culture. On the contrary, he minimized them and achieved a rare sense of unity by his singular ability to exploit class differences, by the emphasis he gave to economic issues. If he was a demagogue—on which epithet everyone could agree—he was the healthiest demagogue the South had known.[38]

Still, that first-rate journalist of the day, the "Unofficial Observer," hit the mark when he wrote in 1935 that Long "has done more than any American in the last three years to make the processes of democracy obviously ridiculous. Yet he continues to grow in power—which again shows that the great masses of people at the bottom look on the processes of government exactly as the big money crowd have always looked at them—not as desirable in themselves, but as means to the attainment of definite ends. That is why Huey is a serious threat to democracy—because he is showing how feeble the devotion to the machinery of political democracy is in comparison to the demand for economic liberty, equality and security."[39]

A sterling apostle of civil liberties or democratic morality Long definitely was not. But neither was he a fascist, nor was his system even remotely totalitarian. The right to organize groups and factions within or outside the Louisiana Democratic Party (there being no other party there except in name) was unimpeded. So was freedom of press and speech and assembly in general. His political opponents might lose their government jobs or elected office; they were never in danger of losing their lives or liberties. As for tampering with elections, a time-honored habit in the parishes, Long was no worse an offender than his rivals and predecessors. Ultimately, there was the fact that his power, immense as it was and so often ill-used, still answered to the federal constitution, was still subject, that is, to hard and fast objective limits. To be a dictator of a state it is first necessary to be the dictator of the nation.

Huey Long sprung rather from the venerable American institution of the political boss, though he occupies a special place in the history of that institution. For no boss ever relied on his own charismatic appeal so effectively as he in prevailing over his enemies, legitimizing his authority, and building a personal organization. He was unique precisely because he was so typical.

JOHN L. LEWIS

From the time he entered politics in 1911 Franklin D. Roosevelt shared the progressive belief that society had an obligation to its workers, those workers especially who were most exploited and least able to care for themselves. As New York governor he plumped for unemployment insurance and factory reform and vetoed bills which labor deemed inimical to its interests. For good reason New York trade unions treated him as a friend and the rank and file gave him their votes.[40]

But his views on unions, to the extent he bothered to think about them at all, were entirely conventional. He sympathized with the union movement, at least with its dominant conservative wing, represented by the American Federation of Labor (AFL), and certainly wished it well in its tug-of-war with capital. Roosevelt looked upon unions—to quote Frances Perkins, who was perhaps closer to him on the subject than anyone else—"as voluntary associations of citizens to promote their own interests in the field of wages, hours, and working conditions." That those citizens might also be "united to one another by unbreakable bonds which gave them power and status to deal with their employers on equal terms" scarcely occurred to him. And the possibility that some of those citizens might advocate class struggle and even a drastic change in the social system was beyond the scope of his comprehension altogether.[41]

Roosevelt might not have been an expert on organized labor, but by the time he was elected President he was as aware as any informed person about the pathetic state of the unions in America. When he served in Wilson's administration during the war they had comprised some four million members, about a fifth of the industrial work force, and they had been a formidable power in the land. By 1933 their numbers had shrunk to well under three million, and, more telling, to well under 10 percent of the work force. Their future was precarious, to say the least. Labor's fear and timidity was reflected in the stodgy, unimaginative, and parochial character of most of the AFL leaders. Babbit could have been their archetype; many of them were dyed-in-the-wool Republicans, indistinguishable philosophically from members of small-town Chambers of Commerce. Only recently, and only under the hammer blows of the Depression, had they abandoned their commitment to "voluntarism" and agreed that the government should assume some minimal responsibility for the welfare of the jobless and the poor in general. (According to the tenets of voluntarism, workers should depend on no one but themselves, winning economic benefits through their union contracts alone. Non-union workers—that is, all others—were simply out of luck.) These hidebound AFL leaders, then, had little to offer Roosevelt and they counted for little in the New Deal's genesis and development.[42]

When he took office the AFL threw its weight, such as it was, behind the Black-Connery-Perkins bill, which proposed to deal with unemployment in a quite radical way—by ordering a reduction of the work week to 30 hours. Though the business community was dead-set against the bill, Congress, desperate for an answer to the unemployment problem and the accompanying threat of social unrest, seemed determined to pass it; the Senate did so by an authoritative vote. Roosevelt, however, took another and much more moderate and comprehensive approach to recovery, one that business could support as well—or at least not oppose. And since neither organized labor nor Congress were inclined to resist Roosevelt in anything he sought during this crisis, the Black-Connery-Perkins bill gave way to the National Industrial Recovery Act (NIRA), which became law practically by acclamation on June 16, 1933, the last day of the special session. It was the centerpiece of the First New Deal.[43]

Even the most conservative union hierarch, whatever his initial misgivings, rejoiced in the NIRA because one of its main provisions, Section 7(a), explicitly guaranteed all workers engaged in interstate commerce the right to join or organize a union of their choice as their bargaining agent with their employers. Never before had the federal government actually sanctioned unionization as national policy. The AFL leaders saw the act as their deliverance, potentially at least, and the gratitude they felt toward the patrician in the White House was boundless.

Now, as they well knew, the object of Roosevelt's industrial policy was not to strengthen the union movement. It was scarcely the object of the brain trusters who drew up the act or of the man Roosevelt appointed to administer it, General Hugh Johnson. Their common object was to bring order and rationality out of the reigning industrial chaos, that is, to reverse the precipitous fall of prices and wages, the intolerably high rate of bankruptcies, the immitigable dog-eat-dog ethic that was tearing apart American economic life. The NIRA would stimulate recovery—so the Roosevelt administration hoped—by getting the segments of each industry to collaborate in establishing, and then to abide by, detailed guidelines on prices, wages, levels of production, working conditions, and allocation of markets. The whole vast enterprise was an experiment in planning that was reminiscent of, and partly modeled on, the wartime experience, complete with patriotic exordia, symbols, parades, and the like. Workers, it was thought, could best fit into this overarching scheme of things by being organized, by being drawn into institutions which would simultaneously represent and control them. The NIRA was not intended to champion the underdog.[44]

No industry cried out for help more insistently than coal. It was a case study *in extremis* of the American malaise. Since the early 1920s cutthroat competition had held sway in the fields from Pennsylvania to Alabama, from Ohio to Kansas. Most operators were on the verge of collapse. Starvation wages, for those lucky enough to find work, prevailed everywhere except in a handful of fields. The condition of the industry was reflected in the condition of the union. In 1919 the United Mine Workers (UMW) counted half a million members, making it the largest and strongest union in the country. By 1933 it had fallen to perhaps 50,000 and was hardly functioning; each local was reduced to working out its own arrangement with the mine owners. When strikes occurred the men were therefore on their own; they could expect little from the beleaguered international. Survival of the fittest, or rather *sauve qui peut,* describes what life was like in the once proud realm of "King Coal."[45]

The UMW boss, John L. Lewis, was the obvious exception to the trade union archetype described above. The other AFL leaders, from President William Green down, were modest men who had risen in their respective bureaucracies through long, patient effort and were rarely noticed outside their accustomed milieus: the shop, the office, the union hall. Lewis also performed and performed mightily in the public arena. There he was able to display his considerable gifts of oratory and repartee, his well-rehearsed and quite pretentious literary allusions, elaborate metaphors and figures, and polysyllabic words.[46] His physical appearance added to the theatrical affects. He was a large man—he stood six feet tall and weighed over 230 pounds of solid muscle, and he looked even larger than his size, thanks to his enormous head, with its thick brown hair (now flecked with gray) parted conspicuously at the middle, beetling eyebrows, cobalt blue eyes, and a massive jaw; a head, in other words, that brooked no challenge.

And he was every bit as overpowering as he seemed. Only a man of great ruthlessness and cunning could have held on to his job during those years of unrelieved decline and defeat. Since taking office in 1920 he had beaten back one foe after another because none of them was as adept as he in the arts of chicanery and deception and the uses of violence. Lewis was vain, pompous, arrogant, cruel, charming when he had to be, and much else besides.[47] He towered above his AFL brethren, and they knew it.

He too voted Republican as a matter of course and subscribed to the same theory of government that animated Harding, Coolidge, and Hoover. He was a thoroughgoing redbaiter, "red" in his lexicon being anyone who opposed him on principle, who could not be bought or intimidated or had no self-serving ax to grind.[48] But Lewis was above all a pragmatist, and he easily adjusted his beliefs and conduct to the winds of circumstance. Taking a hard, realistic look at what was happening to coal, he modified his laissez-faire convictions and boldly came out in favor of regulating the industry along the collaborative lines later set down in the NIRA. Politics aside, John L. Lewis had been ready for the New Deal years before it arrived.[49]

He saw his opportunity in Section 7(a) and he grasped it by the forelock. It was an amazing show of audacity. Exhausting what little money remained in the UMW's exchequer he sent union organizers into the mining communities of America. The men signed up en masse, partly on the assumption that Roosevelt, by now a demigod in their eyes, personally wanted them to do so. The operators must have assumed this too, for they called off the sheriffs and vigilantes and allowed the organizing to go on in peace. And so, overnight, in the early summer of 1933, the UMW unionized the mines of America, including those of "bloody Harlan," synonymous with all that was unendurably brutal in the industry. Lewis, having won his gamble, suddenly was presiding over an institution of 400,000 members, the most it had had since the war. It was all quite startling.[50]

The NIRA codes still had to be negotiated, however, and nothing in the statute compelled the mine operators to bargain with Lewis or anyone else not of *their* choosing. As a matter of fact, the codes governing practically every industry were being drawn up mainly by and in behalf of the employers. The administration went along with this arrangement, General Johnson's high command having itself come from the very businesses it was regulating. The industrial codes, in the words of a cautious scholar, were "designed to defend the position and wealth of business. Organized labor and consumers, meanwhile, had received little from codification."[51] Nonetheless, Lewis managed to best the operators. By a combination of guile, unctuous charm, and threats he got Roosevelt to side with him during the tense, drawn-out negotiations. The operators would have gladly taken on the UMW and probably would have won a fight to the finish; the men could hardly have stayed out long; the union probably would have suffered a catastrophic defeat. But the operators could not take on the President of the United States as well, a President who defined the struggle for economic recovery as the equivalent of a war against a foreign foe. So they conceded in return for government-insured stability.[52]

That Lewis had won a magnificent victory was apparent to everyone when the coal industry codes were announced on September 21, 1933. The miners had never signed a better contract. The companies agreed to deduct, or check-off, union dues from the miners' weekly pay; to provide a huge raise and a basic industry-wide scale for a 40-hour week; to no longer pay miners in scrip or force them to live in company houses and buy in company stores; to send no lad under 17 into the pits; and, not least, to set up procedures for handling grievances. The operators, said one wit, had "agreed to all the things that deputy sheriffs usually shoot people for demanding."[53] The miners themselves must have rubbed their eyes in disbelief, so swift had been the change in their fortunes: only yesterday they were alone and starving.

For Roosevelt, the ordeal of negotiation was something of a learning experience. He noticed that workers, in the midst of their pain and misery, could act together with heroic solidarity, that the union which rallied them bore a mystique of its own, one that transcended calculations of economic self-interest. It was a kind of power he had not hitherto had to take into account.

And he learned firsthand what kind of person John L. Lewis was— how far superior this mere labor chieftain was to the mine operators, and for that matter to most of the industrialists he had had to contend with.

One of Lewis's biographers, Saul Alinsky (admittedly not the most reliable of them), tells the following story. Sometime in the spring of 1933, while the NIRA was wending its way through Congress, Lewis ran into the president of the AFL, William Green, at New York's exquisite St. Regis Hotel. Green was an old comrade; he too had come up through the ranks as a coal miner. While the two men walked along the fashionable East Side streets Lewis stopped to make an important point. Something immense was about to happen, he predicted: the workers of America were soon going to be organized. It was up to the AFL to pour everything it had into the task, the chance of an epoch. Green, the embodiment of caution—it was why he served as AFL president—saw only the problems. "It was that night," Lewis said years later, "that I knew it, and knew irrevocably, that the industrial unionization . . . of the basic industries, would never come of the AFL." The next day he "began to plan the CIO."[54]

The story might be apocryphal. Then again it might be true. The only person who could have contradicted it was William Green, and he said nothing when Alinsky recounted it in 1949. Lewis could very well have been as prescient about the union movement at large as he was about the growth of his own union, and he could even have started planning his future moves while the coal industry and the UMW still lay in shambles and the NIRA was still a dream. But does it matter just when Lewis decided that he was a man of destiny or how he became convinced of it? He might have had a minor epiphany of the sort he described to Alinsky.

Prophetic Lewis might have been, but events caught him off guard, as they did everyone else. There is no indication that he expected American industrial workers to arouse themselves so quickly and forcibly from their long night of exhaustion. The nation was succumbing to strike fever, and the media were reporting daily on the incipient class war. Often, as mentioned earlier, the strikes were led or fomented by radicals of the Marxist-Leninist persuasion. The most astonishing of these broke out in the spring and summer of 1934, in Toledo, San Francisco (and other Pacific ports), and Minneapolis, and in each instance, following a long and bloody struggle, called forth a militant new union. Like other AFL bosses, Lewis did not look kindly on the prospect of welcoming these *soi-disant* revolutionaries as brothers (the new left unions being after all bona fide members of the AFL). But he had to respect their courage and their capacity for leadership in the face of unspeakable adversity. He had to acknowledge the truth: it was they, the unpalatable Marxist-Leninists, not the conservative and timorous representatives of the AFL, who were catching the insurgent spirit of the rank and file.

Meanwhile, his AFL colleagues were giving him more fundamental grounds for disappointment. The issue was the same: how to turn to good account the rebelliousness the American workers were displaying. Countless numbers of those workers were exercising their right under Section 7(a) and signing union cards. They had before them the example of the UMW and what it was accomplishing for the miners. Alas, these optimistic workers discovered soon enough the difference between the UMW and the unions they were joining. The UMW had enthusiastically taken in all workers, no questions asked, and the contracts it signed with the operators covered all of them whatever their skill or function, their race, religion, nationality, etc. The UMW was proud of its tradition as an industrial union, meaning a union that embraced the entire industry and its work force. But those who were enrolling in the other mass-production industries, in autos, rubber, steel, electric, and so on, found to their consternation that the unions had no place for them. They were shunted into receptacles created specifically for them: federal locals, so designated because they were temporarily chartered by AFL headquarters in Washington. There, in limbo, the enrollees waited for assignment to one or another of the existing craft unions, a process that could be interminable—assuming the good faith of those unions to begin with.[55]

In other words, nothing was happening. It became increasingly obvious to the workers that they were getting a runaround, that the unions had no intention of ever taking them in. What was more, they could not then form their own general, or industry-wide, unions because the AFL, which issued the authorizing charters, would not let them. The AFL leaders were not about to permit an alien and possibly hostile element into their organizations.

The crafts had always been suspicious of industrial unionism, which they equated with the revolutionary left. There was a grain of validity in that equation. Historically, the main proponents of industrial unionism had come from the left, the thread of continuity extending from the Industrial Workers of the World in the early part of the century (one could go further back) to the Communist-run Trade Union Unity League of the early 1930s. But the fact that the UMW and the two major garment unions, the International Ladies Garment Workers and the Amalgamated Clothing Workers, were industry-wide and highly centralized proved that the equation contained no more than a grain of validity. These organizations were just about as conservative as those representing plumbers, carpenters, machinists, teamsters, and the rest of the crafts. Industrial unionism, whatever its history, was now affixed to no particular ideology.

But to argue the point with the AFL hierophants was futile. Their conduct can be reduced to this melancholy proposition: better no union than one that might endanger the status quo, or, under the circumstances: better workers in limbo than in opposition and led by radicals.[56]

In self-defense the AFL could and did fall back on the letter of the law. The National Labor Board, an administrative arm of the NIRA charged with settling labor disputes (but utterly lacking the power to do so), had, in March 1934, handed down a landmark decision, approved by Roosevelt himself, stating that the workers of a given company or industry could choose several unions rather than one as their bargaining agents. This decision cut the heart out of the industrial-union principle—the principle, namely, of exclusive or majority representation in a plant or company. This triumph of the craft-union principle left things as they were. For different reasons, then, the AFL and the business community were delighted with the ruling.[57]

In practice, however, it was proving to be as ineffective as it was divisive. Not only were the large corporations able to take advantage of labor's intramural conflicts; they found more and more ways of thwarting the purpose of the law, limited as that was—firing organizers, employing spies and goons and *agents provocateurs,* establishing their own unions, so many shadows of the real thing, and if all else failed, shutting down the plants altogether. The corporations, in a word, were determined to avoid the fatal mistake of the mine operators.

Appalled by the enveloping disorder, liberals concluded that only a comprehensive new labor law—one which granted exclusive representation to workers wishing to join a union and which could be so administered as to prevent corporate sabotage of its intent—could bring labor peace and with it the promise of economic recovery. New York State's Senator Robert F. Wagner (faithful child of Tammany Hall, it will be remembered) and several other like-minded New Deal Congressmen drew up a bill and began the arduous, drawn-out process of seeing it through both houses. Roosevelt, however, gave no assurances that he would back it.[58]

It was from such conditions that John L. Lewis emerged to become the great apostle of industrial unionism in America. He demanded without respite that the AFL mount an all-out drive to "organize the unorganized," regardless of cost. The UMW, whose overflowing treasury was

his to spend, would contribute whatever was asked of it. And his stature
was so immense by now that the AFL executive council, for his sake, did
allow a resolution to go through the November 1934 AFL convention
in San Francisco which appeared to support the drive for industrial
unionism. Actually, the resolution promised nothing concrete by way of
money and resources and so left the important questions unresolved. Yet
the impression went out that Lewis had again scored a victory. It was an
impression the AFL leaders, who knew better, were unwilling publicly
to falsify. Flattering him, appealing to his outsize vanity, was their
technique for restoring him to the fold.[59]

The conflict between them turned ultimately on their reading of the
future. Lewis wagered that labor unrest would continue, the only
question being who would profit by it. In his judgment, the AFL's
procrastination meant abandoning the field to the radicals, the consequences of which he did not hesitate to point out. The AFL council
wagered that the unrest would subside and that the workers in the mass-
production industries—even those warehoused in federal locals—would
shrug off the demagogues and foreign agents who were exploiting their
felt grievances and wait patiently to be accepted into the existing craft
unions. The problem of course was, or would be, determining who won
the wager and imposing the verdict on the loser.

Roosevelt was no mere spectator to the gathering conflict. He
counted on labor support for himself and the Democratic Party in the
years ahead and wanted nothing to disrupt the integrity of the AFL. He
preferred a tranquil John L. Lewis, a team player, not a trade union
version of Huey Long and Father Coughlin, not another mass leader who
preached mass rebellion while, not coincidentally, seeking his own self-
aggrandizement. Lewis too bore watching.

AL SMITH

Most of Smith's biographers sadly note the change that came over him
from about the middle of 1933 on. His response to the New Deal, they
assert, marked a disappointing conclusion to a magnificent political life.
His attacks on government spending and on the numerous and far-
reaching experiments which Roosevelt ushered in grew more and more

querulous and petulant.[60] This despite the fact that the New Deal in many respects enlarged, on the national level and under extreme duress, Smith's own reform program as governor, a fact which he was often reminded of whenever he criticized the Roosevelt administration.[61]

In one of his more reflective, less guarded moments, Smith could sound like a New Dealer himself. "The United States, and particularly states within this country," he wrote in 1935, "have been unusually slow in coming to a realization that a government, in order to carry out its responsibilities to its people, taxpayers and otherwise, must assume a tremendous and direct responsibility for their welfare, both individual and collective."[62] Roosevelt could not have said it more pointedly.

Smith recoiled from the avalanche of government agencies, each with its appropriate initials—"alphabet soup" in his words—that descended on America.[63] He and his conservative friends might not have minded the establishment of emergency and relief offices to help the destitute. What they minded was the extent of the government commitment, its cost and duration. Smith saw an evil motive in the emergence of a gigantic federal bureaucracy: the desire for power, an insatiable desire which expands with the feeding. He could not bring himself to acknowledge that the need for federal assistance was vastly greater than anyone in government had thought possible. But never in Smith's long political experience did he have to confront life-and-death crises requiring lightning moves, each of them precedent-setting. He had been accustomed to operating cautiously, by elaborate accommodations without broadly authorized executive initiatives. There is no question that Roosevelt's behavior, along with the power he exercised, deeply offended Smith's old-fashioned sense of proprieties.

And Smith was again miffed by Roosevelt's failure to consult him about anything, though as ever they maintained the appearance of amity. Smith, according to his daughter, felt rather bitter about being left out in the cold, condemned to sit behind an uncluttered desk as the figurehead president of the Empire State Building Corporation, a venture—the leasing of office space in the recently built 102 story edifice—underwritten by Raskob and the Du Ponts.[64] But if Smith had been appointed to a position he undoubtedly would have tried to exert a conservative influence on the administration from the inside; unable to do so he would very likely have resigned, as so many early New Dealers did when they could no longer support Roosevelt's initiatives. His relations with Roosevelt might have been even more rancorous than they were.

The most rancorous of them turned on Roosevelt's monetary and fiscal measures. To Smith nothing was more reprehensible, both morally and economically, than Roosevelt's apparently cavalier attitude toward the value of the dollar and the size of the national debt. The President's zeal in appeasing Coughlin and Long and their ilk, the self-styled tribunes of the masses, constituted, according to this view, the grossest betrayal of his sworn duty to uphold the very bulwark of society, the good faith and credit of the United States of America. Smith spoke for most bankers and creditors and hard-money interests in general when he stated, in words heard across the length and breadth of America, that he stood "for gold dollars as against baloney dollars . . . experience against experiment." He sounded like the most devoted apostle of Edmund Burke, father of modern conservatism. "If I must choose between the leaders of the past with all the errors they have made and with all the selfishness they have been guilty of, and the inexperienced young college professors who hold no responsible public office but are perfectly ready to turn 130 million Americans into guinea pigs for experimentation, I am for the leaders of the past."[65]

Father Coughlin, dissatisfied as he was with the administration's timidity in devaluing the dollar and facing down the bankers, was not going to suffer such attacks on Roosevelt (who was then still his idol), particularly from fellow Catholics. Leaping into the fray with both feet, as was his wont, Coughlin accused Smith of being the puppet of J. P. Morgan, first among public enemies; specifically, of having visited Morgan's office (accompanied by two bishops, no less), in order to solicit loans for the financially strapped Empire State Building Corporation. Coughlin could not prove that Smith had actually spoken to Morgan or that he had secured the loan. But there was little Smith could do to counter the smear without worsening it. A donnybrook between left and right Catholics ensued, Coughlin's sympathizers springing to his defense, Smith's to his. Roosevelt must have enjoyed every bit of it.[66]

Smith avoided the use of such imprecations as "perfidy" and "deception" in describing Roosevelt, at least in public, but his drift could hardly be misconstrued. To certain ideological purists, Roosevelt, by his heavy spending, by his nationalization of gold and silver purchases—by his attempt, in a word, to "reflate" the economy—did commit an act of monumental betrayal. He had run for President on a platform that explicitly called for a balanced budget, to be achieved by spending cuts in Hoover's programs, and for a sound currency, bedrock of the whole free enterprise system. In his speech to the convention that nominated him, Roosevelt had said of the platform, "I accept it one hundred percent." Yet here he was, with his ever imperturbable countenance, cavalierly violating each of those sacred planks. And because Smith and the other sound-money Democrats had taken him at his word they had contributed to his election drive and campaigned and voted for him. Little did they know his character: he had duped them just as he would dupe anyone who got in his way, adding to his already excessive power.[67] Soon it would be too late for the American people. Smith was intimating dictatorship, and a leftist one at that.

So Smith agreed to join a new organization of large property holders and creditors, one designed to stop the New Deal dead in its tracks and restore the old order of things. The American Liberty League, officially launched in August 1934, consisted pretty much of Al Smith's compatriots—Raskob and the Du Ponts and others like them in oil and steel and autos and banking, men (or rather families) who could be counted on to supply whatever funds were necessary to turn Roosevelt around or, failing that, rid the Democratic Party of him and his whole crowd, not to mention the even more radical types who, if left to their devices, would convert America into another soviet republic.

Roosevelt's response was clever. He commended the Liberty League for speaking up in behalf of one of the Ten Commandments—Thou shalt not steal—an important one to be sure. He was disappointed, however, that it said precious little about another commandment, this from Jesus—Thou shalt love thy neighbor as thyself—precious little, that is, about the plight of tens of millions of fellow Americans who were down and out and looked to the federal government to save them. The nation was mortally ill and Smith and his friends were criticizing the only doctor in attendance. They looked out on the world and judged it according to the quotations on the stock and bond and real estate markets.[68] Roosevelt's implication was clear: Al Smith, beloved of old, had gone "Wall Street."

CHARLES A. LINDBERGH

In the winter of 1933 the United States Senate, with little fanfare, established a special committee to investigate Post Office contracts with airline and steamship companies. The Senate did so because charges were being noised about that President Hoover's Postmaster General had been granting lucrative favors to those companies. The hearings that followed did not exactly enthrall the public; it had other things on its mind during that first critical year of the Roosevelt administration.

The public's interest picked up when the committee began hearing sensational testimony from a reporter whose discoveries—until then suppressed by his employer, the Hearst newspaper empire—had brought the scandal into the open. It was he who found that the Postmaster General had, without competitive bidding, authorized air-mail contracts with the three largest airlines, giving them a virtual monopoly of the business. The trail led the committee directly to Wall Street, where the airlines were headquartered, providing further evidence of the collusive arrangement between the previous administration and the big banking interests. Aviation, said committee chairman Hugo Black, "has ruthlessly taken over from the men who could fly and bestowed upon bankers, brokers, promoters, and politicians." James Farley, Roosevelt's Postmaster General, claimed that the airlines in question had, since 1929, fleeced the government of $46 million. Something drastic, obviously, had to be done.[69]

On February 6, 1934, after consulting with the Senate committee, his cabinet and the Army, President Roosevelt canceled the existing contracts and ordered the Air Corps to carry the mails until further notice. Here was another example of how Roosevelt was using the power of his office to check the rapacity of the special interests. It was, to judge from his popularity, exactly what America wanted him to go on doing.[70]

Criticism of the move came from an unanticipated source— Charles A. Lindbergh, the world-famous "Lone Eagle," the first person to fly non-stop across the Atlantic. On February 11 Lindbergh sent Roosevelt a scathing telegram, which he made sure would be headlined the next day, accusing the President of rash and irresponsible behavior: of acting unfairly, nay, indecently, by condemning "the largest of our commercial aviation without just trial" and failing to "discriminate between innocence and guilt," and of risking the destruction of "the finest commercial airlines in the world." Lindbergh was arguing that the well-being of the country depended on the well-being of the private airlines and that the well-being, or rather existence, of those airlines in turn depended on government subsidies. He went on to predict dark consequences. Because the Army Air Corps was unequipped for the task, so he claimed, its pilots would be subject to tremendous risk. Lindbergh felt so strongly about this issue that he decided to directly challenge Roosevelt and in doing so put his enormous prestige on the line.[71]

He was not, however, in a very advantageous position himself. The committee hearings had brought out the extent of Lindbergh's own pecuniary stake in the welfare of the airlines. As technical consultant for Transnational Air Transport Corporation, one of the chief mail carriers, he had received 25,000 shares of stock, equivalent to $250,000 (which would be reckoned in the millions today), and large amounts in another, Pan American. It also came out that he had been on the House of Morgan's "preferred list" of people who received stocks, really gifts, in a prized holding company at far below market prices. These facts were known, but few dared criticize the great hero.[72] Certainly no one in the administration dared do so. Roosevelt waited under cover until the minor tempest went out to sea.

Roosevelt's luck failed him for the first time since his election. The weather was exceptionally poor for much of the nation late that February and early March. For the Air Corps planes flying the mails through the snow storms and freezing rains it was an unprecedented disaster. Within days after the operation began five pilots had been killed and many others badly injured. Just as Lindbergh had warned, the Army simply lacked the wherewithal to do the job, especially at night. The press eagerly seized on Roosevelt's embarrassment or folly. Nor was there any letup, since Army planes continued to crash with mortifying regularity (12 pilots having died by early April). Roosevelt, seeking to extricate himself from the mess gracefully and expeditiously, had the Secretary of War ask Lindbergh, as a colonel in the Air Corps Reserve, to serve on a committee which would review the training of military aviators. Lindbergh's reply to this peace offer, this attempt to neutralize the issue, was another indignant telegram for public consumption, one that bordered on insult to his commander-in-chief. He would have nothing to do with a committee "whose function," he asserted, was "to assist in following out an executive order." Roosevelt had no choice but to beat a retreat and restore mail delivery to the private airlines (under stricter supervision, to be sure).[73]

That defeat at Lindbergh's hands, writes Arthur M. Schlesinger Jr., cost Roosevelt heavily. It "dented the myth of Roosevelt's invulnerability and strengthened the business community's dislike of what it considered personal and arbitrary action by the New Deal."[74] Roosevelt had been reminded of a fundamental truism in politics: the best professional is no match against a smart, popular amateur.

It was borne in on Roosevelt that this young man was not merely differing with him over a specific deed. Lindbergh, whose stubborn animus was there for all to see, was clearly reacting to Roosevelt himself. Since he knew Lindbergh only by reputation—if they ever met it is unrecorded and at most would have been perfunctory—he might have ascribed the animus to politics, more precisely to the fact that Lindbergh was a Republican who, since his fantastic accomplishment, had moved in wealthy eastern circles. He was married to Anne Morrow, daughter of the late Dwight Morrow, onetime Morgan partner, ambassador to Mexico (where Lindbergh met Anne), and New Jersey Senator.[75]

Roosevelt might also have pondered the irony of Lindbergh's rise to fame and fortune. In 1913, when Roosevelt went to Washington as Assistant Secretary of the Navy, Lindbergh's father was there serving in the House of Representatives as one of its most rebellious members. The elder Charles A. Lindbergh had cut a swath in western Minnesota by denouncing Wall Street and powerful interests in general for threatening to plow under the small farmers of America. Congressman Lindbergh had earned a national reputation as an opponent of American involvement in the Great War and had suffered for it, losing his seat and getting drummed out of Minnesota politics altogether. So Lindbergh had come quite a distance since his lonely, brooding days on a Minnesota farm, driving his father around on the campaign trail.[76]

But politics alone hardly touches the depth of Lindbergh's dislike of Roosevelt. Or rather, he felt as he did toward Roosevelt because to him the man and his politics were indistinguishable. From Lindbergh's standpoint, Roosevelt's outrageous conduct in the air-mail controversy reflected something much more ominous. In Roosevelt, leader of the United States, he found a man who was at once the symbol and the exemplification of a generalized fear. We are taking no liberties in surmising that Lindbergh must have often contrasted his public conduct with Roosevelt's, his virtues with Roosevelt's vices, his idealized America with the America Roosevelt represented in all its misplaced confidence and pride. The contrast deserves elaboration.

From the instant the *Spirit of St. Louis* landed at Paris's Le Bourget airport on May 21, 1927, Lindbergh became the most famous man in the world. Thereafter, uncontrollable mobs galled his every step, as did the equally uncontrollable batteries of reporters and photographers. Heads of state fell over each other to fete and honor this tall, fair-haired, boyishly American youth, barely 25 years old. (President Coolidge was actually voluble in his welcoming speech which announced Lindbergh's promotion from lieutenant to colonel.)* His ticker-tape parade up Broadway drew the largest crowd ever to assemble there, and on that day the staid *New York Times* gave him its first 16 pages in their entirety.[77] That summer, in a whirlwind tour which took him to every state in the union, tens of millions of people and most of America's politicians saw him. One could go on this way and fill a book describing his tumultuous

---

* Lindbergh had graduated from Air Corps training school as a second lieutenant and had flown the mails as a commercial pilot.

international reception (it would, for example, quote from a few of the two million fans who wrote him) and explaining the reasons for it.

Inevitably, the subject of politics did arise. From her inception America had rewarded her heroes with high office, the presidency above all. Though Lindbergh was still too young for *that* office, the ascending path that led to it was his for the taking. Among his new-won acquaintances and admirers he counted the Rockefellers, the Guggenheims, the Lamonts, the Morgans, the Kelloggs, not to mention the Morrows—the men, in short, who comprised the economic sinew and muscle of the Republican Party. Nor was it without significance that during the 1928 election campaign Lindbergh issued a statement ardently backing Herbert Hoover.[78] (His father's ghost on learning of it must have hastened back to its grave.)

But in fact, Lindbergh had no interest whatever in a political career. If he had shown an interest in it a profusion of advisers would have been at his side, grooming and preparing him. They would have taught him how to utilize his hold over the press, how to burnish his image with the adoring masses. He would have become adept at manipulating his appearance and concealing the reality, whatever it might be—his personal feelings, his private life, his true convictions. But all of these stratagems for public success were anathema to him. He thought highly of Hoover because Hoover was so apolitical, because he had been an engineer and businessman and philanthropist who had never run for office before 1928.

In truth, Lindbergh hated crowds, and, from every indication, hated the mass society that gave birth to them. Which is to say, he also hated the press, which acted as their midwife. To Lindbergh, the masses, and by extension the democratic system, represented a descent into mediocrity, a universe without standards and achievements, a universe, more accurately, whose only standard and measure of achievement was the ability to entertain, titillate, gratify low and trivial desires.

Since he was a boy Lindbergh had been driven by the need to perfect himself, to attain absolute self-mastery by conquering every weakness in himself. He once drew up a list of 65 "character factors," as he called them—honesty, vigor, foresight, manliness, enterprise, concentration, zeal, reserve, tact, ambition, etc.—by which he guided his daily conduct. "At night," he later wrote, "I would read off my list of character factors, and those which I had fulfilled satisfactorily during the day I would mark off with a red cross." This ferocious, and in the end victorious, struggle against weakness lasted for years. "I was glad to notice that there was an improvement as I grew older." He never smoked, drank, gambled, womanized, kept late hours, or did anything that might impair his body and mind and so prevent him from springing into action when he had to. These exceptional virtues, plus his phenomenal aptitude with machines and his keen intelligence, made him the best aviator in America.[79]

They no doubt were responsible for his great triumph. He systematically planned every single detail of the flight, from the raising of the money to the most minute specifications of the plane, *Spirit of St. Louis* (named for the city whose businessmen sponsored him).[*] Most important was his performance during the ordeal itself. It was as if all his moral reserves were brought to bear on a single point: staying awake throughout the long, cool night. It was as if this was the ultimate challenge for which he had been priming himself since childhood.[80] His achievements measured the distance between himself and the pullulating masses who, if they could, would reduce him to their level, make him their own. Under no circumstances would he violate the sanctity of the moral code by which he governed himself in order to curry their favor—and precisely because the favor they would bestow on him, if he let them, was so generous, so seductive. The term "Lone Eagle" fit his character perfectly.

Here we should pause to mention his close friendship with Alexis Carrel, a French-born scientist who by every account significantly influenced his outlook on life.[81] Carrel had a laboratory at Rockefeller Institute (now University) in New York City; there years earlier he had discovered how to suture blood vessels (anastomosis) during surgery and had won a Nobel Prize for it. His team of assistants wore long black-hooded robes and worked in rooms with black walls. Carrel wore a black jacket with brass buttons and a white cap pulled down over his ears. To

---

[*] After the war a French-American businessman, Raymond Orteig, had put up $25,000 (quite a sum then) for the first aviator or aviators who crossed the Atlantic nonstop in a heavier-than-air vehicle. Several had already tried it and failed, among them the great French ace René Fonck, and more were preparing for the attempt.

disobey him in the slightest was to call down on oneself the wrath of a tyrant. He had met Lindbergh in 1931 when Lindbergh came to the Institute to develop a machine for pumping blood through the body. Lindbergh's interest had been aroused by the apparent hopelessness of his sister-in-law's heart condition; doctors considered it inoperable because there was nothing to replace her heart's defective pumping action. He and Carrel hit it off at once. Lindbergh regarded Carrel as a genius, a man of great intellectual and spiritual depth. With Carrel as his guide and teacher, he writes in his *Autobiography of Values,* "I felt I had reached the frontier where the mystical and the scientific meet, where I could see across the indistinct border separating life from death."[82]

We have a fair notion of the philosophy which so impressed Lindbergh, thanks to the book Carrel brought out a few years later, *Man, the Unknown.* In it Carrel attempted to disclose the metaphysical truths that underlay scientific method. The book, a runaway best-seller translated into many languages, maunders endlessly through a fog of verbiage and rodomontade, a rehash of Nietzsche and Bergson and William James and Ortega y Gasset, to inform us that life must be seen, or intuited, as a whole, as a force transcending the sum of its parts, separately analyzed and artificially classified. For Carrel it follows that society, to be properly governed, must be run by an elite of men specially attuned to the totality of life and courageous enough to see democracy for the corruption that it is.[83] When he discusses how the elite should be selected we can hear the tumbrels of fascism in the near distance. Carrel would introduce eugenics, the art of sound breeding. "Many living beings," he reminds the squeamish, "are sacrificed at every instant by nature to other living beings." From this is a short step to "euthenics," the art of directly eliminating the unfit—the inveterate criminal, the sociopath, et al.— "humanely and economically." "Philosophical systems and sentimental prejudices must give way before such a necessity," Carrel concludes, applying to society the pitiless ethics of his laboratory.[84]

Did Lindbergh subscribe to Carrel's twisted views? We have no way of knowing since no written exchange of ideas between them is available to us. Such exchanges did occur, of course, for they were fast friends and saw each other daily for long stretches of time. Perhaps Carrel went too far for Lindbergh's homespun American taste; one would like to think so. But it cannot be denied that *Man, the Unknown* did in general body forth Lindbergh's own *Weltanschauung,* his feelings about the built-in defects of democracy—defects which he experienced firsthand and against which his whole being rose up in revulsion.

Even the ineffable trauma of his son's kidnapping could be traced to his desire to escape the leering eye of the masses and their accomplice, the press.

He had built a ten-room house on Sourland Mountain, a secluded area of New Jersey due north of Princeton, about an hour and a half from New York City. With typical assiduity he first surveyed the terrain by air and foot before deciding exactly where the structure would go up. A single road connected it to the world; surrounding it were over 400 acres of grasslands, woods, swamps, and hills. That very isolation helped the culprit (or culprits) make off unnoticed with 20-month-old Charles Jr. on the evening of March 1, 1934.

Of course, the kidnapping became the most sensational news of the day—day after day, week after week, month after month—the press from all over the world descending on the village of Hopewell. And so, on top of their unspeakable suffering, culminating in the discovery of the infant's body on May 12, the Lindberghs had to contend with the ubiquitous, relentlessly prying media. Yet Lindbergh threw himself into the case with the energy and willpower he brought to any technical problem. He worked closely with the police, complied unerringly with the ransom demands, pursued leads on his own, turned his house into a command center. His wife marveled at his composure and equanimity, remarking on how well he slept throughout the ordeal and even how "buoyant" he felt.[85]

It happened that Anne Morrow Lindbergh was pregnant at the time and gave birth to Jon, as he was named, on August 16. It was an event in which the nation rejoiced, but it gave Lindbergh the opportunity to assail the press and therefore the public. "It is impossible for us," he declared bitterly, "to subject the life of our second son to the publicity which we feel was in large measure responsible for the death of the first."[86] If he was issuing a plea to be left alone he must surely have realized that it would fall on indifferent ears. Lindbergh and publicity were irrevocably yoked together. His lot was a cruel one, and he could do nothing but cry out in impotent rage against it.[87]

By his own definition, then, the contrast between him and Franklin D. Roosevelt could not be more pronounced. Roosevelt seemed to thrive on his rapport with crowds, not merely with visible crowds—those that saw and heard him in the flesh, the very crowds from which Lindbergh recoiled wherever he went—but with the invisible crowds, that is, the masses at large, the millions upon millions of people who listened to his honeyed words on the radio, saw him in newsreels, eagerly read about him every day. What stuck in Lindbergh's craw was the fact that instead of disdaining such adulation Roosevelt welcomed and exploited it for all it was worth. Roosevelt's unquestionable talents—the very way he trounced Hoover, installed the hit-and-miss New Deal, and got the American masses to applaud as he gathered up more and more power at their expense—these talents Lindbergh held in deepest contempt because they were the talents of the sly opportunist and the demagogue.

Lindbergh's contempt for the public and the media was proof of his morality while Roosevelt's matchless virtuosity as a politician, his ability to manage public opinion, was proof of his amorality. In that sense, Roosevelt epitomized everything that Lindbergh found objectionable in democracy. It is why Lindbergh's opposition to Roosevelt over the air-mail issue, when it surfaced in the winter of 1934, was so vehement, catching the master politician completely off guard and causing him to fall back in unwonted confusion.

THREE

Roosevelt Triumphant

HUEY LONG

Roosevelt and his political intimates—Louis McHenry Howe, Postmaster General James A. Farley, and the Secretary of Treasury Henry Morgenthau Jr.—concluded in 1934 that the inevitable showdown with Long should come sooner rather than later. The Share Our Wealth movement was obviously no flash in the pan, and Long was developing a national constituency from which to challenge the President should he opt to. And with the New Deal consensus falling apart, as it seemed to be in the second half of 1934, it was a challenge not to be taken lightly. The far left, Communists, Socialists, and lesser revolutionaries, were leading important strikes in the heavy industries, many of them successfully, causing a rift to open up inside the American Federation of Labor, a staunch Roosevelt ally.

The right was experiencing an upsurge as well. Businessmen increasingly registered their horror of New Deal reforms in such organizations as the American Liberty League. On the margins, denouncing Roosevelt as the puppet of the Jews, were the fascist sects, a number of which noisily prepared for violence and wore their own distinctive shirts, black or white or silver or brown.

Roosevelt, it is true, could have taken heart from the results of the 1934 elections. Defying precedent, according to which parties in office lose strength in the off year, and more so if they won the presidency by a landslide, the Democrats actually gained congressional seats, adding to their already swollen majorities—from 310 to 319 in the House, from 60 to 69 in the Senate. But the schisms in America were deepening nonetheless, and there was no telling how they would affect Roosevelt in the crucial third year of his term. The last thing he needed was the indefatigable Huey Long on his back. Having thus made its assessment, the White House decided to bring the conflict with Long to a head.

Morgenthau assumed personal responsibility for tightening the screws. He instructed Treasury agent Elmer Irey to send his men in force down to the sinkholes of Louisiana. From there Irey would report to Morgenthau once a week on his progress. And progress there was. By the end of 1934 one after another of Long's associates, his collectors and keepers and distributors of cash, Joseph and Julius Fisher, Abraham Shushan, and Seymour Weiss (all Jews incidentally), were indicted in federal court for tax evasion. The government of course hoped that at least one of them would turn against the Kingfish to save his own hide.[1]

Roosevelt may have had the big battalions, but Long showed again that he fought best when the odds against him seemed highest. Desperation brought out his most daring qualities of leadership.

For the next several months, while the country looked on with growing interest, Long conducted a series of forays against the Roosevelt administration, suiting his tactics to the occasion and the opportunities at hand. Always he had the ear of the public, for apart from his headline-catching propensities he was able to buy the air time he needed and could count on reaching a national audience.

As usual, he played the martyr's role for all it was worth. Roosevelt, he would claim, was singling him out for destruction because he dared remain true to the principles that Roosevelt had scuttled and so threatened the corporate and banking elite whom Roosevelt served. Or he played the uncompromising gadfly, willing, in the name of those same principles, to discomfit anyone, even his best friends. So he repeatedly held up vital pieces of legislation (for he possessed an uncanny knowledge of the rules) and sometimes filibustered against them, once for 15½ straight hours.[2] So he helped engineer Roosevelt's single biggest defeat to date, one that caught the administration completely by surprise—the Senate's rejection of the treaty that would have brought the United States into the World Court.[3]

Or he played the role of the virtuous inquisitor, alerting the world to New Deal corruption and mendacity. So it was that he accused Postmaster General Farley of having been involved in an illicit building scheme in New York City, and to prove it announced that he had the incriminating evidence. This caused a sensation—a brief one however. For there was no corruption and nothing came of the charges, a Senate committee absolving Farley and the administration in toto, but by then Long had had his innings and moved on to something else.[4]

Or he played the innocent who seeks only to be heard, a role subtly different from, and in many ways more effective than, the martyr's. So he would patiently and temperately reply to attacks by administration spokesmen. In one celebrated exchange, Hugh Johnson—ex-czar of the National Recovery Administration (NRA), and a notorious headliner in his own right, well known for his acerbic tongue—in effect called Long an American Hitler, a "Pied Piper" in Johnson's words, bent on leading the country to dictatorship and spiritual death as he already had Louisiana.[5] Long took the opportunity thus presented to him on a platter—the whole nation, eager to witness a knockdown drag-out fight, was tuned in to his answering speech—to denounce Roosevelt as another Hoover and then, like a lawyer summing up his case, explain in pedantic detail the Share Our Wealth program, his alternative to the wretchedly failed New Deal.[6]

These numerous and shifting roles Long performed masterfully throughout the first part of 1935. He succeeded in keeping the Roosevelt administration off balance and, more important, keeping himself on display as the people's unconquerable champion.

But when all was said and done Roosevelt's strategy did work. He did goad Long into open combat, causing Long to come across as America's paramount critic and naysayer and general obstructionist. And that was because Long allowed himself to be goaded; indeed he welcomed the chance to be goaded. To that extent he and Roosevelt had arrived at an agreement of sorts. Theirs was a tacit collaboration in enmity from which each expected to profit at the expense of the other. Roosevelt assumed that once Americans understood what Huey Long was about they would drive or laugh him off the stage. Long just as confidently assumed that the masses, disillusioned by Roosevelt's treacheries—more politely, his broken promises—would turn to him, Long, for their deliverance.

The issue could not have been posed more sharply.

Roosevelt, however, wanted to push Long only so far and no further. He did not want Long to lose in such a way as to drag Roosevelt and the rest of the party down with him. What Roosevelt did not want, in short, was an extremely popular rival courting Democratic voters in a presidential election in which he, Roosevelt, was going to run. Long's popularity could be measured by the size of the Share Our Wealth movement. It seemed to thrive on its hero's controversies with the administration. Long's chief assistant maintained in 1935 that the organization had almost five million members signed up and accounted for in over 27,000 clubs situated in every state of the union. True, those figures were less formidable than they appeared. The largest numbers were concentrated in Louisiana and adjoining states of the Deep South. And there was no way of knowing if Long could politically mobilize them; all he or anyone else could say was that Share Our Wealth members favored its radical proposals in the abstract, the commitment to it being perhaps as shallow as it was undemanding. Nonetheless, despite every qualification, Share Our Wealth was an impressive affair: it was only a year old and was still growing. Roosevelt and his minions had ample reason for concern.[7]

Long implied, and occasionally stated, that he was thinking of running for President, and not necessarily as a Democrat. The party of Jefferson and Jackson and Bryan, he would say over and over, had been captured by the plutocrats and their toadies. Was he serious? Would he mount a drive to unseat Roosevelt in 1936? He gave no clue, or rather he gave a plethora of clues. This was for him standard operating procedure. Behind the noisy rhetoric, the buffoonery, the contradictory statements, he moved with feline stealth and set purpose. His adversaries were of course familiar with his tactics and were prepared for them. And he naturally took into account their familiarity with them, so that telling them the truth, blatantly and to the point, was yet another act of dissimulation.

By way of emphasis, he wrote a book at this time off the top of his head, entitled *My First Days in the White House.* Sophomoric in style and content and duller even than his autobiography, it sketches a Share Our Wealth paradise under his beneficent leadership. The controversies and partisan differences are now only memories. Faithfully serving him and the country are the politicians whose jobs correspond to their talents: Roosevelt is his Secretary of the Navy, Hoover his Secretary of Commerce, Al Smith his Budget Director, and so on. The fantasy concludes with President Long's tour of America from the rear of a train. At the first stop he asks the crowd, "All right folks, what's wrong?" A chorus of cheers goes up. He repeats the question. Above the din a voice is heard that provides the book's coda: "Nothing! We have just found out how bad [*sic*] we needed you for President all the time."

Much has been written about the secret poll taken by the Democratic National Committee in 1935. It showed that Long, running as a third party candidate in the next presidential election, would receive between three and four million votes, with about as much support coming from the North as the South, from Republicans as from Democrats.[8] The poll in itself, however, did not greatly disturb Roosevelt; it was more impressionistic than scientific, and the election was too far in the future to justify major alarm. What disturbed him was the magnitude of the discontent it revealed—the discontent above all of the progressive groups, inside the Democratic Party and out, who favored the further regulation of industry, the redistribution of wealth, and the guarantee of economic security for labor, small and marginal farmers and businessmen, the unemployed, the poor and handicapped and old; who, in short, favored the radicalization of the New Deal.[9] That discontent had manifested itself in the 1934 election, the main beneficiaries of which, at every level of government across America, were exactly those advocates of a left turn. Long concerned Roosevelt primarily because he did or might command support from the fast-rising progressive bloc.

We have a rare insight into Roosevelt's thinking on just this question from a celebrated letter he wrote early in 1935 to Colonel Edward M. House, Woodrow Wilson's onetime confidant. House had noted a parallel between the 1912 election and the one looming up and had wondered if Huey Long at the head of a third party might, like the first Roosevelt and the Bull Moosers, play the spoiler and bring down the incumbent. In his reply Roosevelt offered a slightly different scenario. He envisioned a four-way race in 1936 between himself, Long, and two Republicans, a progressive and a conservative, in the course of which he, Roosevelt, might conceivably be swept away by the radical upsurge in America. His consoling hope was that "when it comes to show-down these fellows cannot all live in the same bed and will fight among themselves with almost absolute certainty."[10] It was a dubious consolation.

Not fear of Long or Share Our Wealth, then, but the desire to propitiate the emergent force of the liberal-left prompted Roosevelt to launch his Second New Deal, so-called, in the spring of 1935. The strategy of isolating Long, in itself so successful (thanks to Long's complicity), would have backfired, or worked to Long's advantage, had it not accompanied the additional strategy of winning over the progressives in general. In that restricted sense it could be said that Roosevelt felt he must "steal Long's thunder."[11] In response to the schism between right and left that was opening up before him—the schism between, on one side, such disaffected Democrats as Al Smith's Liberty League and traditional Republican conservatives and, on the other side, the forces represented by Long and Father Coughlin and the followers of Townsend's burgeoning old age movement, as well as the La Follettes of Wisconsin, the Farmer-Laborites of Minnesota, and the industrial unionists and their revolutionary allies—Roosevelt chose the left, drawing on its platform of ideas to effect a measurable shift of power in America from the upper to the lower classes. Here is not the place to discuss the farrago of legislation that comprised the Second New Deal. To claim that it made a minor revolution is hardly to exaggerate its accomplishments.

Even Long had to acknowledge, grudgingly, that Roosevelt was moving in the right direction—that is, his direction. To everyone's surprise, for example, Roosevelt in June 1935 sent Congress a revenue bill that would have "soaked the rich," or at least significantly raised taxes on the upper-income strata. Though it cannot be compared to Long's broadly confiscatory plan, the White House revenue bill broke all precedent: it proposed to use taxes for the sake of achieving greater social justice, reducing the inequalities of the classes.

On June 22, before a jammed Senate, Long read a letter of congratulation he had just sent Roosevelt. It is a Longian tour de force, pure Uriah Heep. Roosevelt, he wrote, might be treacherous and vindictive, as witness what he did to his best friends, first Tammany Hall and then Huey Long, yet he, Long, was willing to "submerge every personal feeling and political reaction" toward Roosevelt for the good of America. "My elimination from politics," he went on, effacing himself more and more, "would be the immediate and sure results of your enactment of the Share our Wealth legislation. You would thereby have another complete case for the public's admiration which, cited in contrast with my support of your causes and policies, might give you a measure of added prestige." His smiling words were full of smiling contempt: "Assuring you of my esteem and thanks for courtesies heretofore and hereafter granted, and with good wishes, I have the honor to remain, your sincere friend. . . ."[12]

The sarcastic tone of the letter suggests Long's quandary. He could pick at the New Deal laws as they made their way through the Senate— no man was his superior in the art—but increasingly he appeared to oppose them for opposition's sake. (He in the end rejected the 1935 Revenue Act too as a sellout.) The passage of those laws fastened the alliance of Roosevelt and the progressives, and, to precisely the degree that it did, left Long more and more politically isolated.

If Long was upset by his estrangement from the progressive community he gave no sign of it. His popularity with the masses, once conclusively established, would win over the progressives, and many others as well, to his camp. When it would be conclusively established was the question. On such matters, as noted, he kept his own counsel. T. Harry Williams is convinced that Long by the late summer of 1935 had made up his mind to form his own party the next year, one capable of attracting enough votes from Roosevelt to assure a Republican victory. That would set the stage for his triumph in 1940. "It was a bold plan and also a coldly calculated one. He was willing to let the country suffer for four years so that he could then save it."[13]

This may or may not have been Long's plan—Williams's evidence is rather thin—but in the nature of things, given the swift pace of events, it was pure fancy, the remotest of wishes. Between August 1935 and the campaign season of 1936, Huey Long, brilliant politician that he was, would have changed his plans as often as circumstances dictated. And by then—who knows?—he might have become Roosevelt's most fulsome champion. The switch would have meant nothing to Long, being merely a tactical ploy necessary to achieve his ultimate objective. In 1940 he would have been only 47.

It could also be argued that he had no such long-range plan at all, that he lived for the apocalyptic moment, as it were; to be more specific, that he lived in fear of, and was obsessed with, his own violent death, especially during his last year. He was the victim of a dialectic he himself had set in motion. His enemies resorted to threats on his life more and more openly as his hold over Louisiana tightened, leaving no other way out. And as his mania for security increased so did the number of his bodyguards and the readiness of the state police to use protective force in his behalf, fresh provocations in themselves. But Long surely must have realized that all the security in the world could not save him from the hand of someone who was willing to sacrifice his own life.

Such a person, Dr. Carl Austin Weiss, did confront Long on the night of September 8, 1935. Wiess appeared from behind a column of the Baton Rouge capital building with a gun drawn at close range, and died instantly from a hail of bullets after carrying out his suicidal mission. Long lingered on for a day and a half, time enough to think, incoherently perhaps, on the accuracy of his dark premonitions, and, more painfully yet, on what might have been.

At the memorial service the main eulogy was delivered by one Gerald L. K. Smith. Smith was no closer to the Kingfish than anyone else; no one was close to him. Smith was chosen because delivering a eulogy was his particular metier. He was a minister who specialized in hair-raising oratory, and it was broadly acknowledged that few were his equal in that department. After joining Long early in 1934—he had knocked about for some time before then—Smith was assigned the job of recruiting members into Share Our Wealth clubs. He was a sensation. Long excepted, no one contributed more to the growth of the movement.[14] For certain kinds of audiences Smith was the ideal stump speaker.[15] He worshipped Long, doting on the great man like a pet, even wearing his clothes and occasionally sacking out on the floor near his bed. Understandably, then, Smith in his eulogy seemed to confuse Long with Jesus. "He died for us . . . This untimely death makes restless the souls of us who adored him. Oh God, why did we have to lose him." And so on in this vein.[16]

Smith made the error of thinking that his special relationship with Long and his high-ranking position in the Share Our Wealth organization entitled *him* to claim the right of succession. For without Long he was actually nothing. He threw in his lot with one of the two factions of the Long machine fighting for supremacy. The other faction contained most of Long's Jewish allies, a fact Smith publicly noted in his crudely anti-Semitic fashion. Eventually, he broke with his own group. Repudiated by everyone, Smith was literally thrown out of the state of Louisiana by the police and told never to return; all that was lacking were the tar and feathers.[17]

When the factional struggles calmed down, the Long machine settled into the slough of normality. The jobbery, the self-enrichment, the subservience to the various special interests, oil especially, once again dominated state politics. One of Long's disciples, Richard W. Leche, would say after serving as governor for three years, during which time he accumulated millions, "I swore to uphold the constitution of Louisiana and the United States, but I didn't take any vow of poverty." As for the Share Our Wealth scheme, to quote one observer of Long's epigones: "these gentlemen were interested in getting it, not sharing it." These depredations usually took place in the Kingfish's name, by those who professed to hallow his memory. It was by such means that the structure of reform which he had so painstakingly built collapsed.

Within months of his death the Louisiana Democratic Party, every faction within it, stood solidly behind President Roosevelt. Some contend that Roosevelt had carried out a "Second Louisiana Purchase." This is an exaggeration. Roosevelt was very popular in the state and scarcely needed the support of Long's political heirs. It was simply that the administration had no further motive for punishing them. That was why the restraints on federal patronage and other New Deal subsidies were lifted and the indictments of Abe Shushan and Seymour Weiss dropped (after they agreed to pay their back taxes). Huey Long's ghost had been exorcised.[18]

FATHER COUGHLIN

After Father Coughlin established the National Union for Social Justice, his relations with Roosevelt deteriorated steadily. He became one of Roosevelt's most persistent critics. Sometimes he was devastatingly effective. More than anyone else, Huey Long included, he was credited with sinking the International Court of Justice treaty, which the administration took very seriously. It was his broadcasts on January 27 and 28, 1935, that unloosed the flood of mail and telegrams on Washington and caused enough Senators to change their minds at the last minute to deny the two-thirds majority necessary for passage.[19]

As a result of that stinging defeat, ex-NRA czar Hugh Johnson, at Roosevelt's behest, launched his frontal attack on the "Pied Pipers," Long and Coughlin, accusing them in his radio speech of seeking to lead America to self-destruction. Johnson was not as severe on Coughlin as he was on Long, whom he likened to Hitler, but he was severe enough, the linkage itself implying that Coughlin was a fascist too, a charge that was being made more and more frequently and that he ran the risk of reinforcing in the act of denying.[20]

One can only wonder about Roosevelt's motives in bringing his differences with Coughlin out in the open so acrimoniously. It was certainly true that by placing Coughlin in Long's company Roosevelt was helping to keep them apart politically. Coughlin, who maintained a respectable front, far from party and personal animosities, could hardly afford to be associated in the public mind with the likes of Huey Long, no matter how much they saw eye to eye. They did meet at least once, and beyond taking each other's measure, neither being impressed by what he saw, nothing came of the encounter. "Coughlin," Long was quoted as saying, "is just a political Kate Smith of the air. They'll get tired of him." Coughlin called Long's Share Our Wealth scheme "unspeakable radicalism."[21] Had they nonetheless tried to establish the rudiments of an alliance the world would have at once learned in flaming headlines that the "Pied Pipers" were acting in unison, just as Hugh Johnson had warned. Johnson's speech could be called a prophylaxis designed to prevent an undesirable possibility from coming to pass. Therein lay its ingenuity. That possibility was of course rendered moot with Long's assassination later in the year.

Like Long, Coughlin replied to Johnson over the radio. All of America listened in, the media aspect of the debate, or shouting match, being itself an event. And like Long he dismissed Johnson's arguments and Johnson himself ("a chiseler," "a chocolate soldier," "a creampuff," "a red herring," "a political corpse," etc.) in order to get at the real culprit. But whereas Long concentrated on Roosevelt, Coughlin designated Bernard M. Baruch, Johnson's employer for years and a sometime White House advisor, as the arch-villain of the piece. Baruch already had the reputation, especially in anti-Semitic circles, of being something of a Svengali. Among the several fascist sects in America Baruch, along with Harvard law professor Felix Frankfurter and Henry Morgenthau Jr., belonged to the Jewish cabal that was taking over the country. Coughlin's speech intimated as much.

He wove a tapestry around Baruch's Hebrew sounding middle name, "Menasses." It was Menasses, a prince of ancient Israel, Coughlin reminded his audience, who had the great prophet Isaiah slain for telling the truth about Israel's iniquities. So he, Father Coughlin, would tell the truth about America's iniquities even if he must suffer Isaiah's fate at the hands of this latter-day Menasses and his mercenaries. Coughlin prayed that Roosevelt, whom he claimed still to support in the face of every lapse and show of weakness ("I support him today and will support him tomorrow"), would heed his admonitions in time, before Baruch and the other international bankers accomplished their fell purpose, which was nothing less than the enslavement of the American people.[22] (With scarcely concealed amusement Baruch quietly corrected Coughlin's errors of fact. His middle name, he pointed out, was Mannes, not "Menasses," and he was a stock investor, not a banker.)[23]

For weeks the press enjoyed a field day covering the exchanges between the administration spokesmen—never Roosevelt—and the "Pied Pipers." It was a first-class brawl, no holds barred. Interior Secretary Harold Ickes, who loved the cut and thrust of verbal warfare, called Coughlin a poseur, a man "whose rich but undisciplined imagination had reduced politics, sociology and banking to charming poetry which he distills mellifluously into the ether for the entrancement of mankind."[24] From pro-administration Catholics the cry went up that the church should muzzle the priest, or force him to choose between renouncing politics or the priesthood. Too many people, the argument went, believed he represented Catholic opinion. He was adding to the sum of religious bigotry, drawing out the deep-rooted Know-Nothingness of American culture. But Bishop Gallagher, rising to his defense more emphatically than ever, pronounced him "sound in doctrine" and "able in application and interpretation."[25] Millions of Catholics would have uttered stronger language of approval; their admiration for Coughlin rose in direct proportion to the assaults made upon him.

Meanwhile, enjoying the spectacle was the other protagonist. Roosevelt understood that the longer it lasted and the angrier it became the more he stood to benefit. In an often quoted letter to the old progressive writer Ray Stannard Baker, Roosevelt explained why he would never compete with Coughlin and Long for the public's favor. First, it would turn the "eyes of the audience away from the main drama itself," the affairs of state. And second, that audience must sooner or later grow tired of such men just as it would "a constant repetition of the highest note in the scale."[26] This was shrewdly put, revealing how well Roosevelt knew mass psychology. Roosevelt omitted to say, however, that it was his friends who were largely responsible for eliciting those high notes and for getting them constantly repeated. Hugh Johnson was only one of his *agents provocateurs.*

Roosevelt further provoked Coughlin when, shunning the best advice, he vetoed the Patman bonus bill on May 22, 1935. Now this was a very popular piece of legislation—popular with veterans' groups and the same easy-money interests that so far had dominated Congress. It would have placed over two billion dollars in circulation by granting Great War veterans early payment on the bonuses that were promised to them and due to mature in ten years. In a typical masterstroke Roosevelt went before both houses of Congress to justify the veto, arguing that the bill was inflationary and otherwise fiscally unwise, the budget being too far out of kilter as it was. Roosevelt's aim was to do to his enemies what they had done to him a few months earlier when the World Court treaty had come up for a vote: secure the backing of just over a third of the Senate, thus thwarting a veto override. The tactic worked. The House overrode by a whopping 322 to 98; but the Senate sustained by a comfortable margin.[27]

Coughlin was greatly disappointed. Had the bill passed, Roosevelt would have been twice rebuked, by the votes and by the overrides, and he would have been perceived as both wrong and ineffectual. Roosevelt instead had demonstrated that he was a leader of courage, willing to risk much for his convictions, and that he could hold the citadel against the easy-money hordes who were pressing in on all sides. That Roosevelt might emerge from the veto unscathed, however, was a prospect Coughlin refused to entertain. How could such a prospect be squared with Coughlin's tremendous following, with the very premise on which he had created the National Union for Social Justice? No, devilishly clever though he was, Roosevelt, in Coughlin's opinion, could not escape the long-term consequences of his deed; his betrayal would haunt him.

Roosevelt had no desire to alienate Coughlin more than he had to. His messages to Coughlin remained unfailingly courteous and deferential. And they exchanged pleasantries when they met. On one occasion, the very day Huey Long's death was announced, September 11, 1935, they got together at Roosevelt's Hyde Park house.[28] Coughlin arrived in the morning with his friend Joseph P. Kennedy of Boston, who, as head of the Securities and Exchange Commission, was one of the highest ranking Catholics in the administration. After a companionable breakfast (prepared by Coughlin), Roosevelt came out with it: "Cards on the table, Padre, cards on the table. Why are you cooling off on me? Why are you criticizing the things I'm doing?" Coughlin produced one of the cards. Bishop Gallagher, he said, had learned from a Mexican church official that "a Communist sympathizer" in the Treasury Department had sent a check to a prominent Mexican anti-clericalist, this at a time when the Mexican government was energetically suppressing the clergy. Coughlin had a Photostat of the check in his pocket and showed it to Roosevelt who, caught unawares by this shard of trivia, promised to look into it; he could say or do no more. Coughlin then brought out another card, his favorite one: the crimes of the Federal Reserve Bank and the need to abolish it. Roosevelt replied: "Don't be so innocent to think that the President of the United States can also be the Congress of the United States." The discussion continued into the afternoon. Roosevelt concluded it by stressing how much he and Coughlin had in common and how important it was for them to maintain their united front against the Republicans, especially in the year ahead. Coughlin kept his own counsel.[29]

What he really thought of Roosevelt he disclosed a few months later in a biting letter to his friend Frank Murphy, the ex-mayor of Detroit (now governor-general of the Philippines). "I sincerely feel that Mr. Roosevelt is a socialist of the radical type." Still, he went on, it might be best if Roosevelt were re-elected because only that would bring home to gullible Americans just how dangerous he was beneath the patina of charm and eloquence. The Republicans, too, should favor his re-election, and for the same reason—to ruin him "entirely, together with the hopes of the Tugwells, the Frankfurters and the rest of the Jews who surround him. The plot is deeply laid. . . ."[30] Coughlin, in other words, had given up on Roosevelt. He no longer considered the President a man of good will, duped by plotters; he was himself part of the "plot," a "socialist of the radical type," therefore past praying for.

We have no proof that Murphy informed Roosevelt, with whom he remained close, of the contents of the letter. It might not have been necessary.

Coughlin dropped in at the White House once again early in January 1936 for a chat. It was to be the last meeting and the last show—but only a show—of cordiality between them.[31] For it was soon after that Coughlin denounced Roosevelt in language he normally used against international bankers as a traitor to the innocent faith America reposed in him.

The occasion of their break was the radically agrarian Frazier-Lemke bill. It would have had the federal government assume all farm mortgages and hold on to them at minimal interest rates until the farmers could pay them off. Roosevelt fought the bill as hard as he had the Patman bonus bill, and it was easily voted down. This was a big defeat for Coughlin, its most passionate defender.

In the course of it all Coughlin accused a New York City Congressman and fellow Irish Catholic, John O'Connor, of nefariously sabotaging the bill. Outraged, O'Connor challenged the priest to a fistfight in front of the Capitol. "I shall guarantee to kick you all the way from the Capitol to the White House with clerical garb and all the silver in your pockets which you got from speculating on Wall Street while I was voting for all the farm bills. Come on!" Coughlin gladly accepted and might have gone through with it—he was going to work out in a gym—had Bishop Gallagher not dissuaded him. The public, naturally, enjoyed every minute of the little drama.[32]

What Coughlin had been saying privately about Roosevelt he now said openly to his vast public. The New Deal, finally unmasked, was a covenant with Satan, or rather with Satan as he appeared now in this guise, now in that, now as a Bolshevik or "radical socialist," now as a predatory capitalist or international banker. Satan's genius, like Roosevelt's, was to reconcile such apparent contradictions. Thus Coughlin could describe the New Deal as follows: "While its golden head enunciates the splendid program of Christian justice, its feet of sordid clay are mired, one in the red mud of Soviet Communism, the other in the stinking cesspool of pagan plutocracy."[33] Delicacy of phrase was one of Coughlin's lesser virtues.

But if there was no viable alternative to Roosevelt, what was the point of this kind of rhetoric? It was a question that had occurred to Coughlin.

The opening of the 1936 presidential campaign found Coughlin at the height of his power. With Long dead no one, Roosevelt always excepted, rivaled him as a media star. And with Share Our Wealth moribund or defunct, his National Union for Social Justice was the largest organization of its sort in the country. Even the most skeptical estimates put its membership in the millions, with thousands of chapters throughout America, notably in the Midwest and Northeast, that is, in the farming communities and small towns on the one hand and the Irish-American neighborhoods of the big cities on the other.[34] By March 1936 NUSJ also had its own publication, *Social Justice,* really a mouthpiece for Coughlin's opinions and other matters of lesser interest to the faithful.

His Royal Oak parish furnished the appropriate monument to the power he had acquired. Crucifixion Tower, 180 feet high, overwhelmed the landscape, just as he intended it should. Adorning its base were immense reliefs of the Archangels Raphael, Gabriel, and Michael, the last sculpted in the image of Bishop Gallagher, all "eclipsed," in the words of a *Fortune* writer, "by a monster figure of Christ on the Cross illuminated at night by a battery of floodlights."

The interior was equally impressive. In the basement were the printing facilities; also the army of clerks at their desks who handled the mail and collected checks and money orders and cash, amounting to upwards of five million dollars a year. A store sold photos of Coughlin, religious articles, copies of his sermons, and various tracts, anti-Communist, anti-atheist, anti-Masonic, to the multitude of daily visitors. Coughlin's office was situated high up in the Tower. He reached it by walking up a narrow spiral staircase, then through a succession of doors, each opened by a secret device. (For good measure, he also packed a revolver.) The church proper was awesome in size and ponderous in effect, with its heavy oak walls and marble statuary, a far cry from the tiny besieged wooden building that greeted him in 1926.[35]

Coughlin ran a Sunday school in the church for nicely groomed and well-disciplined teenagers, who after saluting him would recite this vow: "I pledge myself to do all in my power to destroy Communism. If necessary, I will surrender my life . . . rather than obey the dictates of Karl Marx and those who hate our country and our church."[36] Among these last mentioned Coughlin might have been tempted to include the leaders of the American government from the President down.

He was enormously encouraged by the performance of the congressional candidates the NUSJ backed in the April and May 1936 primaries. Exactly how well they did is, retrospectively, open to doubt. The important thing is that the press at the time thought Coughlin's influence counted for much, that his support made a measurable difference in the outcome.[37] Certainly Coughlin thought it did. And that conviction, coupled with his deepening aversion for Roosevelt, led him into his fateful decision: to favor a party that would be consecrated to the 16-point NUSJ program, a party that would in the short run, beginning with the 1936 election, force major concessions from whoever controlled the government, even Roosevelt, and in the long run come to dominate it. Forming a party was a bold move. Coughlin was treading where no Catholic clergyman had dared go before. Alive in everyone's memory was Al Smith's unhappy experience, and Smith was a layman. But with Bishop Gallagher in his corner, and blithely confident that millions of Americans would back him, Coughlin mounted his crusade in the spring of 1936.

Even before the campaign started it was as clear to Coughlin as it was to every other politico that Roosevelt would win the election. The economy was doing too well. The New Deal reforms, including the most controversial ones, had gained general acceptance. And Roosevelt himself still commanded American politics. Only the extent of his victory was at issue. Apart from Jim Farley, whose opinions were dismissed as hyperbolic, few imagined that he would swamp the opposition so completely, that he would reduce the Republican Party to a corporal's guard, locally as well as nationally, and just about wipe Coughlin's effort off the face of the earth.

Coughlin's errors of judgment and defects of character invited the misfortunes that befell him and his choice for President, Representative William Lemke of North Dakota. Lemke had little to recommend him beyond his standing in the radical agrarian community. He was simply out of his depth in the campaign. He had been selected on Coughlin's say so. The NUSJ was not consulted, nor was anyone else in the newly formed Union Party when Coughlin announced his preference in June 1936. At its national convention two months later the NUSJ rubber-stamped the decision already made in its name.[38] Then, and during the rest of the campaign, Lemke, an unpretentious man of rural habits and mien, never got out from under Coughlin's shadow. The same held true for Lemke's running mate, one Thomas C. O'Brien, a Massachusetts union lawyer. It was, at any rate, a balanced ticket.

Coughlin received much more attention on the hustings from the press then his two candidates did. It was his speeches that brought out the crowds and the reporters. Withal he was a disastrous campaigner. He was temperamentally unfit for the hothouse of American politics. His speeches tended to be cataracts of insult, usually designed to show that Roosevelt and his advisors were servants of Communism, bent on surreptitiously creating a Soviet America—the very argument being advanced by the reactionary Liberty League. On this issue of fear of Communism all of Roosevelt's enemies could agree irrespective of their other differences. Coughlin even had to apologize to Roosevelt for calling him such things as a "liar" and "scab President."[39] So far as Roosevelt was concerned the more insults the better.

Coughlin was also deviled by physical encounters, some rather nasty. Once, while speaking in Wichita, Kansas, he suddenly faced a Mr. Woody Hockaday, wearing a red shirt and white pants and Indian headdress, who threw chicken feathers all over him. In the ensuing melee Coughlin and his bodyguards wrestled Mr. Hockaday to the platform floor. As the crowd surged forward Coughlin shouted, "Don't lay a hand on him. . . . Let him alone. I love to talk to Communists." He probably saved the man's life.[40]

Another time, during a press conference, a *Boston Globe* reporter asked him on what basis he accused Harvard Professor Felix Frankfurter and David Dubinsky (head of the International Ladies Garment Workers Union) of being Communists. The question rankled Coughlin, and a few days later, following an exchange of words, he punched the reporter in the face and would have gone on to administer further punishment but for candidate O'Brien's intercession. "If I see that fellow I'll tear him to pieces," Coughlin told the press.[41] His behavior, scarcely calculated to arouse confidence in the Union Party, was a symptom of the embarrassment that was engulfing his whole campaign.

Coughlin did manage, briefly, to send a tremor of anxiety through the political system. That was when he seemed to be teaming up with Dr. Francis E. Townsend's vast and unpredictable movement. Townsend had come up with a scheme to save the millions of destitute old people. It called for a national tax on commercial transactions to fund an "Old Age Revolving Pension" that would guarantee anyone over 60 an income of $200 a month for life. Crackpot or not, the plan had the support of multitudes of poor people, not all of them old. Roosevelt's Social Security Act of 1935 was in part an attempt to co-opt the movement, but the Townsendites condemned the act, so negligible were its benefits compared to what they were proposing, as an insult to older Americans. By a quirk of circumstance Gerald L. K. Smith, the late Huey Long's sidekick, was now Townsend's advisor. Smith claimed that he still ran the Share Our Wealth clubs, a claim that could not be validated or falsified because no one was quite sure of what had become of them since Long's departure. At all events, this improbable triumvirate, Coughlin, Townsend and Smith, might have posed a threat to the status quo, Democrats and Republicans alike, had everything gone right for them—had they gotten along with each other and had they suffered no other misadventures along the way.[42]

But nothing went right for them. The Townsend movement was too fissiparous to be politically viable and Coughlin dismissed it altogether. Smith, an incorrigible buffoon, broke with Townsend and went off on his own crusade against the Jews. It was as though the three of them were determined to act out the roles that respectable society had assigned them—to be what others, those whom they secretly looked up to, wanted them to be.[43] Huey Long, as we observed, had those qualities, so characteristic of the lower-middle-class outsider who admires the very thing against which he rebels. Coughlin gave it away when he wrote, just before the 1936 campaign began, "Take every legitimate means to reduce the sixteen principles of social justice to action. You will be condemned by the modern capitalist as a 'crack-pot' and a member of the 'lunatic fringe' because you do not agree with them that the world is flat. . . . The members of the 'lunatic fringe' and the 'crack-pots' of creation have been those who have forged ahead, digging themselves out of the rut of the commonplace. . . .

"As far as I am concerned, it is an honor to be called a 'crack-pot.'"[44]

So confident was Coughlin when the campaign season got under way that he promised, or threatened, never to speak on the air again if his man Lemke received less than 9 million votes. Lemke received less than one-tenth that number: 891,858. In other words, the Union Party had been repudiated by the very groups to which it appealed—small farmers and the disaffected lower and middle classes. And so, true to his word, and without displaying toward anyone, not even Roosevelt, the bitterness he felt, Coughlin on November 9, 1936, solemnly bid farewell to his radio audience. He had preached to them the moral truths of Christ and they heard only what they wished to hear. The Royal Oak parish was where he belonged and he promised never again to stray from it. He was, after all, nothing more than a humble priest.[45]

AL SMITH

Al Smith and the other Liberty Leaguers were stunned by the results of the 1934 congressional elections, by the clear show of national enthusiasm for the New Deal. The manifest swing to the left frightened the generality of rich folk and strict constitutionalists. They drew back in further shock when Congress in 1935 passed sweeping relief and reform legislation. From the conservative standpoint the Second New Deal was a catalogue of horrors, giving Roosevelt yet more control over the economy, adding yet more agencies to the elephantine bureaucracy—the National Labor Relations Board, the various components of the Social Security Administration, the National Youth Administration, the Works Progress Administration, itself a hydra-headed monster, the Rural Electrification Administration, the Farm Security Administration, to name a few—plunging the government even deeper in the red, and perhaps most outrageous of all, forcing successful Americans to pay for this advancing despotism by a notorious new tax law (which, it will be recalled, had at first met Huey Long's approval). And instead of seeking to suppress the radical elements in America, "that man in the White House" seemed to encourage them, the better to play the demagogue. That was how Al Smith and his fellow Liberty Leaguers explained Roosevelt's unconscionable behavior.

They were convinced he could not go on behaving that way much longer. He could not go on bribing the credulous masses without destroying the whole financial structure on which the nation's future rested, thereby creating a crisis infinitely worse than the one he had inherited. Someday the New Deal would be reviled and denounced as the scourge that it was. The American people would then see through the humbug, the falsity, the fundamental irrationality of the Roosevelt administration. Roosevelt himself would become the victim of his hubris—his having tampered with the laws of nature and nature's God. His fall would be no less spectacular than his rise. Such, in sum, was the premise, the faith, that underlay the Liberty League's existence: such was the inspiration behind its relentless criticisms of Roosevelt throughout 1935.[46]

The League and its wealthy sponsors felt vindicated by the Supreme Court's decisions that year in effect upholding those criticisms, at least as they applied to specific legislation. The possibility even arose that the Court's very narrow conception of the Constitution—and very broad conception its own authority—might pose a danger to the entire New Deal and that in the ensuing conflict between executive and judicial branches most Americans would rally behind the latter. It was a possibility which gave Roosevelt's conservative opponents, most notably Al Smith, reason to hope as the presidential election year drew nigh.

In fact, Smith was maintaining an unusual public reticence on the subject of Roosevelt. Rather than run the risk of appearing churlish, a bore with a predictable message, Smith obviously preferred that Roosevelt stumble and fall over his own mistakes. When the time was ripe he would speak out, and he would be heard.[47]

Now Roosevelt on occasion may have stumbled in 1935—whether through his own mistakes or through obstacles strewn in his path was the question at issue—but he certainly did not fall. His January 3, 1936, Message to Congress was a sharply polemical defense of his achievements. He was proud, he asserted, to "have earned the hatred of entrenched greed," "the unscrupulous money-changers," the "discredited special interests." They and their spokesmen, he feared, sought nothing less than "enslavement" of the people. He invited them to try their best against him. "Let them no longer hide their dissent in a cowardly cloak of generality." If "these gentlemen" want to bring back the past "let them say so."[48]

This was too much for Smith. A few weeks later he delivered a savage riposte before an assemblage of millionaires called together by the American Liberty League in Washington's Mayflower Hotel.[49] The speech, so eagerly awaited,[50] so full of dramatic foreboding, so extensively covered in the press, was a litany of negations and a paean to the good old days when taxes and budget deficits and federal bureaucracies were only a minor irritant. Smith, in other words, fell into the trap Roosevelt had set: he seemed to be justifying the restoration of the *ancien régime,* precisely the thing Roosevelt had warned of. Worse yet, Smith engaged in out-and-out redbaiting. He delighted his Bourbon audience when he equated the New Deal with Marx and Lenin, but it did him and his cause no good, for only the far right believed it. And even fewer would have gone along with the terrible choice he put to America at the close of his speech. What was it to be, he asked, "Washington or Moscow, the Stars and Stripes or the red flag and the hammer and sickle, the Star Spangled Banner or the Internationale?" Until Smith told them, the Communists never dreamed they had so much going for them.

Smith was anathematizing the administration, virtually declaring it un-American. Nor was it a flippant judgment, spoken in the heat of anger. Smith and his Liberty League brethren had already decided to leave the Democratic Party should it renominate Roosevelt. The speech, then, was also a warning, the language of which could not be clearer. "Now it is all right with me if they [the administration] want to disguise themselves as Karl Marx or Lenin or any of that bunch, but I won't stand for their allowing them to march under the banner of Jackson or

Cleveland."[51] If, Smith was asserting, "that bunch" succeeded in capturing the great Democratic Party, he and other *true* Democrats would have to go elsewhere, much as the Hebrews carried the ark of the covenant with them wherever they went.

They were as good as their threat. With Roosevelt's re-nomination Smith and Raskob and the other Liberty League Democrats "took a walk" out of the Democratic Party and threw their support to the Republican candidate, Kansas Governor Alfred M. Landon. No single deed announced more emphatically the distance Al Smith had traveled in his itinerary through life. His quondam associates at Tammany Hall could forgive him everything but this act of apostasy, and they must have joined in the booing and hissing of his name when it came up during the Democratic convention.[52]

Smith, it could be said, conferred still another favor on Roosevelt, his last. He and the Sloans, the Du Ponts, the Pews, the Weirses, et al. enabled Roosevelt to shape the issue on which he ran for re-election—the plausibility of identifying the privileged few with the Republican Party.[53] Had the Liberty Leaguers with their generous pocketbooks stayed discretely behind the scenes, and had Smith spoken only for himself and for like-minded Americans concerned about New Deal experiments, they, the Liberty Leaguers, would not have provided such a convenient foil for Roosevelt, and his 1936 victory might not have been quite so overwhelming as it was, with what consequences for them in particular we will see.

One of Roosevelt's favorite devices during the campaign—it was always a huge hit with the crowds—was to denounce as ingrates the "economic royalists" who opposed him, for they were the people who had the most to thank him for. He drew on a stock of first-rate similes and parables to illustrate the point. For example: "In the summer of 1933, a nice old gentleman wearing a silk hat fell off the end of a pier. He was unable to swim. A friend ran down the pier, dived overboard and pulled him out; but the silk hat floated off with the tide. After the old gentleman had been revived, he was effusive in his thanks. He praised his friend for saving his life. Today, three years later, the old gentleman is berating his friend because the silk hat is lost."[54] Or: "Some of these people really forget how sick they were. But I know how sick they were. I have their fever charts. I know how the knees of all our rugged individualists were trembling four years ago and how their hearts fluttered. They came to Washington in great numbers. Washington did not look like a dangerous bureaucracy to them. Oh no! It looked like an emergency hospital. All of the distinguished patients wanted two things—a quick hypodermic to end the pain and a course of treatment to cure the disease. They wanted them in a hurry; we gave them both. And now most of the patients seem to be doing very nicely. Some of them are even well enough to throw their crutches at the doctor."[55] And, most pointedly because spoken in the heart of Liberty League country, Wilmington, Delaware (seat of the Du Pont empire), this quote from Lincoln: "'the shepherd drives the wolf from the sheep's throat, for which the sheep thanks the shepherd as his liberator, while the wolf denounces him for the same act, as the destroyer of liberty. . . . Plainly, the sheep and the wolf are not agreed upon a definition of the word liberty; and precisely the same difference prevails among us human creatures. . . .'

"Recently, as it seems, the people . . . have been doing something to define liberty, and thanks to them . . . the wolf's definition has been repudiated.'"[56]

Roosevelt's electoral strategy flowed from this characterization of the ungrateful rich. It was to identify the Republican leadership, not the rank and file, with the Liberty League and the economic royalists who had been ejected from the temple. That there was such an identity, or at least connection, between the very rich and the GOP was undeniable, especially after it became known how the Du Ponts alone contributed over half a million dollars to Roosevelt's defeat, an extravagant sum then, with the Pews of Pennsylvania contributing a like amount. It was a connection Republican politicians from presidential candidate Alfred M. Landon down found distasteful, and they were determined to open as much space as possible between themselves and the Liberty League. The 1936 Republican platform, after all, ratified much of the New Deal, and Landon himself happened to be moderately progressive. One can argue that the Liberty Leaguers might almost have been as dissatisfied with

President Landon as they had been with President Roosevelt.[57] Be that as it may, there was no question that they had grown into a large albatross. Smith and his confreres had handed Roosevelt an invaluable gift.

Not, it should be remarked, that Roosevelt could have lost the election under any conceivable circumstances. His campaign theme—that the New Deal had improved the lot of most Americans and held out the promise of improving it further—bore the ring of truth. It was invincible.

Even if Roosevelt were less well liked, even if he were a poor campaigner and Landon an exceptionally good one instead of the reverse, and even if he lacked such useful foes as the Liberty League on the one side and Father Coughlin's minions on the other, he still would easily have won and the Democrats still would have been the majority party in the nation, though perhaps not as much of one as they were. After the election it was widely speculated that the Republican Party, with scarcely a third of the national and state offices, entrenched only in the small towns of the Midwest and Northeast, would soon follow the Federalists and the Whigs into the dustbin of history.

Al Smith fought to the last. He campaigned extensively though he knew that nothing he could say would affect the outcome of the election, but he was no less strident for all that, lashing out at Roosevelt in a most unseemly fashion. Roosevelt, he would asseverate, was leading America down a path marked out by the Communist International. Moscow's master plan was "to conquer America and countries like America that have constitutional law by peaceful means rather than by bloodshed," and under Roosevelt—who, he was quick to add, was himself no Communist—the plan was duly being carried out. Love of America, it followed, meant a vote for Landon.[58]

Thus the melancholy terminus of Smith's political life. He, along with the Liberty League, closed up shop after the election. He was not the kind of man who would go on kicking up a fuss out of personal aversion for the President and his policies. And so from 1937 on he confined himself to doing what no one on earth did better: speaking for charities, bringing religious and ethnic groups together, being the lovable, witty, affable man about town that he had always been. He was citizen Al Smith and nothing more.

JOHN L. LEWIS

On May 27, 1935, the Supreme Court threw out the centerpiece of the First New Deal, the National Industrial Recovery Act. Thrown out with it was Section 7(a) and therefore the legal guarantees, for whatever they were worth, of labor's right to organize and bargain collectively. For John L. Lewis in particular the Court's decision spelled catastrophe, a return to the bad old days of unbridled competition in the coal fields.[59]

But fear of catastrophe bore an ironic result. For one thing, Roosevelt finally gave his blessing to the National Labor Relations (Wagner) Act, and it became law on July 5, 1935. It at last embodied the principle of *exclusive* rather than multiple representation and thus lent industrial unions, wherever they arose, an advantage they never had. It also forbade employers from preventing or obstructing the free exercise of workers' rights by strong-arm tactics and lockouts and company unions. And it set up a board with sufficient power through the federal courts to enforce these sweeping provisions. For another thing, Roosevelt saw to it that the coal industry remained tightly regulated, just as Lewis insisted it should, thanks to the passage on August 30 of the Bituminous Coal Conservation Act ("the little NIRA"), which for all intents and purposes Lewis had drawn up. In the end, the Supreme Court did him a gigantic favor.[60]

He could accordingly be excused his inflated pride. He and Roosevelt were perceived more and more as yoke-mates on industrial policy. Lewis often visited the White House; of no other labor leader, and very few non-politicians, could this be said. He lavished on Roosevelt the most extravagant praise, depicting himself a zealous New Dealer, a devotee of the cradle-to-grave welfare state, a radical reformer who wished to see the whole social and economic fabric redone. In only two years John L. Lewis had undergone a complete transformation. But then so had America.[61]

What Roosevelt thought of Lewis is harder to fathom. Permitting himself to be associated with Lewis in the public mind, or rather tolerating Lewis's use of that association for Lewis's own ends, did not necessarily offend Roosevelt because he found Lewis useful in advancing *his* ends. The question which Roosevelt and his close political aides must have pondered at length was how much further he would have to go before his relationship with Lewis fully crystallized, before an understanding between them was reached once and for all. One did not have to be as politically sagacious as Roosevelt to know that the only limits Lewis respected were those imposed on him by superior strength.

Instead of returning to the fold Lewis was demanding more insistently than ever that his AFL craft-union colleagues follow his lead. They were incensed when he openly sided with the industrial-union rebels who, instead of remaining cooped up within their thinned-out federal locals were forming their own independent unions, defying the AFL leaders in the process. The United Auto Workers, the United Rubber Workers, the United Electrical Workers, and others might have had relatively few members, no more than several thousand in each, yet their leaders were young, bright, and supremely self-confident left-wing rebels. Lewis embraced them as though they were his offspring, and if the AFL executive council did not like it—for, yes, he was unabashedly consorting with known Communists—they could lump it as far as he was concerned.

The council fought back by defeating his every effort to implement the 1934 resolution in favor of industrial unions, rendering it a dead letter. They made it clear to him that no matter how much he encouraged the dissidents before large enthusiastic audiences he would never carry more than a tiny minority of the AFL with him.

So the stage was set for the famous denouement at Atlantic City in October 1935. That AFL convention quickly acquired legendary status. For it was there that Lewis, in full view of the delegates, punched and knocked down the man-mountain autocrat of the carpenters' union and arch-defender of craft unionism, Big Bill Hutcheson, following an exchange of words. And it was there, in defense of his minority report, that Lewis delivered what was probably his best-known speech. His

Chautauquan eloquence was matchless; his similes burst in midair like rockets. He had been "beguiled into believing," he said, that the executive council would soon issue charters for unions in the mass-production industries. "I know better now. At San Francisco they seduced me with fair words. Now of course, having learned that I was seduced, I am enraged and am ready to rend my seducers limb from limb." The craft unions he likened to "mighty oaks" unwilling to shelter the weaker and younger unions from the "lightning and the gale." Reject the minority report, he warned, and "High wassail will prevail at the banquet tables of the mighty." He pleaded with the delegates to "heed this cry from Macedonia that comes from the hearts of men."

But it went without saying that minds had long since been made up, policies long since set. The vote went overwhelmingly against him, as predicted. His repudiation could not have been more pointed.[62]

He had no illusions about what he could accomplish single-handedly. This media personality was addressing the nation, not the convention and certainly not his fellow hierarchs. He was serving notice that the struggle for industrial unionism was about to enter a new phase and that he would be its commander-in-chief and its inspiration both.[63]

Hardly had the convention ended when, as though by prearrangement, he brought together his band of AFL followers, eight trade union leaders in all, the most significant of them being Sidney Hillman and David Dubinsky, the presidents respectively of the Amalgamated Clothing Workers and International Ladies Garment Workers, and created a special "Committee for Industrial Organization." There was no doubt about who ran the nascent CIO. Had Lewis said, "Le CIO cest moi!" he would have been speaking the exact truth. His UMW financed it and his personal associates, men of unswerving loyalty to him over the years, staffed it. The degree of his self-assurance and sense of authority could be measured by the fact that he appointed as the CIO's head organizers several of his erstwhile enemies—for example, John Brophy, once leader of the insurgent Progressive Miners Union, and the likes of Socialists Adolph Germer and Powers Hapgood, both of whom Lewis had once bodily thrown out of the coal fields. No one knew better than he that these men were radicals of the highest integrity and that whatever they thought of him as a human being they would unhesitatingly bury old grudges for the sake of a movement to which they had consecrated so much of their lives.[64]

Lewis and his men welcomed the first challenge that came their way. It enabled them to show what the CIO could do, to advertise the fact that a true labor movement had been born.

In mid-January 1936 Lewis traveled through the industrial heartland and talked to large and voluble crowds. Nowhere was he hailed more exuberantly than in Akron, America's great rubber and tire production center. He was at the top of his bent there, denouncing the rubber barons, above all Goodyear's fearsome president, Paul W. Litchfield, for unfair labor practices, specifically for threatening to restore the eight-hour day. The workers were gravely upset by this prospect, the six-hour day having become a tradition since it was introduced in 1931 as a method of spreading around the available jobs. Their mood was obvious from the brief sit-down skirmishes they had already fought against two lesser companies, Firestone and Goodrich. But these were only skirmishes.

On February 10 Goodyear dismissed two tirebuilders for refusing to work for lower rates, the prelude, it was generally believed, to the imposition of a longer day. Soon hundreds of tirebuilders, the skilled tradesmen of the industry, were not only refusing to work; they were refusing to leave the plant, thus simultaneously going out on strike and drawing maximum attention to the rebellious act. Their effectiveness was evident a week later when Goodyear workers voted with scant opposition to strike the huge factory complex, this during one of the bitterest cold snaps on record. To Goodyear's amazement all but a few of its 14,000 employees stayed out, and by mass picketing confounded every attempt to resume operations. As the weeks dragged on the CIO organizers and other radicals who flocked to Akron from all corners of America helped maintain rank-and-file discipline and advised the young and inexperienced union leaders on how to keep control in the face of every imaginable vicissitude. The demonstration of iron resolve compelled the imperious Litchfield to bargain with the United Rubber Workers and yield to its demands, even though he refused formally to recognize it or sign a contract with it. (Not until 1941 would he do so.) The empty gesture only underlined the fact, apparent at once in the boardrooms and factories of America, that Lewis and his fledgling CIO, not to mention the United Rubber Workers, had won an extraordinary victory.[65]

But in the nature of things Akron was no more than a dress rehearsal for the battle on which the outcome of the whole war probably hinged. The rubber industry, vital as it was, constituted a secondary objective. The citadel, dominated by the twin colossi of their great industries, General Motors and United States Steel, still lay in the far distance. To storm it required from Lewis and his entourage the most careful preparation.

Especially so since his enemies were not standing idly by. Showing decisiveness for once, the AFL expelled the United Mine Workers and the other CIO unions from its ranks, declaring to whoever would listen that John L. Lewis and the men surrounding him were a danger to the republic and should be shunned, resisted, and if necessary suppressed.[66]

Meanwhile, the major industrial companies were doing exactly what the Wagner Act proscribed, were indeed spending more and more on illicit measures to prevent unions from gaining a foothold among their employees. They did have a case: they expected the Supreme Court to deal as summarily with the Wagner Act as it had with the NIRA and a host of other New Deal reforms. Why, then, should these brash, upstart new unions, led by revolutionaries, be permitted to hide behind the skirts of a manifestly unconstitutional law? From Lewis's standpoint the best way to field that question—in itself valid, perhaps, given the composition of the Court—was to bring public opinion to bear on it. That was why he worked so closely with the Special Senate Committee on Violations of Free Speech and the Rights of Labor, chaired by Wisconsin's decidedly pro-union Robert M. La Follette Jr., whose sensational hearings, beginning in the fall of 1936, brought out in horrendous detail what some of the largest and most respected corporations were up to—the very corporations, it so happened, that the CIO was set to organize.[67]

Lewis needed to secure two other fronts, both of them political, before his forces could launch a full-scale attack on the citadel of capital. Ever the pragmatist, he made a deal with the strongest of the radical groups, the once hated Communist Party. In return for Communist assistance, especially for his recently formed Steel Workers Organizing Committee (SWOC)—still only the germ of a union, its whole leadership and structure having come out of the UMW—Lewis promised to protect Communists throughout the CIO from their numerous foes, left and right both, and to appoint and promote them wherever justified. After some debate the party's Political Committee ratified the arrangement. Despite their misgivings about Lewis, a brute of an enemy for so long, they were eager to pursue the Popular Front, or anti-fascist, course laid down the year before at the Seventh Party Congress in Moscow. Forming alliances with progressives was their first and paramount order of business. To that end class antagonisms were muted, ancient enmities abandoned, improbable friendships forged. The agreement with Lewis, then, involved no big issue of principle.[68]

The Communists went on to carry out their part of the bargain. Their organizers were instrumental in signing up foreign-born and black steel workers for SWOC, two substantial components of the steel industry's labor force. Lewis, good as his word, saw to it that no redbaiting divided the CIO and that talented Communists were appointed to high positions. There was, as Lewis told the editor of the Communist *Daily Worker*, "room for everybody."

Roosevelt's re-election was the other political front he needed to secure. Without Roosevelt at the helm the CIO campaign, for all its preparations and brio, might collapse. And so, in fact, might Lewis's own UMW, despite its hundreds of thousands of dedicated members, its millions of dollars in yearly dues, its aura of invincibility. This possibility was startlingly brought home to him in 1936 when the Supreme Court threw out the Bituminous Coal Conservation Act ("the little NIRA"), thereby plunging coal into the throes of anarchy for the second time in a year. And for the second time, or rather third if one goes back to 1933, Roosevelt came to the rescue by getting through Congress yet another stabilization act for coal (the Guffey-Vinson

Act).[69] Roosevelt's indispensability to Lewis could not be clearer. Moving with his accustomed temerity, Lewis formed a CIO political action committee (misnamed the Labor Non-Partisan League) and set aside nearly $600,000 for Roosevelt and other candidates in the upcoming election, this on top of the million or so already given to SWOC and the CIO. Such amounts seem negligible today, when some campaigns for a single U.S. House seat may cost much more. In the 1930s they were considered huge—Roosevelt gratefully thought so— and Lewis could, with a modicum of truth, regard himself as the Mark Hanna of the election. That Roosevelt regarded himself as its William McKinley may be doubted.[70]

Roosevelt's great victory buoyed Lewis and the rest of the CIO militants, giving them a sense of omnipotence. They would hardly have taken such extreme chances if they did not now believe that the future was theirs to possess and that America stood firmly with them as they poised to do battle.

Looking back after all these years we realize why the General Motors strike has lost none of its power to astonish. It is as if the whole vast concatenation of events revolved around the doings of a few adventurous radicals, Communists mostly, in the city of Flint, Michigan. The story, often told, sometimes expertly, has acquired mythic dimensions. Well it should, for it describes or celebrates nothing less than the decisive engagement of the great labor wars of the New Deal era.[71]

On December 30, 1936, hundreds of members of the United Auto Workers suddenly ousted the supervisory personnel from General Motors' two Fisher Body plants in Flint and locked the doors behind them. Strikes were also closing other GM factories across America but the ones in Flint were particularly harmful to the company because Fisher supplied the bodies for its cars, whatever the division (Pontiac, Oldsmobile, Cadillac, etc.). GM faced the prospect of complete paralysis. Yet the sit-down, for all its momentary effectiveness and elan, seemed futile, little more than a heroic statement, perhaps an act of martyrdom. GM was simply too big. With 250,000 employees and 110 factories coast to coast it completely dominated the automobile market, earning sizable profits even in the slough of the Depression. It was the pride and envy of the industrial world.

That was why the tiny United Auto Workers union, sustained by the CIO, put so much effort into seeking out GM's vulnerabilities—the vulnerabilities of a goliath. The organizers, most of them Communist auto workers, for months had been mapping out the strategy of assault, laboriously recruiting men who were willing to do whatever was asked of them. The leaders had settled on the tail end of the year for the move partly because Michigan's new governor, Frank Murphy (who had introduced Father Coughlin to Roosevelt in 1932), a deep-grained liberal, was about to take office, and partly because a strike begun earlier would have deprived the men of their Christmas bonuses. Nor, on the other hand, could the strike start much later given the fact that union militants everywhere were restless, straining to march without waiting for official approval. And there was the fact or rumor that GM was stealthily preparing to move Fisher Body machinery from Flint to another and safer city. It was then or never.

The strike could be likened to a drama in three acts, each set off by a violent and successful defense of their position by the men, each marked by a significant enlargement of the conflict.

The first act was rather subdued. The men who struck Fisher Body numbers 1 and 2 developed a community of their own, winning in the process the admiration of more and more workers otherwise neutral or even unsympathetic to the strike. The UAW's immediate object was to legitimate a patently illegal deed, the seizure of private property, a deed, however, which caused no physical harm—this in contrast to the only alternative, mass picketing. The union's ultimate object, of course, was to gain recognition as the GM workers' sole bargaining agent. GM had no intention of recognizing the existence of the fledgling union, much less bargaining with it, since it represented an insignificant fraction of the workers, was a nesting ground for Communists, and as if these were not enough, was guilty of a dreadful crime. By dealing with such an organization GM would not only be sanctioning lawlessness, it would be letting down the rest of corporate America and all Americans who valued private property and established order. The two sides were girding for a fight to the finish.

GM clearly got the worst of the public relations contest. For one thing, the La Follette committee was just then informing the country of pervasive violations of civil liberties in the auto industry. For another, GM appeared to encourage crude vigilantism by backing a company union, the Flint Alliance, which, it was revealed, had been arming itself for an eventual shoot-out with the striking UAW. And for yet another thing, GM committed an embarrassing gaffe when it asked for and received an injunction against the sit-down strikers from a judge who, it was learned, owned considerable GM stock.

The second act opened on January 11, 1937, with the "Battle of the Running Bulls," a legendary event in labor lore. The police, exasperated by the standoff and their impotence, did something foolhardy on that fiercely cold day: they tried to break into Fisher Body no. 2, using tear gas for the purpose. After being routed with some ignominy, the police fired into a crowd of pickets that had just gathered, wounding several. As a result of the violence Governor Murphy ordered state troopers to Flint, not to dispossess the strikers—who vowed resistance against no matter what authority—but to maintain the status quo. In effect, Murphy was throwing a cordon of protection around the two plants and their occupants. He wanted to avoid driving them out as long as possible, to use them as leverage in bringing GM and the UAW together. Roosevelt felt as Murphy did that it would be an unforgivable mistake to force the workers out of the factories merely because they were trespassing. Through Secretary of Labor Perkins, Roosevelt kept abreast of the negotiations, doing whatever he could to advance them from behind the scenes. Such were the larger consequences arising from the Battle of the Running Bulls.

Murphy did finally get the parties to come to terms. The UAW agreed to call off the strike and evacuate the men. GM promised not to start up production or shift machinery from the Fisher plants during the collective bargaining. But just as the agreement was about to be ratified the UAW discovered that GM was secretly negotiating with the Flint Alliance. The UAW cried betrayal—which it certainly was—and ordered the sit-down to continue. Henceforth it would trust only GM's written word.

The crisis had grown too big for Murphy to handle alone. Roosevelt now entered as one of the central protagonists. John L. Lewis took over from the UAW, and GM's legendary chairman, Alfred P. Sloan, whose genius had made the company the colossus it was, came in too, but only reluctantly and at Roosevelt's personal request. For Sloan there was nothing to discuss: the government's responsibility was to uphold the Constitution and punish its violators, the handful of outlaws who remained in the plants. Sloan was of course intimately connected to the Du Ponts, who controlled about 40 percent of GM stock, and therefore to John J. Raskob and Al Smith, all of them mainstays of the now defunct Liberty League which had tried to unhorse Roosevelt in the election. Sloan, then, saw Roosevelt and Lewis as leaders of a vicious anti-business cabal. And while he could not refuse the President he could and did refuse to sit with Lewis. To Secretary Perkins, Sloan laid down his minimal condition for participating in the talks: the immediate departure of the strikers from Fisher Body numbers 1 and 2. Lewis was equally adamant: first a contract with the UAW, then their removal. Roosevelt, for all his charm and powers of persuasion, was unable to do anything.[72]

The nation was looking on with heightened interest as the lead actors competed for its favor. On January 21 Lewis held a crowded press conference in Washington. His point was that Roosevelt now had a chance to repay his debt to those who helped him beat back "the economic royalists of General Motors" in the 1936 election. "The same economic royalists now have their fangs in labor," Lewis went on, "and the workers expect the Administration in every reasonable and legal way to support the auto workers in their fight with the same rapacious enemy."[73] Exactly what he expected Roosevelt to do was left unsaid. How could Roosevelt compel General Motors to submit?

If Lewis was hoping to win the public to the side of the strikers he certainly failed. The press came down heavily on him and on Roosevelt too. Here was a swaggering, despotic labor boss—so he was universally depicted—ordering the President of the United States to fulfill his part of an implied, perhaps explicit, arrangement between them. The middle class had had enough, and its gorge was visibly rising.[74] Lewis's press conference, moreover, gave Sloan his pretext for being done with the whole sordid affair and returning to New York City. Roosevelt at his own press conference said that Lewis's statement was "not in order." A few days later he also criticized Sloan's petulance.[75]

Some historians trace the enmity between Lewis and Roosevelt to these exchanges. In fact, there was scarcely a trace of enmity in them. What one does notice is that Lewis by his deliberate gaucheries had done Roosevelt and himself a good turn. He had allowed Roosevelt to distance himself from him and the sit-down strikers, thereby enhancing Roosevelt's status as honest broker. Like Murphy he was being denounced in conservative circles for his refusal to at least clarify the issues by condemning the takeover of the plants as illegal and wrong. This he and Murphy could not do. Roosevelt's spat with Lewis, or rather the public's perception of a spat, could be interpreted as an intelligent tactic, serving as it did to improve Roosevelt's position as an arbiter in the next round of negotiations.[76]

For a while it appeared there would be no further negotiations. Against a background of burgeoning violence in one strike-bound community after another, GM chose to pursue a tougher line. It sought a renewal of the injunction, this time from a judge whose rectitude was beyond cavil. Once such an injunction was handed down could the governor fail to do his duty? The forces of suppression were closing in on the strikers.

Their response, which began act three of the drama, was more daring and defiant than anything that had gone on before, and they pulled it off with a display of virtuosity that military strategists would have admired.

It occurred on the very day the Court heard GM's plea for an injunction. The strikers' plan was to seize Chevrolet plant number 4 in Flint, the jewel in the company's crown, producer alone of a million engines a year. It was of course heavily guarded against such a possibility. So the chief organizer of the strike, a young Communist named Robert Travis, thought up a ruse. On January 31 he held a secret meeting of UAW functionaries to announce in strictest confidence that an adjoining (and much smaller) Chevrolet factory, number 9, would be taken the next day. Travis knew that the information would instantly end up in the hands of GM and the police. Even the media were present the following afternoon when workers arriving on the swing shift struck Chevrolet no. 9. GM's security personnel, many of them withdrawn from the other plants, were waiting in force. After a brief scuffle, in which tear gas was used, the strikers were subdued and evicted. But they had held out long enough for the real event to unfold—the union's easy capture of unguarded Chevrolet no. 4. The feint had worked masterfully. The media, the cheering pickets, the dejected security forces, all rushed to the site of the latest UAW coup. This further defeat for General Motors, the leviathan of American capitalism, was not lost on the employees, few of whom, it should be repeated, belonged as yet to the union.

The maneuver seemed to take the fight out of the corporation, though the world did not yet know it. Perhaps GM's top executives concluded that too much blood would flow before the plants could be regained and that the public, meaning millions of consumers—at a time of explosively high sales—might blame the company for having caused it. Nor could the cost from damage to the machinery be minimized, machinery that might take years to replace. There was no alternative to negotiations with the hated UAW.

The culmination had its own *sturm und drang,* at the heart of which, naturally enough, stood the granite figure of John L. Lewis.

The talks got under way in Detroit under considerable pressure. More troops than ever surrounded the three struck plants. The judge who had handed down the injunction would not be put off much longer, and on February 5 he ordered the county sheriff to clear out the strikers. The union, breathing fire, in effect dared the sheriff to try. The political leaders could not waste an instant; the hammer was on the anvil. Roosevelt worked on Sloan and the Du Ponts and other corporate statesmen. Murphy worked on Lewis, who stated unequivocally that he would never ask the men to leave the plants until their basic terms—recognition by GM of the union—had been met. It was still a stalemate.[77]

Murphy squeezed harder. On February 9 he read Lewis a letter penned in anguish the night before, the gist of which was that unless Lewis yielded, he, Murphy, would see to it that the "occupied plants" were returned at once to "their rightful owners." He had no choice. We have evidence of Lewis's reaction to the letter from two sources. One is from a journalist who claimed to have overheard Lewis tell Murphy the following: "I am not going to withdraw these sit-downers under any circumstances except a settlement. What are you going to do? You can get them out in just one way, by bayonets. You have the bayonets. What kind do you prefer to use—the broad double blade or the four-sided French style? I believe the square style makes a bigger hole and you can turn it around inside a man. Which kind of bayonet, Governor Murphy, are you going to turn around inside our boys?"[78]

The other is from Lewis himself and therefore may be a richly embellished version of what actually happened. The best account of it (for there are several worth re-telling for their own sakes) is to be found in Saul Alinsky's hagiographical study.[79] Alinsky writes:

> Lewis fixed a stony stare upon the Governor and then began in a very low voice. "Uphold the law? You are going to do this to uphold the law? You, Frank Murphy, are ordering the National Guard to evict by point of bayonet or rifle bullet the sit-down strikers? You, Frank Murphy, are giving complete victory to General Motors and defeating all of the hopes and dreams of these men. And you are doing this you say '*to uphold the law!*'"Lewis continued with his voice rising with each sentence. "Governor Murphy, when you gave ardent support to the Irish revolutionary movement against the British Empire you were not doing that because of your high regard for law and order. You did not then say, 'Uphold the law!' When your father, Governor Murphy, was imprisoned by the British authorities for his activities as an Irish revolutionary you did not sing forth with hosannas and say, 'The law cannot be wrong. The law must be supported. It is right and just that my father be put in prison! Praise be the law!' And when the British government took your grandfather as an Irish revolutionary and hanged him by the neck until dead, you did not get down on your knees and burst forth in praise for the sanctity and glory and purity of the law, the law that must be upheld at all costs!
>
> "But here, Governor Murphy, you do. You want my answer, sir! I give it to you. Tomorrow morning, I shall personally enter General Motors plant Chevrolet No. 4. I shall order the men to disregard your order, to stand fast. I shall then walk up to the largest window in the plant, open it, divest myself of my outer raiment, remove my shirt, and bare my bosom. Then when you order your troops to fire, mine will be the first heart that these bullets will strike!"
>
> Then Lewis lowered his voice. "And as my body falls from the window to the ground, you listen to the voice of your grandfather as he whispers in your ear, 'Frank, are you sure you are doing the right thing?'"

Actually, the negotiations were drawing to a close when, presumably, Lewis uttered these words; only the details of an agreement remained to be discussed. Those details were important to be sure, for they concerned above all the vexing question of how much time should elapse between the settlement and the vote by the workers on whether or not the UAW would represent them. GM wanted the least possible time, the union the most; both assumed that the more time the union had to present its case to the rank and file the better its chances of winning a majority and receiving certification. GM's other concessions already amounted to a huge victory for the UAW. No more than three months, said GM. At least six months, Lewis insisted. The Roosevelt administration got GM to give in. On the night of February 10 Lewis received the news of the capitulation, while lying in his hotel bed with the flu, from the lips of GM's chief counsel himself.

The next day the strikers victoriously marched out of the factories to the cheers of the thousands who were on hand and the millions who were not. The drama in three acts was over 71 days after it began.

GM's direst apprehensions came to pass. In one factory after another, even those that had been the most adamant in resisting UAW organizers, GM employees signed up with the union that had against all odds humbled their great and terrifying boss. Now it was the UAW which appeared all-conquering, and it had little trouble winning over the lesser auto and auto-parts manufacturers, among them Packard and Studebaker and, after a brief and tempestuous sit-down strike, Chrysler, third biggest in the industry. That a majority of GM's workers would vote for the union in August was by then a foregone conclusion, and GM accepted the verdict, when it came, with surprising equanimity. Bad as the results were from its point of view, the resumption of war would have been infinitely worse.

The larger strategy that underlay the GM strike quickly redounded to the advantage of Lewis and his minions. Even as the strike was going on the chairman of the board of United States Steel, New York financier Myron C. Taylor, was surreptitiously meeting with Lewis to arrange a deal whereby the company would recognize the Steel Workers Organizing Committee (SWOC) as the steelworkers' union. Taylor was one of those capitalists for whom Roosevelt and the New Deal, and indeed the emergent CIO, held no terror. To him, industrial peace and stability was the main desideratum, and he was willing to pay a price—namely, break with hidebound open-shop (union-free) principles—to achieve it. The agreement, announced on March 2, 1937, caught everyone by surprise, even Lewis's and Taylor's own associates.[80]

It was a *fait accompli.* SWOC members had no voice in the contract, generous as it was to U.S. Steel's employees. The union's officers were chosen from above, that is, directly or indirectly by Lewis. In form and structure SWOC was no less autocratic than its parent, the United Mine Workers. It was headed by Philip Murray, for years Lewis's most faithful lieutenant and best friend (if Lewis can be said to have had a close friend outside his immediate family), the only man allowed to call him Jack.[81] What could not be gainsaid was that Lewis had scored his most spectacular victory. With a stroke of the pen some 200,000 members joined the union's rolls, and Lewis and Murray could look forward to increasing that number several times over: few doubted that the rest of the giant industry would soon follow its leader.

Within a couple of months, then, the twin citadels of American business enterprise had fallen to the CIO, one of them having surrendered without a struggle. There had been nothing like such an upheaval in the annals of American labor. Industrial unionism, once a distant dream, or fantasy, had come with a great rush and was now, by the spring of 1937, a powerful presence in the sprawling, company controlled mill towns of the East and West, comprehending as no movement ever did America's diverse religious, ethnic and racial groups and such a range of disparate and even conflicting ideologies, from far right to far left. The newly risen CIO was a force to reckon with. And so, manifestly, was its leader.

The euphoria induced by its early triumphs could not of course last indefinitely. The Ford Motor Company was proving more obdurate than anticipated. Instead of being swept along by the UAW machine, old man Ford rallied his army of security toughs, led by the redoubtable Harry Bennett, and the union after a while had to end the campaign and admit total defeat.

More serious was the outcome of the war between SWOC and "Little Steel," the smaller companies—Bethlehem, Jones and Laughlin, Republic, among others—which refused to follow Myron Taylor's example and insisted on retaining the open shop in their considerable portion of the industry. Overconfidence was certainly one of the reasons SWOC lost the strike. It was overconfidence born partly of the Supreme Court's April 12, 1937 decision upholding the Wagner Act, a decision freighted with symbolic meaning, the defendant having been Jones and Laughlin, one of the mainstays of Little Steel. Would the companies fail to heed the Court's ringing endorsement of unioniza-tion and collective bargaining? Yet it can also be argued that no amount of preparation and intelligent leadership could have enabled SWOC to beat Little Steel. The murderous resolve of those companies was brought home to the rank and file early on in the strike—Memorial Day 1937 to be exact—when the Chicago police slew 10 pickets in cold blood and wounded countless more near one of Republic's mills. The strike, thus ill-fated from the start, dragged on for about a month before SWOC gave up.[82]

Labor historians and Lewis's biographers make much of the tension that arose between Lewis and Roosevelt during the Little Steel strike. The consensus among them is that their alliance, not to mention their friendship, deteriorated from this moment on, that Lewis never forgave Roosevelt for his treachery. Certainly the public assumed at the time that they had fallen out. This was obvious from the sequence of events.

Lewis and Murray had pleaded with Roosevelt for help, meaning that he should pressure Little Steel to negotiate with SWOC as he had pressured GM to negotiate with the UAW. But at a news conference on June 29, as the strike was petering out, Roosevelt said, with appropriate emphasis: "A plague on both your houses."[83] Two months later, Lewis, in a Labor Day speech broadcast to the nation, issued a stinging reply, one that could have come only from him: "Labor, like Israel, has many sorrows. Its women weep for the fallen, and they lament for the future of the children of the race. It ill-behooves one who has supped at labor's table and who has been sheltered in labor's house to curse with equal fervor and impartiality both labor and its adversaries when they become locked in deadly embrace."[84]

Whether Roosevelt and Lewis would break completely or had already broken was a subject that occupied the press and the political columnists for a season.

But, as Lewis's best biographers, Dubofsky and Van Tine, inform us, there was no proof of a break, a falling out, or even demonstrable hostility between them. Lewis may have chided Roosevelt for failing sufficiently to distinguish his friends from his enemies. That hardly affected the resiliency of their working alliance. The very appearance of hostility was, again, almost calculated to benefit Roosevelt. The little Steel Strike caught Roosevelt at a very inopportune moment. He was just then experiencing his own fiasco over the Supreme Court-packing bill. Opposition to that bill had called forth a viable anti-New Deal coalition, dissipating much of the promise of Roosevelt's election only a few months before. With his unexcelled ear for public attitudes, he saw how injurious it would be for him to be identified as an uncritical ally of John L. Lewis and the other troublemakers who seemed to be shutting the country down with impunity whenever they liked. More and more Americans were turning against labor, were angered by the long strikes, the seizure of property, the ominous sense of class warfare abroad in the land. Roosevelt's remarks, therefore, may have struck just the right note.

Nor did it hurt him to be reproved by Lewis—as Lewis well knew. Despite the contretemps, each depended on the other as much as ever: the shift to the right brought Roosevelt closer to organized labor. As we already pointed out, Lewis needed, and received, Roosevelt's help in restoring yet again the Coal Conservation Act. No, the alliance was intact, though now it was less open and demonstrative than before.[85]

Setbacks and all, Lewis was indisputably the man of the hour. He was the lion of Washington society, the most sought after of its celebrities. His press conferences were occasions. He was, next to Roosevelt, perhaps

America's most quoted figure. His successes spoke for themselves; the horn he tooted so loudly in his own behalf was not an empty one. His audacity had been entirely vindicated. The mass-production industries were wholly or partially organized. His CIO now comprised 29 unions, with a total membership of over three million, a number roughly the same as the AFL's. And he had no doubt that this militant new institution, bursting with zeal and optimism, would under his tutelage carry everything before it; it would draw millions more into its fold, including those who belonged to existing AFL unions, soon to be a pile of whitened bones. The age of the CIO had arrived, and John L. Lewis was its master.[86]

FOUR

THE ISOLATIONIST IMPULSE

FATHER COUGHLIN

In January 1937 Father Coughlin returned to the air, barely two months after vowing never to do so again. Millions again tuned in to the familiar voice at the accustomed time. He broke the vow, he explained, because the beloved Bishop Gallagher had, on his deathbed, asked him to resume the broadcasts for the sake of Christ. That promise had to be kept.[1]

It did not take long before Coughlin found himself in hot water. The chief target of his animus now was John L. Lewis and the CIO, an organization he had once embraced. In one broadcast after another and in the pages of *Social Justice* Coughlin denounced the CIO as subversive of Christianity, a partner in the enveloping Communist conspiracy. As for Roosevelt's complicity in its rise—his friendship with Lewis and the other leaders, his refusal to intervene in strikes—that spoke for itself, providing further evidence, as if any were needed, of which foreign ideology he served.[2]

Gallagher's replacement as bishop of Detroit, Edward Mooney, happened to sympathize with the CIO. So did many other prominent Catholics, in and out of the church, among them the governor of Michigan, the same Frank Murphy who had brought Coughlin and Roosevelt together and whose own refusal to forcibly open the occupied

General Motors plant had saved the day for the striking workers and therefore the union. Though he left Coughlin alone, Mooney often let it be known where *he* stood. Coughlin thus found himself in an uncomfortable position. In one September 1937 broadcast he argued that for Catholics to belong to the Communist-run CIO was equivalent to their worshipping in a mosque. This was too much for the bishop. He publicly chastised Coughlin and stated that membership in the CIO was perfectly compatible with devotion to Catholicism and that no priest had the authority to say otherwise. Undeniably, Mooney continued, there were Communists in the CIO, but there were more Catholics in it and the Catholics would sooner or later defeat the Communists.

In a fit of pique Coughlin canceled his remaining broadcasts.[3] This elicited a flood of mail, much of it abusive, most of it descending on poor Bishop Mooney; protest meetings were held; petitions were circulated. So loud was the uproar the Vatican was forced to announce its support for Mooney, and Coughlin had to ask his fanatical devotees to cease and desist. And again he vowed to be silent as a tomb.

But again he broke the vow, this time evidently at the express wish of the Vatican, or someone in the Vatican Council, perhaps from the Pope's Apostolic Delegate to the United States who, it is known, met with Coughlin on December 11, 1937.[4] Coughlin himself said many years later: "I had lots of friends at the Vatican, people who could not agree with me publicly. But they knew I spoke the truth. They knew that I recognized the Communist threat to the church."[5]

He was referring to what can only be called a major policy decision by Pope Pius XI. It amounted to this: the church must support, and even align itself with, any positive force in the world, however unpalatable that force might be in itself, which would contribute to the destruction of the paramount evil, Communism. The church felt that the time had come to take sides, for the Communist threat, broadly construed, was rising. The church was under siege in Mexico, where it was being ruthlessly suppressed; in France, where the government was a Popular Front of Communists and Socialists; and worst of all in Spain, where the

civil war was raging unabated between the devoutly anti-clerical Republicans, or Loyalists, and the Fascists, or Rebels, led by General Francisco
Franco, who among other things favored restoration of Catholic privi-
leges. From the church's standpoint the Spanish Civil War focused the
global character of the struggle between good and evil. Could it be
accidental that assistance for the Loyalists came mainly, one could say
entirely, from the Soviet Union and the Comintern, while Hitler's
Germany and Mussolini's Italy gave massive assistance to Franco's army?
Finding virtue in the likes of Hitler and Mussolini was perhaps an
unpleasant necessity for Pius XI (though he had already embraced, and
with a good deal of enthusiasm, such pro-Catholic dictators as Dollfuss
of Austria, Salazar of Portugal, and Horthy of Hungary), but he found
it anyway, and the church naturally followed suit.[6]

In his encyclical *Divinis Redemptoris* the Pope was indistinguishable
from Father Coughlin. A "powerful factor in the diffusion of communism," according to the encyclical, "is the conspiracy of silence on the
part of a large section of the non-Catholic press of the world. We say
conspiracy because it is impossible to explain otherwise how the press . . .
has been able to remain silent so long about the horrors perpetrated in
Russia, in Mexico, and even in a great part of Spain, and that it should
have relatively little to say concerning a world organization so vast as
Russian communism. This silence is due in part to short-sighted political
philosophy, and is favored by various occult forces which for a long time
have been working for the overthrow of the Christian social order."[7]

Vatican policy was soon reflected in the American church, among
leaders lay and clerical. Anti-Communism was their order of the day, and
by anti-Communism they meant what Coughlin meant, though they
hesitated to go as far as he did by painting anyone on the left who failed
to share their convictions in shades of red. Under this sweeping criterion
even some of the faithful—the publishers, editors, and writers of the liberal
Catholic magazine *Commonweal,* for example—were suspect. What else
could account for the fact that they sided with the enemy, the Spanish
Loyalists, whose bastion of support was the international Communist
movement? These recusants, however, represented a tiny minority of the
faithful, and if by chance a clergyman agreed with them he kept his own
counsel.[8] That Roosevelt and his liberal administration were suspect went

without saying. Roosevelt did scrupulously adhere to a neutral course in foreign affairs and publicly took no sides in the Spanish Civil War. But he did so out of compulsion, because the American people would countenance no other course. It was well known that he reluctantly went along with the January 1937 joint congressional resolution which banned the export of munitions to Spain, thereby increasing Franco's advantage. Roosevelt showed where his heart really belonged in his famous speech of October 5, 1937, calling upon the United States to join with like-minded nations to "quarantine" aggressors, the aggressors of course being Italy, Germany, and Japan (though he mentioned no names), all of them, it so happened, front-line powers in the struggle against the Soviet Union, all of them signatories to the Anti-Comintern Pact, two of them, Italy and Germany, being Franco's indispensable allies.[9]

Taking their cue from the Pope, and going along with Coughlin, the American clergy resented Roosevelt's hand-wringing concern about Fascist misbehavior and his indifference to the, in their opinion, much greater Communist or Communist-inspired crimes. Nor did they count it accidental that American reds and their crimson-hued friends now looked upon Roosevelt and the New Deal benignantly, as co-participants in the Popular Front against Fascism. It was no accident and certainly no secret that the Communists backed Roosevelt in 1936, even though they ran their own presidential candidate, and that Roosevelt had become something of a hero to them. Under the circumstances many liberal Catholics, hitherto staunch New Dealers, began to change, to reassess the whole character of the administration. They now judged liberalism from a different, and it could be said more Coughlinite, angle of vision.[10]

We therefore can appreciate the reasons why Father Coughlin received so much encouragement from his fellow churchmen when he returned to the air on January 9, 1938. It was useful to have this Peck's Bad Boy say openly—and, yes, outrageously—to his enormous audience what they, his fellow churchmen, were discussing privately. In truth there was no one like him.

If in the years past Coughlin was attracted to the fascist system he had let few know about it; occasionally he had even denounced it as un-

American, though of course nothing so un-American as Communism. Now he was finding much to rejoice in Fascism. Increasingly, he expressed his disappointment with democratic institutions, resting as they did on the weight of sheer numbers, the absence of standards, the failure to distinguish, and hence reward, the more desirable groups, the inexorable tendency to lawlessness and disorder. Coughlin talked instead of "corporate democracy," a political way of life from which party conflicts would be banished. Drawing on the accomplishments of the Austrian, Italian, and German regimes he would turn America into a semi-syndicalist state, one in which political representation would be accorded not to individuals in the form of "mobocracy," but to economic collectivities or syndicates—farmers, businessmen, workers, et al. Coughlin emphasized that he was not laying down a blueprint, only suggesting a guideline for overhauling the Constitution so as to bring it into conformity with the best the modern world had to offer. The Constitution must either ride the wave of modernity or sink without a trace.[11]

How thoroughly he adopted the fascist formula he made all too clear in the summer of 1938. It was then that he fully and proudly launched his ferocious anti-Semitic campaign, though he denied that such an odious word could ever apply to him.

He did so in the course of establishing a new political action outfit, the Christian Front, his patriotic and Christian version of the Communist-inspired Popular Front. For some time Coughlin had been urging militant Christians to form "Social Justice Platoons" at the neighborhood level. These, he now said, would constitute the nuclei of the emergent Christian Front, much as Communists cells were the nuclei of the Popular Front.[12] His hope was that the Christian Front, numbering in the millions one day, would influence the 1938 congressional and the 1940 presidential elections, when Roosevelt would be gone and with him the Jews who ran the administration. No, Coughlin asserted defiantly, the Christian Front did not fear "the word 'fascist,' because it knows the word 'fascist' is bandied about as part of Communism's offense mechanism." Nor did it "fear to be called 'anti-Semitic,' because it KNOWS the term 'anti-Semitic' is only another pet phrase of castigation in Communism's glossary of attack."[13]

But the phrase did fit perfectly, as he well knew, once his journal began publishing the notoriously anti-Semitic *Protocols of the Elders of Zion* in July 1938. He admitted that the *Protocols* might be fraudulent. No matter. The important thing for him was that the Jews, as both bankers and Communists, were scheming to bring down America and Western civilization.[14] And that scheme, he claimed, was advancing on schedule. "Is it not true," he asked, "that the synagogue of Satan, under the leadership of anti-Christ, has hindered and hampered the activity of the Mystical Body of Christ? . . . Is it not true that a force, over which we Christians seem to have no control, has gained control of journalism, motion pictures, theatres and radio? . . . Is it not true that some unseen force has woven the threads of International banking to the detriment of civilization; that a godless force is dominating industry, . . . that gold, the international medium of exchange, has been concentrated in the hands of a few private individuals while nations languished, poverty-stricken, with want in the midst of plenty?"[15] And so on and on he traced the curse of the modern world to the infernal Jew.

He was presenting a line on the "Jewish question" similar to the one espoused by the Nazi regime and echoed by its numerous hangers-on and friends in the United States. Subscribing to that line also, no doubt, was a large proportion of the estimated 13 million folk who listened to Coughlin every Sunday evening. For his information, for the details of Jewish maleficence, he relied heavily of Dr. Josef Goebbels's fecund propaganda mill.[16] Coughlin's most blatant canard was that Jewish investment bankers, chief among them New York's Kuhn Loeb Company, had financed the Bolshevik Revolution and that it was therefore hardly accidental that all but one or two leading Bolsheviks, from 1917 to the present, were Jews. Coughlin proved this fabrication by revealing their real names, so egregiously Jewish sounding (Leon Trotsky, Lev Bronstein, etc.).[17] For that matter, whenever referring to a public figure who happened to be Jewish he would conspicuously note the fact. He would repeat verbatim the lies Goebbels had been spouting, without acknowledging their source, of course. Not that it bothered him when the press divulged the source, dark and hideous as it was, or when the alleged participants in the conspiracy— Kuhn Loeb, Kerensky, Russia's pathetically weak premier before the Bolshevik uprising, and Trotsky, then in Mexican exile—refuted the charge. Coughlin could not have cared less: for him as for Goebbels ideology alone defined the standard of truth.

But he was in a tight situation. He was borrowing from the Nazis precisely when the Nazis were falling into increasing disfavor with the American public. They were embarking on a new round of anti-Semitic persecutions, the culmination of which was the monstrous *Kristallnacht* affair of November 9-10, 1938, the pogrom sponsored by the German government which destroyed vast amounts of Jewish property, gutted synagogues, and brutalized and killed scores of people, after which the government held the Jewish community financially liable for the losses incurred. In protest, the United States recalled its ambassador to Germany. Coughlin could have distanced himself from the Nazis, asserting that his views on the Jewish question had nothing in common with theirs. Instead, in one broadcast after another, he served as their apologist. He compared what was to him minor persecution suffered by some German Jews to the massive persecution suffered by all Christians in Russia and elsewhere at the hands of Communists. And scarcely any Jews, he complained, protested against *those* persecutions, leading one to suspect that maybe they approved of them.[18]

Moreover, he continued, the German Jews shared the blame for their fate. They had failed to root out the Communists in their midst. That was why their loyalty to the German nation was in doubt, why excesses, deplorable to be sure, were committed against them. But they were excesses that must be understood dispassionately, indeed sympathetically. "Simply as a student of history," Coughlin said, giving Hitler's minions the benefit of every outrage, "I am endeavoring to analyze the reasons for the growth of the idea in the minds of the Nazi Party that Communism and Judaism are too closely interwoven for the national health of Germany."[19]

He criticized American Jews by the same rules of logic. If, he stated over and over, there was anti-Semitism in the United States the Jews should look to themselves. From their loins sprung the enemies of the people, the bankers and Communists and the like, and they by their silence or indifference must be held accountable. Coughlin went on to advise the Jews of America on how they could redeem themselves and so avoid the anti-Semitism that was sure to come, the German events being a harbinger of what lay in store for them here. They must pass a political test he took the trouble to draw up in their behalf—such was his concern for their welfare. They "must repudiate atheistic Jews and international Jews." They must "fight Communism as vigorously as they fight Nazism," for, to quote Christ, "'You are either with Me or against Me.'"[20] He appealed to "the highly intelligent Jews of America who recognize these truths. . . . I humbly admit your influence in banking, press and radio. And I humbly suggest, for your own sakes and the sakes of the less informed members of your race, that you, too, will recognize that there is no anti-Semitic question in America, but that there is an anti-Communist question which cannot be solved except your genius and your assistance are thrown into the battle on the side of God and country."[21]

The implications could not be more clearly spelled out. Father Coughlin, self-proclaimed spokesman for Christian America, was warning the Jews, humbly, as their friend, that they would go on being tolerated as long as they obeyed the canons of behavior which he was prescribing for their "race." They had to be made to realize that as outsiders they were welcome only on sufferance. They still had a chance to save themselves, but only if they demonstrated that they were not a force for ill to those who, like Father Coughlin, had their true interests at heart. And should they persist in their recalcitrance America's Christian charity and forbearance might run out. "My fellow Jews," he counseled them, "please understand our Christian attitude toward all of this. You are a minority—a small but powerful minority. We are a majority—an easygoing, paternal majority—but a majority always conscious of our latent power."[22]

Now why did Coughlin resort to such virulent anti-Semitism at this time? Most scholars, to the extent they bother to raise the question, contend he did so for opportunistic reasons, to keep or enlarge his radio audience and with it his political influence. But this obviously begs the question: Why did his opportunism, if that was his motive, take this particular form and no other?

Consider the world situation as Coughlin perceived it in 1938, when he openly espoused Fascism. The strongest and most resolute opponent of Communism was incontestably Adolph Hitler. If there was any force on earth that might extirpate the evil root and branch it was Hitler's Germany, the democracies being notable only for their pusillanimity. Hitler had liquidated the largest Communist Party in the West and had destroyed the rest of the German left. He was boldly intervening in Spain, underwriting Franco's imminent victory. He was relentlessly mobilizing Germany and her friends for the great crusade to come. And who could deny that his rule so far had been a succession of triumphs? His armies had marched into the Rhineland, taken over the Saar, annexed Austria, and grabbed part of Czechoslovakia, all in a little more than two years. Hitler's unfolding new order might have been imperfect from Coughlin's point of view—his violent methods could not always be condoned and his treatment of the Catholic Church left much to be desired—but his Germany was embarked on a heroic endeavor, and for that alone he deserved the uncritical applause of right-thinking Christians.[23]

The benefits of Hitler's emergent new order might soon be felt in America as well. That at least was what Coughlin was betting on. Should Fascism dominate and transform Western civilization, a likely prospect, what would America's destiny be? So far as Coughlin was concerned nothing could be more salutary than America's own transformation. He assumed that modern Communism, or "Jew-Bolshevism," was merely an extension of traditional liberal values, the ideology of enslavement being the inevitable outgrowth of hostility to established churches, the repudiation of original sin, the belief in human perfectibility, etc. Coughlin could now, in a fascized world, envision a corporate-Christian America which would suppress Jews and radicals of every stripe, along with atheists, Masons, international bankers and plutocrats, these and all the others against whom he had been inveighing for the past 12 years. However, unlike American fascists in general—the Nazi Bund, the Silver Shirts, the Black Shirts, for example—Coughlin did not say what measures should be taken against these assorted un-Americans, that is, exactly how the international new order would come to the United States. Such details, presumably, could be left to the future.

Coughlin's American dream, it is worth observing, bore a rather close approximation to the nativist utopia of recent times. This is something of a paradox, since the nativists were invariably anti-Catholic, Coughlin himself, in his early years at Royal Oak, having once fought them tooth and nail. But his quarrel with them turned not so much on their larger objective of a purified white Christian society as their means of achieving it. Coughlin was more pluralistic than, say, the Ku Klux Klan. His variant of the nativist-fascist model made room for *all* Christians, irrespective of their social and national origins and mode of worship. (And perhaps the color of their skins. Coughlin expressed no discernible hostility towards blacks. Neither did he defend them; he simply accepted the status quo in race relations.) For the rest, he was hardly distinguishable from the nativists.

His bellicose anti-Semitism offended many Catholics. No one was more critical of him than his coreligionists, high and low, from Cardinals Mundelein and O'Connell down. They made it plain that he spoke for himself, as a citizen, not as a Catholic. Their main objection to him, it should be emphasized, was that he drove things to their extreme, thereby weakening an otherwise perfectly valid argument and driving away potential allies. Now the clergy may have deplored his heavy-handedness and pro-Fascism, as we have seen, but, they also regarded Communism as the mortal evil of the day. And they were compelled to admit that he was, with all his faults, useful in matters affecting church policy.

Just how useful was evident in January 1939, when the Roosevelt administration asked Congress to relax the neutrality law, the part of it especially which imposed an embargo on military goods to Spain, so that the United States might better deal with aggressors, meaning the Fascist powers. The Catholic Church, Generalissimo Franco's undying friend, denounced the administration and launched the "Keep the Spanish Embargo Committee" to collect petitions and lobby Congress.[24] Every Sunday evening Coughlin preached in behalf of the committee. It was the internationalists, led by the world Jewish conspiracy and working through the Popular Front of Communists and liberals, he informed the country, who were behind the move to lift the embargo. Should they succeed, he warned, they would end neutrality altogether and entangle the United States in European and Asian conflicts. "America's destiny is not woven with the destinies of the empires abroad. By fighting for them we are fighting for neither peace nor democracy, but for the perpetuation of an obsolete financial slavery operated and controlled by the Sassoons, the Montefiores, the Rothschilds, the Samuels [all Jews of course] and the litany of those flagless citizens who have obstructed justice, practiced usury and used the peoples of the world as their own pawns upon the chessboard of exploitation."[25]

His friends and enemies alike conceded that his efforts were instrumental in killing the attempt to repeal the embargo and in reinforcing the nation's commitment to strict neutrality. To Coughlin the results were doubly sweet. The Popular Front had been decisively rebuffed. He had shown that he was still someone to reckon with.

In the months that followed, as the war clouds thickened over Europe, Coughlin drew still closer to the Fascist powers. Their achievements exhilarated him. The Nazi conquest of Czechoslovakia and annexation of Memel and Franco's occupation of Madrid, all taking place in March 1939, along with Mussolini's invasion of Albania a few weeks later and Japan's seizure of further Chinese territory—these had Coughlin's whole-hearted endorsement. "It should never be forgotten," he reminded the readers of *Social Justice* on April 3, "that the Rome-Berlin axis is serving western Christendom in a peculiarly important manner."

The premise on which Coughlin's politics rested was this: the Axis, or anti-Comintern, countries would one way or another bring down the Soviet Union, epicenter of anti-Christ; their historic mission done, they would rejoin the comity of nations, much as a group of vigilantes become normal citizens again when they have brought the outlaws to heel. Events, however, went awry. If Hitler was going to vanquish Communism he had an odd way of doing so. On August 23, 1939, to everyone's surprise, he signed a non-aggression pact with Stalin, which included a secret provision to divide up Poland between them should either one of them be at war with her. A week later Germany attacked Poland and the division was duly consummated. Britain and France then declared war on Germany, as they promised they would in the event of such an attack. So it was that the vigilantes had conspired with the outlaws and were themselves waging war on the community they were supposed to defend. The Soviet Union could watch bemused as the nations of Western Christendom fought it out once again among themselves.

Far from being disillusioned Coughlin fell over himself in his haste to back the Führer. The pact with Russia was a tactical ploy, an expedient, he maintained. Once Germany settled accounts with Britain and France the apocalyptic struggle would begin in earnest. Coughlin's attitude toward American foreign policy thus stayed the same: to oppose any assistance to the democracies, to preserve neutrality uncompromisingly at all costs.

If Coughlin had had a sense of humor he might have appreciated the irony of his situation. His closest political companions just now happened to be none other than the Communists. For like him they justified the Hitler-Stalin pact on grounds of expediency. Like him they condemned Roosevelt for openly siding with Britain and France, bastions of imperialism, and for seeking to materially assist them and indeed bring the United States into the war. The cream of the jest is that Coughlin and the Communists were no longer combating each other's ideologies; they were content to concentrate their fire on the same enemy, President Roosevelt, leader of the interventionists, who wanted the country to side with the Allies, no matter what the consequences. Coughlin and the Communists, or, more generally, the Fascist right and the revolutionary left in America, had entered into a most extraordinary popular front of their own.

The term was no misnomer. National sentiment throughout 1939 and early 1940, the eight months of the "phony war," remained overwhelmingly isolationist. Americans on the whole might have favored the Allies and even gone along with Roosevelt's desire to help them. But Roosevelt, master politician that he was, understood the limits of his possibilities. He could not allow himself to be perceived as an interventionist, or worse, a warmonger, the label his enemies to a man sought to pin on him. Such a perception would have been fatal to his administration. On this issue, all things being equal, his opponents had the advantage.

Coughlin, meanwhile, was Hitler's unfailing apologist. He welcomed the fall of France and the advent of the puppet Vichy regime. He condoned the *Luftwaffe*'s attempt to bomb England into submission. He applauded the new dispensation that the Axis powers were bringing to Europe and Asia. These views, bodied forth with the familiar hyperbole, were more than his radio audience, much of it at any rate, could abide, and it melted away, leaving behind only a hard core of devotees. One by one the stations dropped him, and by the end of 1940 the great voice was stilled. He continued to publish *Social Justice,* but it was a pathetic reminder of days long gone.

The behavior of the Christian Front, the organization Coughlin had formed in 1938, led to the public's further disenchantment with him. While most American's knew scarcely anything about the Front, those who lived in cities with large Irish-American and Jewish populations knew all too much about it. The Front went in for direct action: brawls and head bashings. Its toughs, drawn from Irish districts, would go into a Jewish neighborhood and provoke fistfights by delivering anti-Semitic tirades on its main thoroughfares.[26] Front members bought weapons and drilled for combat. Their New York captain, John F. Cassidy, a lawyer, announced loud and clear: "We are prepared to say to the Communists that they lay down their arms or we will meet their arms with our arms—firearms. War is declared in New York on Christianity. We must be prepared to defend Christianity." To which Coughlin added, in a July 30, 1939, broadcast, "the Christian way is the peaceful way until—until—all arguments having failed, there is left no other way but the way of defending ourselves against the invaders of our spiritual and national rights. . . ."[27]

But the country had more to worry about than occasional free-for-alls in city streets or wild statements by fringe groups. It was when the FBI, on January 13, 1940, made a highly publicized arrest of 17 top Christian Fronters in Brooklyn, Cassidy among them, and charged them with plotting to kill Congressmen and seize the Customs House, the central post office, and major armories, that the country took notice. (Director J. Edgar Hoover himself led the arrest.) The FBI displayed the captured weapons and ammunition and explosives before the cameras of the world. To be sure, the evidence was thin given the enormity of the charges, conspiracy being hard to prove, and after ten weeks the trial jury found none of the Fronters guilty.[28] By then, however, Coughlin's name had been repeatedly dragged through the mud, the charges against them having become attached to him, their persistent defender, their seeming apologist in sedition.

His opposition to Roosevelt's increasingly bold moves was now entirely ineffectual. No longer was he a serious adversary. Few paid attention to his vicious attacks on the Lend-Lease bill, passed on March 11, 1941, which provided credits for Britain and any other nation at war with the Axis. Or for that matter his fulminations against Roosevelt for extending Lend-Lease to the Soviet Union following Hitler's invasion on June 22. The depth of Coughlin's rage can only be imagined. Here at last German armies were about to stamp out the abomination for good and the American government was attempting to thwart them.[29] What better proof—it was all in the open now—of Roosevelt's subservience to Stalin? But even those Americans who might have agreed with Coughlin in general now ceased to take him seriously.

JOHN L. LEWIS

The November 1938 CIO convention, held in Pittsburgh, ran true to form. Lewis was absolutely in control of the proceedings. All attempts to reunite it with the AFL, some initiated by Roosevelt, had failed, and the CIO (now the Congress of Industrial Organizations) officially declaring itself separate and independent, ratified its own constitution, and unanimously elected Lewis its president and Sidney Hillman and Philip Murray its vice-presidents.[30]

"Stagnant" is the word that best describes its condition at the time, less than two years after its smashing triumph. There was the "Roosevelt recession" which had struck the country with terrific force in August 1937, to the detriment especially of the basic industries, those the CIO unions represented. Far from renewing the failed struggle against Ford and Little Steel and other such opponents the CIO was content merely to hold onto what it had without further losses.

And there was the amazing recovery of the AFL. The hierarchs on whom Lewis poured so much scorn were learning how to fight back—that is, how to use the bugbear of the CIO to their own advantage. They offered employers their safer kind of unionism. To offer such an alternative, however, they had to cease quarreling with each other over jurisdiction, to cease the practice of keeping workers in limbo until the various crafts saw fit to take them in. AFL unions issued charters right and left to any group of workers who applied, even if they were unskilled and were in direct competition with CIO unions. Had the AFL acted with comparable dispatch and concern in 1933-34 there would have been no CIO. So it was that the AFL made sizable advances while the CIO was going nowhere.[31]

What was more, the American political climate had definitely turned against the left-liberal principles of the CIO. The Pittsburgh convention took place precisely a week after congressional and state elections which saw the Republicans inflict heavy blows on the Democrats. The conservative coalition which henceforth dominated Congress marked the death of New Deal reform. The drift of public sentiment had actually become clear months earlier, during the primary season; that was when Roosevelt had sought to affirm the liberal character of the Democratic Party by actively opposing, or "purging," several conservative incumbents and had failed badly, all but one of them having won re-election handily. Here was conclusive evidence, if any were needed, of Roosevelt's lame-duck status. That fact undoubtedly weighed on the minds of the convention delegates.[32]

What the CIO and the left in general could expect had also been foreshadowed by another ominous event that dominated the headlines in the second half of 1938. A special committee of the House of Representatives, chaired by Martin Dies of Texas, an enemy *tout court* of New Deal liberalism, had been established to investigate "un-American" activities by "extremist" organizations. The most sensational part of the hearings dealt with allegations of widespread Communist power and influence in American life. Of particular interest were charges, aired by high-ranking AFL officials and broadcast daily in bold headlines, of how Communists had taken over much of the CIO. The AFL wanted the country to believe that Communists and their stooges, acting on Soviet instruction, were responsible for the schism in the labor movement and for the National Labor Relations Board's recent rulings in favor of the CIO.[33]

The AFL's demand that the Wagner Act be changed and its administration cleansed of radicals helped bring about the creation of yet another House committee, this one under an egregiously anti-labor conservative, Representative Howard Smith of Virginia, to inquire into the conduct of the red-tinctured NLRB and suggest remedial legislation.[34] From the CIO's standpoint, a sort of counterrevolution was gathering momentum. Lewis's rhetoric sounded brave, and to his credit he stuck to his side of the bargain, defending the rights of Communists in his organization, but the most he and the CIO could hope to do was ward off the blows that were soon to fall.

Why then did Lewis, giant among the captains of labor, fall away from Roosevelt at this instant, just when he appeared to need him so much? This question has given rise to much speculation. Some authorities, as we saw, trace the hostility between them to the Little Steel strike and even further back to the Flint sit-down days. We also saw, however, that these conjectures are very weak since the two men collaborated and maintained cordial relations right through 1938. Irving Bernstein, dean of labor historians, speaks for many in ascribing it to the inevitable clash of strong personalities: "each insisted on being No. 1."[35] But this truism fails to explain why, the personality factor being constant, they parted ways when they did and not sooner (or later) and why over one set of issues and not another.

Lewis's most exhaustive biographers, Dubofsky and Van Tine, argue that foreign policy differences estranged Lewis from Roosevelt, that as Roosevelt gave up on domestic reform and coquetted with Republicans and conservative Democrats who backed his interventionist approach so Lewis gave up on him. These biographers place a good deal of stock in Lewis's commitment to isolationism; it was, they claim, a deeply held conviction with him, a "consistent set of beliefs."[36] A plausible explanation on its face, but in advancing it the biographers seem scarcely aware of their own inconsistency. They spend many pages of their fine book documenting very persuasively just how void of principles, how completely opportunistic, Lewis was throughout his public life but fail to say why isolationism meant so much to him.

And even if we grant the validity of their argument we are still left with the essential question—why Lewis developed an aversion to Roosevelt so profound that it caused him to act curiously out of character, so curiously it bordered on self-destruction. Since Lewis gave no reasons for his behavior at the time—as distinguished from retrospective apologias, which he supplied in abundance—we are thrown back on our own inferences.

Now two things can be stated with a fair amount of certainty. First, Lewis was a ruthlessly unsentimental man; a man who suffered no failure of weakness in others; who admired power, even (and often preferably) in those on the other side of the class divide; who was not the sort to go down in glorious defeat for a noble cause. Second, Roosevelt by early 1939, following the congressional elections and the apparent burial of the New Deal, had become precisely the kind of spent and vanquished force that Lewis unhesitatingly wrote off. Roosevelt's magic had departed, and the ex-magician himself would soon enough depart from the scene. Lewis was already looking beyond Roosevelt to such other possibilities as might benefit the UMW, the CIO, the labor movement—and, not least, himself.

A third thing can be stated with less certainty, but in the end might prove the most important in explaining Lewis's relations with Roosevelt. We can infer from everything Lewis was and did that he never cared for Roosevelt the man. Roosevelt was simply not the kind of leader he respected—the kind exemplified by such strong personalities and oaks of integrity as Herbert Hoover and Myron Taylor and Thomas Moses (boss of the Frick Coal Company and an ancient antagonist), the kind he looked up to as role models. Roosevelt, by way of contrast, came across as weak, temporizing, disingenuous, even duplicitous, qualities he hardly concealed by his breezy, egalitarian manner and lubricious charm. Lewis did respect, and readily exploited for his own advantage, Roosevelt's political skills, his ability to captivate the masses. But now the emperor was standing naked before those same masses (or so one might gather) and Lewis's contempt burst through the overlay of self-interest that had contained his feelings for so long.

We can accordingly appreciate why Lewis reacted to Roosevelt with such vehemence when their foreign policy differences arose. Was it conceivable that Roosevelt might again weave his magical spells? It was indeed conceivable, and his detractors, Lewis prominent among them, could not abide it.

Consider the situation from Lewis's angle of vision. Since the end of the Great War the American people had affirmed isolationism as the credo of their national purpose. They had been fooled by Woodrow Wilson, well meaning though he was, and by the war profiteers and economic royalists who wanted the flag to protect their foreign ventures. Let the nations of the world take care of their affairs or not as the case may be. America's responsibility was to her own well-being. Isolationism, thus defined, was so popular few dared challenge it. Roosevelt had challenged it, gingerly, in his "quarantine" speech of 1937, an eloquent if ambiguous statement of concern about the rising level of aggression and the need to deal with it, but Congress, obviously reflecting public wishes, steadfastly refused to weaken the neutrality acts. More than ever, it seemed, Americans sought to isolate themselves form the awful contagion that threatened to spread across Europe and Asia. There was little Roosevelt could do about this attitude.

Until, that is, the war in Europe began. This gave him the chance to recoup his losses, regain his popularity, and become again a great leader. On September 3, 1939, a few days after Hitler's armies marched into Poland, setting off the war, Roosevelt spoke out: "This nation will remain a neutral nation, but I cannot ask that every American remain neutral in thought as well"—meaning that he intended to aid Britain and France, if he could get away with it, thereby repeating the experience that led to our entry into the Great War. Roosevelt then proclaimed a national emergency and called a special session of Congress to repeal the arms embargo.[37]

Lewis found this entirely unjustified. Roosevelt, he said, was manufacturing a crisis out of whole cloth, was subjecting the country "to an overdose of war propaganda," was creating "the illusion that when war breaks out in Europe, the United States in some mysterious fashion will forthwith be involved," was in a word practicing "a monumental deception." Roosevelt, master manipulator, was at it again, and Lewis saw through him at once. Roosevelt's ultimate aim was transparent: "War has always been the device of the politically despairing and intellectually sterile statesman. . . . Labor wants the right to work and live—not the privilege of dying by gunshot and poison gas to sustain the mental errors of current statesmen." Lewis's play on the word "statesman" was designed of course to convey the opposite impression—that of a clever, scheming politician who for the sake of his own ambitions was willing to sacrifice the youth and the workers of America.[38]

Speculation over Roosevelt's plans supplied more grist for Lewis's mill. Would Roosevelt run for a third term, thus smashing one of America's revered traditions? Roosevelt said nothing to diminish the speculation. Should he decide to run it would vindicate Lewis's view. It would prove that Roosevelt had been plotting all along, crying wolf—to be blunt, warmongering—in order to get himself re-elected. Such was the burden of Lewis's numerous and extensively covered speeches throughout the winter and spring of 1940. His denunciations of Roosevelt could be reduced to simple ideological terms: internationalism was the death of social reform, the immediate victims being the poor, the unemployed, the oppressed blacks, the working class, the future victims being the young men who would be sent to foreign climes, and their loved ones. Dubofsky and Van Tine correctly describe Lewis "as the angriest man on the American left, the most outspoken and effective critic of the New Deal's domestic failures."[39]

In this role he received a good deal of encouragement. Liberal-minded isolationists liked what he was saying, though he might have been a mite too radical for their tastes. Conservative isolationists and Roosevelt-haters in general, while categorically disagreeing with Lewis on every specific issue, urged him on in the hope that he would help bring down the Democratic edifice. His most vociferous support came from the Communist Party and its friends. Ever since September 1939, Hitler and Stalin having signed their non-aggression pact and partitioned Poland, the Communists were following the neutralist line and condemning Roosevelt for favoring the "imperialists," Britain and France.

This was a sudden switch. Until then the Communists had applauded Roosevelt as the leader of the American "popular front" against Fascism. Now they were condemning him for siding with the imperialists. "The Yanks Are Not Coming" was the artful way they put it. Lewis could not have said it better.[40]

How nettlesome Lewis could be to Roosevelt was graphically illustrated one cold wet day in early February 1940. Roosevelt, at his wife's behest, spoke that afternoon to a delegation from the American Youth Congress who had gathered on the White House lawn. Assuming the parental mode, Roosevelt told them that they did not know enough about foreign affairs to criticize his conduct of it (they had passed a resolution condemning his support of the "imperialist" countries) and were too young to realize how intractable the unemployment problem was (they had also passed a resolution condemning his abandonment of the struggle against unemployment). He further informed them, rather gratuitously, that they had the right to espouse Communism or any revolutionary doctrine so long as they obeyed the law.[41]

The young radicals then headed over to the Labor Department building to hear the other distinguished speakers, among them John L. Lewis and Eleanor Roosevelt, whose solicitude for them had made the event possible. She was on the stage, therefore, when Lewis launched a booming rebuttal of her husband's talk on the White House lawn. Lewis was at his most acerbic. "Some answer!" he said, alluding to the fact that the youngsters had stood in the freezing rain hoping that the President would address their concerns. "How many years, how many years can you stand to be without a job? . . . to live the normal life of the normal citizen?" As to their alleged ignorance of foreign affairs Lewis had this to say: "After all, who has a greater right to protest against war or any part of war, or the diplomatic intrigues of war, or the subtle policies preceding war, than the young men who in the event of war will become cannon fodder." And after lambasting Roosevelt for going after "Fifth Columnists" rather than the racists who prevented black Americans from voting, Lewis invited the American Youth Congress to affiliate with his own

Labor Non-Partisan League, creating the basis of a new coalition that would be at once isolationist and radical. According to Eleanor Roosevelt's biographer Joseph Lash (himself a youth leader), "bedlam ensued." Lewis was their hero.[42]

Roosevelt uttered not a single word of reproach against Lewis publicly. Dealing with Lewis in such a way as to render him *hors de combat* was another matter.

Like Father Coughlin, Lewis gravely miscalculated the shape of things to come. The credibility of his isolationist position rested on the conviction that the new war in Europe would drag on indefinitely, as the Great War had. And until April 1940 so it seemed. But then in the next seven weeks the *Wehrmacht* overran Norway, Denmark, Belgium, Luxembourg, and the Netherlands, defeated France, and drove the English army, or what remained of it, back across the Channel. Nearly all of western Europe lay in Hitler's hands (Mussolini being by now his junior partner). With the exception of out-and-out Nazi apologists, or the Communists, who had their own ax to grind, hardly anyone could reasonably assert that Roosevelt was inventing the crisis. The crisis might be explained, interpreted, attempts might be made to understand it, to give it an ideological spin, but the fact, overwhelming in its import, could not be denied. So organized opposition to Roosevelt's policy of aiding Britain, which stood alone against Hitler, was on the defensive by the time the Democratic nominating convention met in mid-July 1940 and chose Roosevelt, even though he had until then expressed his reluctance to break historic precedent and seek another term. To Lewis, of course, Roosevelt's reluctance was pure humbug, a stratagem to help him win the election.

In continuing to oppose Roosevelt, Lewis labored under definite constraints. Roosevelt was taking on the trappings of a war president, gathering up tremendous new powers over the economy. One of the most important quasi-war agencies was the National Defense Advisory Council, consisting of representatives from trade unions, industry, and government, whose task was precisely what the title suggests—to develop ways of mobilizing the nation's resources for defense. Appointed to the council in May 1940 was CIO vice-president Sidney Hillman. His apostasy—for so Lewis regarded his acceptance of the post—should not have come as a surprise since he agreed totally with Roosevelt's foreign and domestic policy; if anything, Hillman would have gone further in siding with Britain.[43] Nor was Hillman alone. Roosevelt carefully cultivated the friendship of other CIO leaders, above all Philip Murray, head of SWOC, and chief organizer John Brophy. Lewis was thus isolated within his own innermost councils. True, the Communists were his stalwart allies, and they carried some weight in the CIO, but they were vulnerable themselves, increasingly so, and he held them in contempt too.[44]

Those who misread the shape of things to come can, by taking corrective measures, by rolling with the punch as it were, recover their equipoise and be none the worse for the experience. Lewis had committed grave mistakes in his long career as a labor leader. But his ability to compromise, his vaunted pragmatism, or opportunism, had enabled him in every instance to survive them. This time, in his battle royal with Roosevelt, he did the opposite: like Ahab he stayed on his disastrous course to the end, though his crew, unlike Ahab's, had long since abandoned him to his fate. It was as though Lewis's deepest flaws of mind and temperament had conspired to make him a figure in a minor tragedy.

First, there was his provincialism. He was the type of small-town American who had switched from idealism to cynicism—who, having concluded that foreign intervention in the name of democracy was a racket and a fraud, told himself that he would never again be deceived, least of all by fast-talking college-educated salesmen. If Lewis was beyond his depth that fact could never be conveyed to him because he reduced every problem to fit the narrow frame of his prejudices. The heavens might fall (as in a sense they did after 1939); he would not be moved.

Second, there was his egomania, which rendered him completely impenetrable. He genuinely felt that on every important issue he spoke for America's industrial workers and that America's industrial workers controlled America's destiny. Their power, he believed, when organized and directed, was indomitable. It was their votes which determined how the pivotal states—New York, Pennsylvania, Illinois, Ohio, Michigan, among others—and therefore the nation would go in elections. Whether or not Lewis was right is beside the point. What matters is his assumption that he could deliver those states to whomever he wished. He came to imagine himself—such was the reach of his vanity—a latter-day Warwick. Kings come and go; the Warwicks endure.

That is why the tale of his own political pretensions is not as incredible as it seems. Frances Perkins, in her memoir, recounts a conversation Roosevelt had with her and Daniel Tobin, Teamster president, early in 1940, shortly after Lewis had paid a visit to the White House. Roosevelt, she claims, told them that Lewis had insisted that he run again, that he, Roosevelt, had demurred because "it would be very hard going politically," and that Lewis had said, "'those objections would disappear'" if "'the vice-presidential candidate happened to be John L. Lewis. . . . A labor man would insure full support, not only of all the labor people but of all the liberals who worry about such things as third terms.'" He then had asked Roosevelt, who was speechless, "'to think it over and give it consideration.'"[45]

Some have questioned the veracity of Perkins's account. Her reason for presenting it was to show why Lewis was so harsh and unrelenting in his assaults on Roosevelt. Dubofsky and Van Tine dismiss it, in effect calling it a fabrication.[46] But there is no warrant for such an extreme judgment. Perkins's reliability as a source has never been questioned. The most one can assert is that she did not get the details precisely right. And since the matter of veracity is raised, why not lay the guilt at Roosevelt's feet? That he might have been the culprit is a possibility Lewis's biographers fail to mention. But since, in any case, we have no evidence to the contrary—Lewis himself did not deny the Perkins story—we can assume that it might have happened pretty much as she, quoting Roosevelt, said it did. Lewis could easily have believed that without him on the ticket Roosevelt would surely lose the election and that Roosevelt saw the ominous truth as clearly as he did.[47]

And third, there was Lewis's consummate hatred of Roosevelt, a fact already touched on. Nothing but an insensate wish to bring Roosevelt down, irrespective of consequences even to himself, can explain Lewis's bizarre conduct in the 1940 presidential campaign.

We saw how Lewis came forward as the darling of the left, the champion of the poor, the blacks, the youth, the dispossessed, et al., all those on whom Roosevelt presumably had turned his back. Though Lewis failed to win over the liberals, whose support of Roosevelt never wavered, they could at least applaud his sentiments, his passion for justice. And so how astonished they and the public at large must have been when they learned that Lewis's choice for further liberalizing American society and rescuing its insulted and injured was none other than ex-President Herbert Hoover, symbol of conservative inaction while America lay prostrate, and relentless critic of the New Deal, its labor policy included. Rewriting history, especially his own part in it, Lewis now exonerated Hoover retroactively, contending that Hoover's policies had begun to work when, alas, an uninformed electorate kicked him out of office and that the Great Depression was in fact Roosevelt's fault, high unemployment having become a permanent feature of American life since 1933. Lewis then went on to recommend that the Republican Party nominate Hoover for President at its June convention. Speaking for labor in tones of papal infallibility Lewis personally guaranteed Hoover's election.[48] The Republicans of course paid no attention to Lewis's fantasy and chose dark horse Wendell Willkie as their candidate.

That summer and fall Lewis unceasingly condemned every move Roosevelt made in Britain's behalf and in preparing America for the possibility of war. Roosevelt's moves were popular because they came while the great Battle of Britain was taking place. If there was any doubt about Nazi fiendishness the bombing attacks on defenseless cities between August and October—the very months of the presidential campaign—dispelled them once and for all. Lewis took no sides, not openly at any rate. Willkie was himself too internationalist to suit him, though as the campaign wore on Willkie's fortunes appeared to improve when he raised the war issue and promised never to send American boys abroad, forcing Roosevelt to offer a similar promise of his own. As the race tightened Lewis's position grew stronger. Both candidates gave credence to Lewis's boast that he could deliver millions of votes in the big, crucial states. Roosevelt was concerned enough to call him to his private White House chambers on October 17 in hopes of effecting a rapprochement, minimally an agreement which would assure his neutrality.[49]

That he was dead set against any kind of rapprochement or agreement he immediately made clear when he charged President Roosevelt with ordering the FBI to tap his phone and demanded that this violation of his constitutional rights cease forthwith.[50] The charge naturally ended any further exchange between them. This, obviously, is what Lewis intended. If he had a desire for a quid pro quo with Roosevelt he would hardly have let the existence of wiretaps stand in its path. The image of John L. Lewis as an apostle of civil liberties—he who had committed every outrage against civil liberties in his career—is one of the droller pieces of hypocrisy. Which is not to deny that his rights were as precious as the most ardent and angelic civil libertarian.

Yet the truth is, Roosevelt was justified in wanting Lewis monitored. The British Empire, let it be remembered, was about to fall—few gave it much of a chance against Hitler—thus deepening the crisis which enveloped the United States. And it was well known that the German government favored Roosevelt's defeat in the election and would do whatever it could to bring it about. We have fairly solid evidence that Lewis was one of the people the Reich believed should be encouraged in his anti-Roosevelt endeavors. This is not to suggest at all, as spymongers might conclude, that Lewis conspired with the Germans; to suggest such a thing would be an unconscionable affront to his name.[51] But Lewis did receive contributions in 1940 from a friend of his—one William Rhodes Davis, an oil magnate—who dealt extensively with the German regime and who, at Reichsmarshal Hermann Göring's behest, worked to beat Roosevelt. In other words, Roosevelt had a legitimate concern in knowing if Lewis was somehow being used by the evil men in Berlin. Lewis naturally assumed that Roosevelt was having him shadowed and bugged for selfishly political reasons, because he, Lewis, posed such a huge threat to Roosevelt's nefarious plans.[52]

Lewis would have opposed Roosevelt no matter who ran against him. Willkie, as it happened, stood on the liberal side of the ideological divide and accepted the New Deal reforms as permanent. This he made explicit immediately after conferring with Lewis. "I stand with Abraham

Lincoln," Willkie said. "Labor is . . . the superior of capital." Conservative Republicans did not care for these words, and indeed they hardly cared for Willkie, but like Lewis they would have supped with the devil to be rid of Roosevelt.[53]

By the time Lewis delivered his hour-long speech in Willkie's behalf before all the major networks on October 25 (the cost of which was largely borne by William Rhodes Davis), Roosevelt was clearly headed for victory. Lewis knew it. Did he think he could turn the election around by his dramatic announcement? That the workers of American and their wives, a fourth of the electorate by his estimates, would rally to his standard? Perhaps. That may explain why he issued his incredible ultimatum: should Roosevelt win it would mean that the CIO rank and file had "rejected my advice and recommendation," and he would have no choice but to retire as CIO president at its November convention. Some contend that Lewis had been eager to quit all along and was looking for a pretext. If so, how odd that such a shrewd man would risk humiliation in the course of doing what he was going to do anyway.

There is a better explanation—that he was goaded to this extremity by his detestation of Roosevelt. He had to show by more than words how wounded he would be by the perfidy of the working people for whom he had sacrificed so much. He would yield up to the friends of his enemy, to the very men he had lifted from obscurity, the organization he had sired and raised. He would orphan his own child.[54]

This act of self-maceration was in fact consistent with the rest of his amazing performance. Most of it was a sustained philippic against the man he abhorred. Roosevelt's election, he feared, meant giving a blank check to a warmonger, a dictator, a prevaricator, and cruelest cut of all, "an amateur, ill-equipped practitioner in the realm of political science." It would, in sum, "be a national evil of the first magnitude." The speech was an accurate index of an obsession. Only an inveterate, unappeasable Roosevelt-hater could fail to see how unbalanced, hence how self-defeating, his remarks were. Not many Americans who tuned in to Lewis that night recognized the object of his detestation. Roosevelt aroused passionate animosities, but few regarded him as a stage villain. One has the sense reading the speech that Lewis was interested less in convincing his audience than in getting something off his chest, that he was addressing his obsession, not them.

As for Willkie, he was almost an afterthought, worthy of no more than the briefest notice. Even where Lewis praised him it was for the purpose of running down Roosevelt. After mentioning Willkie as a "gallant American," whatever that meant, Lewis said the following: "He is not an aristocrat. He has the common touch. He was born in the brier and not to the purple. He has worked with his hands, and he has known the pangs of hunger." All of which was true, as Americans by now were undoubtedly aware. It was also true that Willkie was a rich lawyer. Lewis, in his heavy-handed encomium, was only drawing attention to Harold Ickes's brilliant gibe at Willkie, "the barefoot boy from Wall Street."[55]

According to Robert E. Sherwood, the prospect of discrediting Lewis gave Roosevelt more satisfaction than vanquishing Willkie, whom he came to like personally.[56] It was doubly satisfying to him because he won every industrial state but two, Michigan and Indiana, both traditionally rock-ribbed Republican, and these by the narrowest of margins at that. Among workers of every kind, industrial and craft, organized and unorganized, his margin of victory was overwhelming. Sweetest of all, perhaps, was the fact that the mine workers were with him completely. Lewis, to put it bluntly, had made an ass of himself.

As for his resignation from the CIO, Lewis sedulously kept his own counsel. His opening speech to the convention (held in the same Atlantic City auditorium where he punched Big Bill Hutcheson on the jaw) on November 18, 1940 was ambiguous on the question. Playing himself with rare skill, Lewis intimated that yes, he was through. The tears glistened in his eyes and his deep voice broke as he told the hushed delegates, "Some great statesman once said that the heights are cold. I think that is true. The poet said, 'Who ascends the mountain's top finds the loftiest peaks encased in mists and snow.' I think that is true." But neither, he went on, can we "stop to weep and wear sackcloth because something that happened yesterday did not meet with our approval or that we did not have a dream come true. . . . You know when you first hired me I was something of a man, and when I leave you in a day or two I will still in my own mind be something of a man." And so on and on went the panegyric to his manliness.[57]

Or was it a panegyric? Was Lewis up to his old deviltries and, the lachrymose display notwithstanding, inviting a draft? He had not yet resigned, and momentum was building to re-elect him. To prevent this from transpiring was now CIO vice-president Sidney Hillman's specific task—Hillman's, and it might be added, Roosevelt's, who kept abreast of everything at Atlantic City and was in constant contact with him. Hillman was himself a first-class performer, clever, quick, resourceful, and as opportunistic as Lewis. These were qualities he would need to call up from the depth of his soul if he—with Roosevelt's unfailing assistance—was going to head off the movement to draft Lewis that was being engineered by the talented cadre of Communist labor leaders.

In his address to the convention Hillman was clever indeed; it was as if he plucked a leaf from Roosevelt's book. He took Lewis's resignation—never formally proffered—to be an accomplished fact, a fact he, Hillman, greatly regretted of course (but then one also had to respect "a man who in a crisis stands by his guns"), and proceeded to nominate the enormously popular Philip Murray, head of SWOC, as Lewis's successor. Lewis later delivered a nominating speech for Murray full of laudations, and the CIO had a new president. Hillman, the "fox," had, in Irving Bernstein's words, "outsmarted the lion."[58]

Lewis was now what he had been before his vertiginous rise—with this difference, however, that he was no longer a welcome guest at the White House, that if he did come for reasons of expediency it was as his host's avowed adversary.

CHARLES A. LINDBERGH

Nothing Charles Lindbergh and his family ever experienced compared to what awaited them when the putative killer, Bruno Richard Hauptmann, was arrested, tried, found guilty, and executed, the interminable process lasting from mid-September 1934 through all of 1935 and into the spring of 1936, during which time they were plunged again into the maelstrom of worldwide publicity and were forced to relive, in detail and before the whole of humanity, the nightmare from which they had barely awakened.

And so the three of them sneaked off to England, the only passengers on a slow freighter. The American people learned of their departure, or rather escape, when they were far out to sea, beyond the reach of the press.[59]

The Lindberghs stayed in Europe for three years, settling first in England and then in France, before returning to the United States when the war in Europe seemed imminent. Lindbergh was no passive bystander to the catastrophic events that engulfed Europe in the years of his exile. It was his deep engagement in those events that prepared the way for his fateful encounter with Franklin D. Roosevelt.

Lindbergh first visited Germany in the summer of 1936 at the invitation of the American military attaché there, Major Truman Smith. Smith, impressed by what he saw of Germany, and indeed sympathetic to it, thought Lindbergh might like to "inspect the new German civil and military air establishment" and assured him that the German air ministry and its famous boss, Reichsmarshal Hermann Göring, were eager to show him around. Smith was confident Lindbergh would be impressed too.[60]

One can understand why Lindbergh would leap at the invitation. Like everyone else he was extremely curious about Germany. In the three and a half years since Hitler took power Germany had miraculously changed. From a nation that had been paralyzed by conflict and depression and hopelessness Germany was now united as never before in her history, was prosperous, thanks to vast military and public works programs, and was the focus of world attention. She bore no resemblance to the Germany that had been crushed and humiliated by the Versailles Treaty. It was no secret that she intended to be a great power again. Hitler was proclaiming it in every speech, and he in effect dared the Western democracies to try to stop him. He proved how correct he was—this in defiance of his general staff—when in March 1936 his army occupied the Rhineland despite the provisions of the Versailles Treaty, and Great Britain and France did nothing. The governments of those countries believed that Hitler might be useful—that if he was bent on war he would unloose it on the Soviet Union. His maniacal anti-Communism, the bottomless evil which it was his specific mission to extirpate from the face of the earth, encouraged them in that belief.

Lindbergh was reasonably familiar with the goings-on in Germany. They were featured in newspaper headlines; few made better copy than Hitler. They were the incessant topic of conversation in England among the upper-crust people the Lindberghs knew socially. But if Lindbergh had any thoughts on the subject of German restoration, Hitler, Nazism, the destruction of civil liberties, the official anti-Semitism, the murder, torture and imprisonment of opposition leaders, and so on and on, he kept them to himself. The portions of his journals and his wife's diaries that have been published reveal not a sign of interest in these questions on his or their part before they flew to Berlin.

They immensely enjoyed the ten days they spent in Germany. He was warmly embraced by Reichsmarshal (and former war ace) Göring, received from Lieutenant General Milch the German Aero Club insignia, inspected planes and training facilities, delivered an eloquent speech at Flier's House on the unity of civilization and aviation, and was an honored guest at the opening of the Olympic Games—and these without ever having to contend with pestiferous crowds and reporters and photographers.[61]

He was more than impressed; he was inspired. Then and there he came to view the German cause sympathetically. Now it is true that someone like Lindbergh, who condemned demagoguery and the revolt of the masses, who held Roosevelt in such low esteem, could scarcely fall in with Hitler and his machine. Nor could Lindbergh have been indifferent to the brutality that had become institutionalized in German politics and culture. But these he conceived to be the excesses endemic to a brash new society, overflowing with energy, still struggling to find itself. He had no doubt that once Germany was secure in her strength and fully self-confident, her "fanaticism," by which he meant Nazism at its apocalyptic extreme, would moderate, and she would become a force for good in the world.[62] In plain language, Lindbergh became a fellow traveler. Now the term "fellow traveler" has fallen on bad times and today it even implies disloyalty. Yet there is no substitute for it. The fellow traveler plays a unique role in life-and-death ideological struggles, the outcome of which may depend on how we, the uncommitted, the neutral, the apolitical, incline one way or the other. The fellow traveler persuades us—and through us our neighbors, friends, community, government—to support a country or party whose views we may not share and whose behavior we may not even approve of. The ideal fellow traveler is himself one of us, a non-partisan, open-minded and independent as we are, and is in addition universally respected for his achievements or status. Charles A. Lind-bergh was an ideal fellow traveler.

For the fundamental question he posed to whoever would listen was this: how could the Western democracies help Hitler's Germany, with all her faults, become a force for good in the world? Lindbergh's fellow traveling consisted in placing the burden of that terrible question on the shoulders of others, Britain and France in particular, and lifting it from Germany's. To be useful, in other words, Germany must be appeased, propitiated. She must not be "ignored, trampled on," as Anne Morrow Lindbergh wrote in a letter to her mother soon after their return to England, or she "could be a horribly destructive force." She added: "There is no question of the power, unity and purposefulness of Germany. It is terrific. I have never in my life been so conscious of such a *directed* force. It is thrilling when one sees it manifested in the energy, pride and morale of the people—especially the young people. But also terrifying is its very unity—a weapon made by one man but also to be used by one man. Hitler, I am beginning to feel, is like an inspired religious leader, and as such fanatical—a visionary who really wants the best for his country."[63]

No one but a convinced Nazi would now, in the 1990s, argue that Hitler's Germany could have been a force for good. In the 1930s, however, Lindbergh was hardly alone in thinking so. As a pro-German fellow traveler he differed from the vast congregation of fellow travelers only by his fame, popularity, and ingenuousness. Like them he favored appeasement on the grounds that the new Germany was the West's protection against a twofold barbarism: the barbarism from the East and the barbarism of revolution, both springing from the same Communist root. Lindbergh and the generality of fellow travelers feared Communism because it sought to activate the benighted, impoverished masses of the earth, black and brown and yellow and red as well as white. Its rallying cry was the overthrow not only of the European ruling classes but of the empires over which they presided.

For without those empires how could the Asiatic and African hordes be kept at bay?*

Hitler, like him or not, was manning the farthest outpost of Western civilization. And that was why expansionist Germany, vulgar and beastly as she often was, deserved the benefit of every doubt.

Lindbergh's racial philosophy should be mentioned because it was so central to his thinking on other issues. He was a racist of a particular kind. He should not be equated with the garden variety of American white supremacist. We have no indication whatever that he thought ill of American blacks or justified Jim Crow laws. Less so can he be equated with Nazi racists, with their Aryan fixation, their murderous hatred of Jews, their lunatic hierarchy of superior and inferior peoples, masters and slaves. In contradistinction to them Lindbergh felt that the white race had its specific genius and should be left alone to exercise it. Other races should be left alone to pursue theirs as well. The world being what it is, however, the whites had to defend their way of life. And that, perforce, meant keeping non-whites, the rest of humanity, in their assigned place.[64]

Many years later, long after the Second World War, long after the obliteration of Nazism and the whole system of empires, Lindbergh gave a modified version of his philosophy to historian Wayne S. Cole. He was ready to admit that racial prejudice is a curse, but he still reminds us of the fellow traveler of the 1930s. "As to superiority," he stated, "I think that can be claimed validly only in relation to the framework of the race claiming it (as a carpenter is superior to a bricklayer in the field of carpentry). It seem to me that the average intellectual superiority of the white race, for instance, is countered by the sensate superiority of the black race. Even though I was born and live in the framework of the white race, I believe it is quite possible that the black race will achieve a better balance eventually. I believe that each race must protect its own

---

* Lindbergh's close friend Alexis Carrel, in the 1939 introduction to *Man, the Unknown*, included this dire warning: "Europe and the United States are thus undergoing a qualitative as well as quantitative deterioration. On the contrary, the Asians and Africans, the Russians, the Arabs, the Hindus, are increasing with marked rapidity. Never has the European race been in such a great peril as today. Even if a suicidal war is avoided, we will be faced with degeneration because of the sterility of the strongest and most intelligent stock."

security, territorially and otherwise, and that it would be unfortunate for mankind if any one race obtained too great predominance."

In another letter to Cole, Lindbergh expanded on these remarks, pointing out that "certain races have demonstrated superior ability in the design, manufacture of machines," these being the North Americans, British, Germans, Dutch and Swedes. "The growth of our western civilization," Lindbergh continued, "has been closely related to their superiority. Whether or not it will be advantageous to our people is yet to be shown."[65] Back in the 1930s he did not have to be shown anything. Their "superiority" was for him an article of faith.

It is one thing to be a fellow traveler who from personal convictions seeks to influence or convert others. It is altogether another thing for a fellow traveler to allow himself to be used and deceived. Lindbergh was thus used and deceived by the Germans, and it is doubtful that he ever realized the extent of it.

Since it was generally acknowledged that a future war would turn on air power nothing so concentrated the minds of the general staffs elsewhere in Europe as the size and competency of the *Luftwaffe*. The Nazis knew this of course. If, they reasoned, it could be established on good authority that the *Luftwaffe* was already the best in the world and constantly getting better—for who could doubt German resolve and technique?—the governments of Europe might be too intimidated to fight when the showdown came. Each success would brighten the nimbus of invincibility that enveloped Hitler. Here is where Lindbergh proved so valuable to the German cause. He told the British and French politicians and military what the Nazis wished them to be told, namely, that Germany did possess by far the best air force in the world and was improving it by the day and that it would be an almost insuperable task for their air forces to catch up, even if they acted in concert.

Lindbergh, moreover, was doubly impressed during a second whirl-wind visit to Germany with his wife in the fall of 1937. "The growth of German military aviation," he confided to a friend immediately after, "is, I believe, without parallel in history; and the policy in almost every instance seems laid out with great intelligence and foresight." He also discerned "a sense of decency and value which in many ways is far ahead of our own." We do not have to spell out what he meant by "a sense of decency and value."[66]

It was this predisposition that made it so easy for the Nazis to fool him. Overwhelmed by what he saw firsthand he uncritically accepted the statistics the German Air Ministry showed him, leading him to think he was privy to secret data. The report he and Truman Smith wrote estimated than Germany was producing up to 800 planes a month, with about 10,000 already built and operational, a quantity five times larger than the number produced by Britain and France *combined*.[67] How effectively he was taken in has by now become clear. According to Leonard Mosely, who examined German military archives, the *Luftwaffe* in 1940, two years after Lindbergh's report and a year after the war had begun, possessed only 1,711 bombers, 424 dive bombers, 354 escort fighters, 1,356 pursuit planes, and 830 reconnaissance and other planes. And the output was correspondingly lower than Lindbergh claimed: only 300 bombers and 125 fighters a month. The Germans themselves later admitted how scandalously inefficient their system of aircraft production was. Ernst Udet—chief of the Air Ministry's Technical Department, like Göring a renowned war ace, and one of the Germans Lindbergh admired so extravagantly—had the job of escorting Lindbergh about, sharing confidences with him, and conning him in the process. Udet took his life in 1941 after his dismissal for gross incompetence. If, as Mosley contends, Germany's production failures may have cost her the war it must count as one of the happiest ironies in history.[68]

That Germany was on the move by the spring of 1938 no one, not even the most hidebound fellow travelers, could deny. Their rationale was that Germany must be permitted to fulfill her destiny, whatever it was— Lebensraum, hegemony over Central Europe, etc.—or there could be no peace. Within limits, as we noted, the governments of Britain and France accepted the argument and gave Hitler carte blanche to annex Austria in March. But a few months later, when Hitler demanded the Sudetenland, the mostly German-speaking part of Czechoslovakia, they balked. The

Soviet Union went further and offered to join the Western democracies in militarily opposing Hitler. The issue thus rested squarely with them.

As the threat of war approached so Lindbergh became more and more entangled in the coil of events. He was the indisputable expert on aviation in general, German aviation in particular. That expert knowledge he offered wholeheartedly to the cause of peace; that is, to Hitler's cause. Lindbergh could imagine nothing more calamitous than a war of Western nations which would result in the further encroachment of the East, the further expansion of Communism. To sacrifice a province of Czechoslovakia, perhaps all of Czechoslovakia, was, under the circumstances, a painfully necessary cost to bear.[69]

Lindbergh was thus a very busy man in that critical month of September 1938, when momentous decisions hung in the balance. He delivered his by now familiar message to France's Minister of Air, Guy LaChambre—that the *Luftwaffe*'s size and proficiency gave Germany a tremendous advantage—and to top officials of the British Air Ministry and Air Staff. He was also in touch with America's ambassador to Britain, Joseph P. Kennedy, himself a German fellow traveler at this point, and like-minded members of the English aristoi. Kennedy, hardly a paragon of diplomacy, had said that Hitler should have a free hand in the "East and South East." Lindbergh's sentiments exactly.[70]

These messages Lindbergh incorporated in a letter he sent Kennedy on September 22 and which Kennedy passed on to Secretary of State Cordell Hull and President Roosevelt. Not only did Lindbergh provide the familiar analysis—that compared to the *Luftwaffe* the rest of the European air forces was pitifully inadequate—he threw in his own opinions, couched in hackneyed phrases, the effect of which was to bring him directly into the policy arena: "A general European war would, I believe, result in something akin to Communism running over Europe and, judging by Russia, anything seems preferable. I am convinced that it is wiser to permit Germany's eastward expansion than to throw England and France, unprepared, into war at this time." And further: "We must recognize the fact that the Germans are a great and able people. Their military strength now makes them inseparable from the welfare of European civilization, for they have the power either to preserve or destroy it. . . ."[71] Who, faced with such a choice would fail to act as Lindbergh suggested?

He therefore may have had something to do with the democracies' capitulation at Munich on September 29, 1938, by any reckoning one of the great blunders of all time. For within a year Britain and France, led by the same governments, were at war with Hitler, and they were at war alone, the Soviet Union in the meantime having signed its non-aggression treaty with Germany. Exactly how much Lindbergh influenced events is unclear. The French took his gloomy estimate of German strength seriously, yet they would have been willing to fight if Britain had been. To what extent Prime Minister Chamberlain and his advisors took Lindbergh's views seriously is impossible to ascertain. We know that Chamberlain read a summary of Lindbergh's letter to Kennedy just before he, Chamberlain, saw Hitler in Munich. We also know, however, that British Air Ministry officials regarded Lindbergh as a purveyor of German propaganda and believed they possessed a more accurate understanding of the situation than he did.[72] Lindbergh, it could be said, contributed to the Munich fiasco by confirming and justifying a decision that Chamberlain and French Premier Daladier had already arrived at.[73] Political, not military, considerations led to the sellout of Czechoslovakia. The democratic governments still assumed, or hoped against hope, that Hitler, most militant of anti-Communists, could be a force for good in the world.

But Munich was about as far as those governments could go in appeasing him. By their submission the democracies were defining a hard-and-fast limit—*their* limit. Hitler was the recipient of *their* magnanimity. *They* remained as ever the arbiters of Europe's fate. Implicit in the Munich agreement, then, was the assumption that Hitler could not transgress his limit without challenging Britain and France for hegemony over western Europe. For them to do nothing in the face of such a transgression would be equivalent to accepting German hegemony, the ultimate act of appeasement, or rather obeisance.

Now many fellow travelers were willing to accept German hegemony, even welcome it, as the resolution of the problem. Lindbergh was emphatically one of these fellow travelers. Munich reinforced his conviction that only Germany, with its vitality and discipline, could be relied on to guard the ramparts of civilization. He was more convinced than ever that the major democracies were too weak, too decadent to do so and would open their gates to let in the Asian hordes. France he wrote off as fractious, pleasure loving, fickle; England as incurably old-fashioned and set in her spinsterly habits, blithely indifferent to the fact that modern technology was passing her by. Apart from Germany, he had little faith in Europe.[74]

Munich inspired him to offer his own plan for peace. He came up with a proposal, as fantastic in retrospect as it was improbable at the time, under which France and Germany would agree to help each other out militarily: in exchange for receiving badly needed Daimler-Benz 601 plane engines France would give Germany her highly praised Desvoiture 520 bodies, the details to be worked out by Lindbergh. The French were "astounded" when he broached the scheme to them, but Premier Daladier was intrigued by it. So too were *Luftwaffe* Generals Udet and Milch and Reichsmarshal Göring. Lindbergh was sufficiently encouraged to hope he might just bring off this miracle, this step in the quest for permanent peace among the nations of the West.[75]

He was meanwhile growing more and more fond of Germany. He said he felt freer there than anywhere else. He and his wife during their October 1938 trip to the Third Reich even decided to live in the gorgeous Berlin suburb of Wannsee. When for complicated reasons they could not buy the house they sought, the German government promised to build them one according to Lindbergh's blueprint and under the supervision of no less a personage than Albert Speer, Hitler's chief planner (and himself an architect). Whether the Lindberghs could live in Germany depended, however, on the success of his mission, which is to say, on the future of the world.

One day during that October trip the American ambassador to Germany, Hugh Wilson, hosted a stag dinner in Lindbergh's honor. Present were high officials from the aviation and diplomatic communities of Berlin. Ambassador Wilson was pleased because he, unlike his extremely anti-Nazi predecessor, William E. Dodd, strove to improve relations between the United States and the Third Reich. As expected, Göring dropped by. To everyone's surprise he suddenly drew a medal from a red box. It was the Service Cross of the German Eagle—four little swastikas on a cross of gold—the supreme award to a non-German "who deserved well of the Reich" (Henry Ford having been the only other American to receive it). Göring "by order of the Führer" then proceeded to bestow it on Lindbergh. That was that. No one gave any further thought to the brief ceremony.[76]

It became an incident later, following the hideous *Kristallnacht* pogrom of November 9 and 10, launched and largely carried out by the Nazi regime. President Roosevelt, to his credit, denounced the pogrom as an outrage against "twentieth century civilization" and recalled Ambassador Wilson, in effect breaking diplomatic relations with Germany.[77] Criticisms could now be heard across the international landscape. Lindbergh's acceptance or retention of the medal came to symbolize his warm feelings toward the German government and its works and, more broadly, his desire to appease it. Secretary of the Interior Ickes, waiting for a chance to get in his licks, asked, in a widely quoted speech, how an American could be decorated "by a brutal dictator who, with that same hand, is robbing and torturing thousands of fellow human beings."[78] With such attacks mounting, even some of Lindbergh's friends advised him to return the medal as a sign of his own indignation toward the Nazis.

That he was indignant is obvious from his journal. On November 13 he wrote: "I do not understand these riots on the part of the Germans. It seems so contrary to their sense of order and their intelligence in other ways. They undoubtedly had a Jewish problem[!] but why is it necessary to have it so unreasonably? My admiration for the Germans is constantly being dashed on some rock such as this."[79]

Yet even if he wanted to publicly rebuke the regime he could not because of the delicate and secret negotiations in which he was engaged. His indignation stemmed more from the difficulties the Germans were creating for him than from the wrongs they were committing. Besides, he never conceived that Hitler and Göring and responsible leaders like them were at fault; others were or might have been, Himmler and Goebbels perhaps. Lindbergh's ignorance of the situation, in other words, was appalling. As he confided to his journal, he tried on subsequent visits to "obtain a better understanding of the German mind" concerning "the Jewish problem"—why so many Germans had come to resent Jewish capitalists, Jewish debauchers of innocent German girls,

Jewish Communists, etc.; Lindbergh took Nazi propaganda seriously enough to weigh its charges on the scale of plausibility.[80]

His friends must have known he would not return the medal, assuming even that the thought of doing so crossed his mind. Lindbergh was a very stubborn man, particularly under pressure. And he would never allow it to appear that he noticed, much less took to heart, what his critics were saying about him.

Lindbergh was meanwhile traveling back and forth between Paris and Berlin in pursuit of his sacred mission. By mid-January 1939 he was confident it would succeed, an official of the French Air Ministry actually having met Generals Udet and Milch to arrange for the purchase of the Daimler-Benz engines. To his dying day Lindbergh was convinced that the French Foreign Ministry sabotaged the deal just as it was being consummated.[81]

The more reasonable assumption is that it never stood a chance, that it was wrongheaded from the start. For even if it had succeeded and met every expectation it still would have failed. Lindbergh's motive for initiating it, remember, was to aid the cause of peace, the pax Germanica to which he subscribed. What finally rendered his project or any other such endeavor useless at this time was the inexorability of the war; to be more exact, the insatiability of Hitler's appetite. Hitler had sworn at Munich that the Sudetenland was all he coveted and that the rest of Czechoslovakia was safe. On March 15, 1939 he devoured the rest of Czechoslovakia. (Lindbergh's journal, incidentally, carries not a word of regret over this tragedy.) A week later Hitler annexed Memel and demanded access rights to Danzig through the Polish Corridor. The British and French governments then pledged to help Poland should her independence and territorial integrity be threatened; they gave the same pledge to Rumania and Greece, both of which stood in danger of attack following Mussolini's invasion of Albania. There could no longer be any doubt that war was coming. Under the circumstances, who in the chancelleries of France and Germany gave a second's thought to Lindbergh's desperate plan?

There was nothing left for the Lindberghs in Europe. His place was in America, despite the horrors of the past and probably those to come. He would carry on the same struggle. "I felt I could exercise a constructive influence in America by warning people of the danger of the Soviet Union and by explaining that the destruction of Hitler, even if it could be accomplished through using American resources, would probably result in enhancing the still greater menace of Stalin."[82]

These words were written in the 1970s. Back in 1939, however, he had regarded Hitler not as a menace but as a force for good.

When his boat docked in New York harbor on April 14, 1939 Lindbergh found himself in a familiar setting. Bedlam engulfed him as packs of reporters, photographers, policemen, and others shouted, jostled, and pulled and camera bulbs exploded all around.[83] In fact, media interest in him and his family (who joined him a few weeks later) died down perceptibly, as they soon discovered to their relief. They were pretty much left undisturbed in their North Shore Long Island retreat. In themselves, the Lindberghs were rather dull. It was just that things had a way of happening to them.

Lindbergh performed an extremely valuable service for the United States government on his return. He told Army Air Corps chiefs everything he knew about German aviation, explaining how and why it was so much more advanced than America's or any other country's. As a member of the National Aeronautics Advisory Committee, a high-level body set up to recommend policy changes, he was instrumental in getting the administration to propose, and Congress to legislate, a vast increase in expenditures for airplane research and production. Back again on active duty, Lindbergh toured the country, flying from one facility to another in a new-model fighter the Army placed at his disposal, seeing with his own eyes where the shortcomings lay. His reports, read in the highest echelons of the War Department, helped upgrade the standards of military aviation in what proved to be a critical moment for America. Probably no one but Lindbergh could have brought off those results.[84]

Even as he was giving valuable assistance to the government in technical matters Lindbergh was laboring to countervail its anti-Nazi bias. He regularly met in Washington with a group of militantly isolationist, Roosevelt-hating businessmen, journalists, politicians and officials, among them Major Truman Smith, now with Army Intelligence at the top level of the command structure, and ex-ambassador Hugh Wilson, who was openly blaming American Jews for the administration's wrongheaded European policy (and German Jews for Nazi excesses).[85] In consulting with these men Lindbergh was not only trying to reinforce a point of view, he was priming himself for a showdown with the President himself, should the occasion arise—that is, should war break out.

Roosevelt's hostility to Hitler was of long standing and well known to Lindbergh. From afar Roosevelt had sought to encourage Britain and France to stand up to German expansionism. Ideologically, he took a position absolutely antithetical to Lindbergh's, and both of them were aware of that fact.[86]

When the war did break out on September 1, 1939, the day Hitler attacked Poland, Roosevelt proceeded to act just as Lindbergh feared he would. Roosevelt immediately announced what he thought America should do. Though formally committed to neutrality—this went without saying—he made it clear where America's sympathies should lie and where its economic and military aid should go once the arms embargo was repealed.[87] Roosevelt had two objectives in mind, short-range and long-range, minimal and maximal. The short-range or minimal one was to persuade the American people—and no one was more persuasive than he—that Nazi Germany and to a lesser extent Imperial Japan and to a much lesser extent Fascist Italy constituted a great evil in the world, an evil ultimately directed against them, the American people. The long-range or maximal objective was to do something about that evil, namely to begin mobilizing the nation for the possibility of war, remote as it then seemed. Obviously, to achieve his long-range objective Roosevelt first had to secure his short-range one: to win over public opinion. So it was that public opinion served as the battleground on which he and his opponents fought their terrible struggle in the fall and winter of 1939-40.

On the evening of September 15 Lindbergh delivered a speech over all the major radio networks. It dealt with the burning issue of what

America's response should be to the European war. Roosevelt learned of the speech shortly before it was delivered, and he was displeased to say the least. He had a fair idea of Lindbergh's appeal, and the prospects of crossing swords with an adversary who could inflict grave wounds, yet was as elusive as a ghost, daunted the President, who had enough trouble moving America in his direction as it was.

The day Lindbergh went on the air Truman Smith conveyed to him an amazing offer from the President. Would Lindbergh be willing to serve as Secretary of Air, a new cabinet post to be established specifically for him? The motive behind the offer was transparent: to co-opt, compromise, and thus silence Lindbergh, or, what amounted to the same thing, neutralize the content of his speech. Lindbergh indignantly said no. "This offer on Roosevelt's part," he wrote in his journal, "does not surprise me after what I have learned about his Administration. It does surprise me, though, that he still thinks I might be influenced by such an offer." Lindbergh's already low opinion of Roosevelt sunk lower, and he was resolved more than ever to speak out, to avoid temporizing, whatever the consequences.[88]

We have presented Lindbergh's version of the affair. Even if it is correct—as far as it goes—his smug righteousness and accusatory tone are hardly justified. Whether he realized it or not he was entering the political lists. On that turf the moral certitudes he took for granted did not so readily apply, and the relations of means to ends and ends to means was hopelessly entangled. Under the circumstances, Roosevelt's attempt to silence Lindbergh was proper and justifiable; he perceived Lindbergh as an emergent antagonist over a matter of greatest import. Except by asking Lindbergh's price he had no way of knowing who he was dealing with, what kind of antagonist he might be up against. Now he knew.[89]

Lindbergh's indignation, in any case, was misdirected: it should have been (and perhaps was) aimed at himself for engaging in politics and thus for having to court the good will of the masses and, irony of ironies, the press. To this extremity had he been reduced!

His September 15 speech was, as Roosevelt feared, no one-shot affair. During the next seven months he spoke repeatedly over the radio to large audiences and wrote two broadly discussed articles, one for *Reader's Digest* ("Aviation, Geography, and Race"), the other for

Atlantic Monthly ("What Substitute for War?"). These were not polemics or impassioned harangues in the style of Huey Long and Father Coughlin. They were well-reasoned, clearly written opinions by someone who had given a good deal of thought to the central question that occupied the nation's mind: How did the European war affect American interests? Roosevelt's answer to that question set the agenda for the debate that followed. Roosevelt, whose political sense rarely betrayed him, had had a premonition that Lindbergh would be one of his most effective critics.

The thrust of Lindbergh's argument can be stated simply: The European war is not, as Roosevelt and his votaries maintain, a war between the children of light and the children of darkness, between democracy and Nazism, between the decent, law-abiding peoples and the ogre Adolph Hitler, who is bent on ruling the universe. Nothing of the sort. It is a war between the haves and have-nots. Or, to phrase it differently, it is a contest between the enervated and declining and the dynamic and rising states of Western civilization. The "democracies"—Lindbergh enclosed the word in quotation marks whenever he referred to Britain and France—of course comprise the former, and Germany (and later Italy) the latter. The world is a jungle where might prevails and right tags behind to legitimate it. "There is no adequate peaceful way for a nation to expand its territory and add to its colonies—no international measure for the right of birth rates, virility, skill, and all the innumerable factors that enter into the rise and fall of nations, of empires, of civilizations. And therefore, where a strong people become dissatisfied with its position through negotiation and agreement, it turns to that primeval 'right' of force—as we did with the American Indians and with Mexico, as England did in Africa, India and America, as Italians did in Ethiopia, as Germany is doing today." And so it follows with ruthless logic that "the war in Europe is not so much a conflict between right and wrong as it is a conflict between differing concepts of right—a conflict in which the 'defenders' are represented by the static, legal 'right' of man, and the 'aggressors' by the dynamic, forceful 'right' of nature."[90]

Lindbergh, however, was no detached political scientist affecting a show of impartiality. The point of his analysis was to depict Germany as the aggrieved party and the "democracies" as the wrongdoers. Germany, in his view, was exercising her inherent, nature-given power; the "democracies" had declared war in retaliation. By Lindbergh's logic, they had become the aggressors and Germany the victim. He detailed the reality behind the appearance, the truth underlying the fine-spun rhetoric.

He did not have to spell out what he was driving at, the fact that Germany needed to dominate Europe, whether or not Britain and France liked it. Nor did he conceal his sympathy for this happy verdict of history. Germany, not the "democracies," was facing the "Asiatic hordes"; and Germany was occupying the "intangible eastern border of European civilization," as indeed she had done for thousands of years. But the threat from the east had never been so great, thanks to the Soviet Union and Communism. The possibility that the "democracies" might be defeated did not in the least disturb Lindbergh's equanimity. Nor should it disturb America's in his view. If anything, he would welcome it as the triumph of nature over debilitation and loss of nerve.

Whatever the outcome, Lindbergh argued, the war was a tragedy fraught with danger. He again faulted Britain and France. They had obfuscated the issue that shaped modern history, and that issue was purely and simply race. Nothing on earth could be more foolish than what the Europeans were doing to each other, fighting a war "in which the White race is bound to lose and the others bound to gain, a war which may lead our civilization through more Dark Ages if it survives at all."[91]

Lindbergh would have had America—if she were led by a statesman instead of a confidence artist—bring the combatants together in common defense of beleaguered white peoples. "Oriental guns are turned westward, Asia presses toward us on the Russian border, all foreign races stir restlessly." In Lindbergh's prose one hears unmistakably the echoes of Nazi racial philosophers and geopoliticians, the likes of Houston Chamberlain, Alfred Rosenberg, and Karl Haushofer. "Our civilization depends on a united strength among ourselves, on a strength too great for foreign armies to challenge; on a Western wall of race and arms which can hold back either a Genghis Khan or the infiltration of inferior blood;

an English fleet, a German air force, a French army, an American nation, standing together as guardians of our common heritage, sharing strength, dividing influence."[92]

The preservation of world order—American dominion over the Western Hemisphere, European dominion over Asia and Africa, German dominion over Europe—this, in sum, was the majestic task to which the white race should dedicate itself lest it expire in a conflagration of its own making.

But, Lindbergh went on, bringing the argument full circle, if America could do nothing to end the European war in no way should she meddle in it. It must be permitted to take its own course. Neutrality, absolute and unconditional, must govern American policy. In other words, Roosevelt, meddler par excellence, must be prevented from meddling on behalf of the "democracies."

It is hard to measure the effectiveness of Lindbergh's campaign of counter-persuasion. It should be understood that he began with something of an advantage. When the war got under way the United States was already deeply committed to neutrality and isolation. To sustain that commitment was certainly easier than changing it, even taking into account Roosevelt's ability to use his office as a bully pulpit. The law of inertia applies to nations too.

But Lindbergh's main problem was not Roosevelt; it was Hitler. If the Germany Lindbergh was discussing in his speeches and articles were led by an ordinary mortal—by a Bismarck, say, or even a Kaiser Wilhelm— he would have been more convincing. The fact is, Hitler terrified Americans who, all things being equal, were as isolationist as Lindbergh. Hitler drove many people who only vaguely sympathized with Britain and France into the arms of the interventionists—those espousing all assistance to Britain and France short of war—converting them into anti-Nazi activists. Most Americans could not bring themselves to equate, as Lindbergh did, Nazi Germany with Western civilization. If Germany was their bulwark against the ravenously Communist East, why did she, a week before the war, sign a non-aggression pact with the Soviet Union, thereby enabling Stalin to seize part of Poland and the Baltic countries? And if, as

Lindbergh claimed, Germany was the protector of the white race, why was she allied with Japan, a country which was in the process of challenging or displacing the Western empires throughout Southeast Asia? So it was that the American people, despite their adherence to neutrality, despite the patient hearing they gave Lindbergh and lesser isolationists, in the end willingly accompanied Roosevelt. In early November 1939 Congress repealed the arms embargo by a sizable margin and allowed the belligerents, meaning Britain and France, to buy military goods, unlimited amounts of them, on a "cash and carry" basis.[93]

Nonetheless the advantage was still Lindbergh's. A majority of Americans followed Roosevelt provided he did not advance too far ahead of them, a fact of life Roosevelt appreciated all too well. As long as the situation remained the same, as long as the "phony war" that followed Hitler's conquest of Poland continued, America could intervene in it no further than she already had.

The *Wehrmacht's* invincibility in the spring and summer of 1940 must have surprised even Lindbergh, who could justifiably say, I told you so (though he would be the last person to say it). History had seen nothing like it.

But only the most blatant apologist could now call Hitler a defender of Western civilization. He was, on the contrary, its greatest scourge. Defeating mighty France was one thing; conquering such small and innocent countries as Norway, Denmark, the Netherlands, Luxembourg, and Belgium quite another. Had Hitler's armies invaded the British Isles, that too would have been fair as one defines fairness in war. What was brutally unfair, by the standards America took for granted, was the *Luftwaffe's* daily bombing of English cities, many of them free of military or industrial facilities, week after week, month after month. Americans cheered British heroism and defiance, personified by Prime Minister Winston Churchill and embodied in the Royal Air Force, which, at fearful cost to itself, beat back the assault, giving Hitler his first major defeat and persuading him to turn his attention to the east.

In his journal Lindbergh hardly referred to this remarkable episode, one which should have interested him hugely, eliciting from him commentary and insight. His reticence may be explained by the fact that the Battle of Britain contradicted his belief, raised to mythic proportions, in German air superiority and England's congenital inability to assimilate advanced technology. He uttered not a syllable of applause for the English performance. He assumed it was a waste in any case, a prolongation of the agony.

Roosevelt did not have to rely on rhetoric and personality to prove his point. That Germany, along with Italy (which joined the war on June 10, 1940) and Japan, constituted a potent threat to the United States had become obvious enough. Obvious too was the necessity to prepare for the worst. Roosevelt had no trouble imparting a sense of crisis to the nation during that fateful spring and summer. Congress appropriated vast sums for defense, enough, for example, to produce 50,000 planes a year, an unheard of number. Greatly increased aid went to Britain, whose collapse—so Roosevelt asserted and so America feared—might bring the hated Nazis to the New World: better that Britain fought them there (Churchill: "Give us the tools and we will do the job") than America here. Avoidance of war justified these measures, and Roosevelt would not have been re-elected in 1940 had Americans concluded otherwise.

A large number of Americans, however, did conclude otherwise. Roosevelt's response to Hitler's astonishing success gave rise to a counter-response, a mass movement consecrated to the principle of isolationism. It was a disparate and heterogeneous movement, a most improbable mélange, one that only a crisis of this magnitude could have thrown up. At one end of the spectrum resided the Communists, a considerable presence in several of the big cities, who condemned Roosevelt for siding with imperialist Britain and whose phrase "The Yanks Are Not Coming" struck a chord. Not so far to the left were the remnants of the Socialist Party, led by its seasoned warrior Norman Thomas, who claimed that an America at war would engender a fascism of its own. Some liberal critics of the administration—the La Follettes of Wisconsin, a host of western Senators, Chester Bowles of Connecticut, the writers Stuart Chase, Charles A. Beard, Harrly Elmer Barnes, among many others— did not go quite that far, but they envisioned under Roosevelt the death of reform and the sellout of the country to the special interests. Marching in the isolationist ranks, for obvious reasons, were representatives of some of the important ethnic groups, German- and Irish- and Italian-American chief among them. On the conservative side of the spectrum could be found the congeries of Roosevelt's enemies, ex-President Hoover, Senator Robert A. Taft of Ohio, William Randolph Hearst, the publishers of the *Chicago Tribune* and the *New York Daily News,* the heads of such corporations as New York Central, Inland Steel, Sears, Roebuck, Eastern Airlines, Swift, Fleischmann's Yeast, Ford Motor, etc., all of whom denied that conditions abroad warranted any enhancement of Roosevelt's power, already far too great for the country's good. Further to the right were the legion of anti-Semites who did not doubt for an instant that Roosevelt was acting at the behest of the Jews. At the far end of the spectrum, worthy only of a passing glance, were the out and out Nazis and Fascists, an embarrassment of sects and cults too numerous even to begin to mention.[94]

From this extraordinary potpourri one significant group or coalition of groups did emerge as the locus of resistance to Roosevelt's foreign policy. This was the American First Committee, which formed in the summer of 1940 and quickly grew into a major organization, capable of bringing the isolationist case to the public through newspaper ads, articles and books, radio talks, rallies, etc. Since anyone was free to join America First it attracted a fair share of anti-Semites and Nazi and Fascist sympathizers and, on the other side of the ideological divide, some left-wingers as well, but it was dominated and run by straight and proper wealthy types who contributed the bulk of its money, occupied its executive positions—from its chairman, Robert S. Wood (president of Sears Roebuck), down—and made sure that elements of the lunatic fringe played no conspicuous role in its affairs. At its peak in the early months of 1941, historian Wayne S. Cole estimates, America First had some 450 chapters and subchapters and a membership of about 800,000, two- thirds of whom lived in the upper Midwest, most of the others in the German, Italian, and Irish quarters of Northeastern cities. America First was the cutting edge of the loyal opposition.[95]

For a long time Lindbergh, as was his wont, joined no formal organization. The Lone Eagle spoke as an unfettered individual for the isolationist movement in general. Exactly where he fit into that move-ment was unclear. He was no anti-Semite, though he accepted some of the standard anti-Semitic canards of the day, for example, that Jews dominated much of the press and most of radio and movies. While he would never have been caught dead in the company of Black Shirts, Silver Shirts, Nazi Bundists, and their ilk, he was as much a fellow traveler of the Third Reich as ever and often took counsel with like-minded people.

It would have been unseemly of him now, with Hitler's victories trumpeted daily in the press, to go on proclaiming Germany's greatness. Instead, he adopted the fatalist approach. Nothing, he said, could stop Germany from reaching her goal of European hegemony. She was "The Wave of the Future," the title of the famous essay arguing the same point that Anne Morrow Lindbergh published in 1940. Germany, she then claimed, was "the dream that is coming to birth."[96] Lindbergh thus dismissed Britain's heroism as preposterous, an exercise in futility. The war for all intents and purposes was over. The United States, it followed, should come to terms with reality and ride the crest of the wave that was washing over mankind. The United States should recognize the legiti-macy of Germany's power; more than recognize, embrace it. Which was why, in Lindbergh's opinion, the United States must be rid of President Roosevelt and the values he epitomized: they represented the tyranny of the dead over the living.

Lindbergh thus leaped into the thick of a controversy—the 1940 presidential election—that went beyond Roosevelt the man and leader. For the fact is that a considerable body of Republicans who had no love of Roosevelt supported his interventionist foreign policy. In the summer of 1940 two prominent Republicans joined his cabinet, as Secretaries of War and the Navy. The strongly interventionist Committee to Defend America by Aiding the Allies was made up largely of Republicans, most of them drawn from eastern financial, corporate, and legal circles, the very circles in which Lindbergh himself moved. His wife's family, her mother, sister, and brother, were all resolutely pro-British and pro-interventionist.

Her diary discloses the strain she felt as she and her husband found themselves increasingly ostracized, cut off even from those she loved and respected. She laments: "we are exiles, exiles for good. For we are exiles in *time*—not in space. There is no place for us today and no people." But though she herself had reservations about Lindbergh's views, her loyalty to him and his ideas never wavered. "I am not on the side of evil," she writes while the Battle of Britain raged, "I want evil to be vanquished as much as they—only my mind tells me, perhaps wrongly, that it cannot be done the way they think it can."[97] A variation on the "Wave of the Future" theme.

Inevitably, Roosevelt set about defeating this enemy, removing this thorn from his side. Unlike his other enemies, from Al Smith to John L. Lewis, Lindbergh had few or no apparent vulnerabilities and no vices. And the President was definitely not going to debate the young hero publicly. Nor was it Roosevelt's style to directly engage his opponents; he would get cabinet members who had a talent for polemics to do so, or he would subtly provoke his opponents into injuring themselves. Only as a last resort would he launch a frontal assault in full view of the nation. Lindbergh was to experience each of these treatments before Roosevelt was done with him.

What Roosevelt thought of Lindbergh we learn from a letter he wrote on May 21, 1940: "when I read Lindbergh's speech I felt that it could not have been better put if it had been written by Goebbels himself. What a pity that this youngster has completely abandoned his belief in our form of government and has accepted Nazi methods because apparently they are efficient."[98] In that speech Lindbergh had taken aim at Roosevelt's recent appeal for funds to build 50,000 planes a year. "The power of aviation," Lindbergh had said, "has been greatly underrated in the past. Now we must be careful not to overestimate this power in the excitement of reaction. Air strength depends more upon the establishment of intelligent, consistent policies than upon the construction of huge numbers of planes."[99] Roosevelt could hardly be blamed for his anger at remarks such as these. All along Lindbergh had been preaching the gospel of air power and now that it was being acted on he was preaching the gospel of restraint. It sounded suspiciously like apologetics, and so Roosevelt and others understandably concluded that Lindbergh had "abandoned his belief in our form of government."

Around this time the White House learned that Army Intelligence officer Truman Smith had helped Lindbergh prepare his speech, that Smith, to quote Roosevelt's press secretary, "was known to be pro-Nazi," a blatant misstatement. Smith was promptly transferred from Washington to Fort Benning, Georgia. Lindbergh was in a fury. Roosevelt, he complained, was once again "out to 'get' him."[100] The validity of the complaint does not minimize Lindbergh's bad faith in asserting it. Did he actually expect the President to stand by and merely wince while an Army officer was collaborating with, perhaps even giving valuable information to, the President's political adversary? Lindbergh wanted to play the political game yet enjoy immunity from its conditions and consequences. This syndrome was apparent earlier when he indignantly rejected the offer of a cabinet post.

Lindbergh testified as an expert nonpareil before committees of both houses of Congress against Roosevelt's most ambitious attempt to assist Britain, the Lend-Lease bill (H.R. 1776), according to whose provisions any country deemed crucial to America's security could "lease" unlimited amounts of arms and equipment and pay for them in the future. The initial outlay was to be seven billion dollars, a staggering figure in 1941. Lindbergh's argument was the familiar one—that Britain could not survive, that American help would achieve nothing but prolong the suffering and involve the United States in a conflict for which she was wholly unprepared, that her best strategy was an improved air defense from one end of the continent to the other. And since the United States controlled the air lanes of North America she would by his reckoning possess total security, though Germany and Japan between them might soon dominate the Eastern Hemisphere and the oceans as well. This, in a nutshell, was the isolationist strategy for Fortress America.[101]

That it was not the strategy America favored Congress amply demonstrated when in May 1941 it approved Lend-Lease by a lopsided vote. The majority of Americans, in other words, felt that the best way to achieve isolationist objectives, keeping America out of the war and avoiding entangling alliances in general, was by Roosevelt's means. They thus established an equilibrium between their profound sympathy for the victims of German, Japanese, and Italian aggression and their profounder desire for peace, between their fear of inhabiting a world subjugated by Fascism and their greater fear of joining the struggle to stop it.

But it was a fragile equilibrium. What would become of it if Britain were defeated while Germany and Italy continued to advance in every direction? Would the American public then come around to the isolationist view, that is, write off Europe (and maybe Asia), withdraw into its own hemispheric carapace, and reach a modus vivendi with the Axis nations? The awful truth confronting Roosevelt was that Lend-Lease and all the other assistance to Britain (and China) were having only a marginal effect on the war. They failed to stop Hitler's armies from resuming their march in the spring of 1941. Greece and Yugoslavia were conquered with ease and the huge British force that defended Crete was routed. At the same time, the Afrika Korps under General Rommel was sweeping across Libya after smashing the British army there and entering the precincts of Egypt, gateway to the Middle East and beyond. Hitler's submarine fleet, meanwhile, was interdicting the North Atlantic sea lanes, sinking with impunity the merchant ships that carried American goods to Great Britain. Nazi hegemony over Europe was complete, and, it would seem, permanent. Under the circumstances, there was every reason why American public opinion might find the temptation of isolationism irresistible. This was Roosevelt's nightmare.

He was particularly disturbed, therefore, when Lindbergh in April 1941, with much fanfare, joined the America First Committee. Roosevelt's attitude toward America First may be gauged by the fact that he had the FBI check into its contributors to see if it was a bona fide organization; Roosevelt suspected, and hoped to discover, the presence of German gold or advisors. But J. Edgar Hoover found nothing to incriminate America First or any of its leading members.[102]

At any rate, to mark his recruitment into the organization Lindbergh delivered a series of stinging broadsides against the administration that were widely publicized. He accused it of deliberately leading the country into a war which could not be won, and against the wrong enemy at that, the Communist East being the only threat to civilization.

At this point Roosevelt determined to bring him down, or better, provoke him into bringing himself down.

On April 13 the administration's *provocateur* par excellence, Harold Ickes, referred to Lindbergh in a speech as "America's number one Nazi fellow traveler," "the first American to raise aloft the standard of pro-Nazism," among other choice epithets. Ickes also went after Mrs. Lindbergh, calling her book, *The Wave of the Future,* the "Bible of every American Nazi, Fascist, Bundist and appeaser."[103] Despite these cuffs below the belt Lindbergh wisely said nothing in reply.

The master himself then took a hand. On April 25, after reading about Lindbergh's latest criticisms, Roosevelt held a press conference at which reporters were encouraged to ask questions concerning Lindbergh because they could expect good copy if they did. One reporter asked Roosevelt why Lindbergh had not been called up for active duty when so many other reserve officers had.

Roosevelt's answer was a parable drawn from American history. Weeks before, he had asked a journalist friend, Jay Franklin, to find what he could about the Copperheads, the Northerners who opposed the Civil War out of sympathy for the South. This Franklin did, singling out for special mention the leading Copperhead, Ohio Representative Clement L. Vallandigham. "Vallandighams," Roosevelt asserted, were men whom the government could not for obvious reasons rely on, whatever their merits. He explained that these Vallandighams "urged immediate peace" on Lincoln in the belief that the war could not be won. And for good measure Roosevelt brought up the case of the "appeasers at Valley Forge" who pleaded with Washington to quit, because the revolutionary cause was hopeless. If the reporters wanted the patriotic view on quitting in adversity he suggested they consult Tom Paine.

As though the parable were insufficient a reporter than asked Roosevelt point blank, "Are you still talking about Colonel Lindbergh?" Roosevelt, according to the account, gave "A simple and emphatic affirmative."[104]

This was provocation with a vengeance. The papers were full of how the President in effect accused the famous aviator of treason. Everyone knew about Valley Forge. Most remembered Paine's characterization of "the summer soldier and the sunshine patriot" who failed his country during the "times that try men's souls." The allusion to Vallandighams required some explaining. Roosevelt came in for much criticism, even by friends who thought he was being unfair, using language inimical to civil liberties. The United States, after all, was not at war, as she had been in 1863 and 1776, and Lindbergh, like any American, had a perfect right to his opinions on what the national interest was and should be.

Had Lindbergh again kept his own counsel, or had he responded to Roosevelt thoughtfully and temperately, he undoubtedly would have won the public's sympathy. He might even have humbled Roosevelt into making an apology.

Instead, he fell for the bait. It took him two days to compose his letter to Roosevelt, though one would not infer that from its brevity and curt, businesslike tone. All he did was announce that he was resigning from the Army Air Corps because his "President and superior officer" had impugned his "loyalty," "character," and "motives." "It was," as Leonard Mosely puts it, "a fatal move to have taken." While Americans were being drafted under the recently enacted Selective Service Act Lindbergh was yielding up his commission, shirking his duty to his country. Nothing Roosevelt said about him justified such a reaction, if he was the patriot he claimed to be. This, at any rate, was the conclusion many Americans drew from his letter of resignation.[105] He had let his rage break through the wall of self-discipline that had usually protected him so well. It was the opening Roosevelt sought.

The affair reinforced Lindbergh's perception of himself as a martyr, a reluctant martyr to be sure, but a martyr nonetheless. And by all the objective criteria he *was* a martyr. He had no personal interest in the cause he espoused. His motives were entirely selfless and dispassionate. Far from gaining anything material, he, who detested publicity, called forth the most outrageous denunciations, from the President of the United States down, and even from erstwhile friends. Almost as unpalatable to him was the work he had to accomplish: to speak before large, raucous crowds, and often in the company of pacifists and left-wingers like Norman Thomas. Lindbergh felt nothing but contempt for pacifists, yet necessity compelled him to embrace them as fellow isolationists. In a moment of exasperation he wrote: "Sometimes I feel like saying, 'Well, let's get into this war if you are so anxious to. Then the responsibility will be yours.' In comparison to the work I am now doing the fighting will be fun. But my mind tells me that we better face our problems and let Europe face hers without getting mixed up in this war. . . . I have an interest in the type of world my children are going to live in. That is why I will probably stay on the stump with the pacifists. . . ."[106] Martyrdom could ask for no more.

His wife certainly knew what he was going through, and her admiration for him—for his willingness to suffer for the truth—was boundless, to judge from the parts of her diary that she has published. She attributed his effectiveness on the platform to his purity and goodness. She wrote in early May 1941, following an America First rally:

> The crowd, galvanized by him, silenced, turned to him. And when he started to read, slowly, with emphasis, I felt his great strength and power and watched that crowd looking at him, with faith, with undivided attention, with trust—leaning on that strength (which was really unexpressed—not whipped, not asked for. He was not using his strength or his power *intentionally*. This has always been so with him, always. No—it was simply there—*in him*). I kept thinking of Tennyson's Sir Gallahad. "My strength is as the strength of ten because my heart is pure."[107]

But Roosevelt had introduced a dollop of original sin into Lindbergh's soul—the sin of personal vulnerability, of hurt pride. The intimation of his disloyalty gave him a deeply felt stake in the outcome of the great controversy between isolationists and interventions and, closer to the bone, between himself and the President of the United States. Lindbergh's language on the stump grew more strident, at least toward Roosevelt, whom he pictured either as an egomaniac bent on shaping world history or as the servitor of an "organized minority" that favored war. Lindbergh actually compared America under Roosevelt to Germany under Hitler. Before a cheering America First audience at Madison Square Garden, he stated that in the 1940 election the people had had as much free choice over foreign affairs "as the Germans would have been given if Hitler had run against Göring."[108] Roosevelt was beginning to obsess him.

Hitler's invasion of the Soviet Union on June 22, 1941 made Lindbergh more strident yet, especially when Roosevelt announced that the United States would extend Lend-Lease assistance to the Communist state. To Lindbergh and most isolationists this was the most demonstrable proof of Roosevelt's un-Americanism, exposing his administration for what it was and always had been. For Lindbergh it was more important than ever that the United States remain neutral. The war, he predicted, would soon be over and the curse of Communism exorcised at last. This would have happened years ago—so went his argument, advanced without a scintilla of proof—but for the vanity and ignorance of the democracies. If, that is, Britain and France had not come to Poland's defense Hitler would have attacked Russia much earlier. And if Roosevelt had been less hostile to Japan she unquestionably would have attacked Russia too. Lindbergh reflected broad isolationist sentiment when he asserted categorically that he "would a hundred times rather see my country ally itself with England, or even with Germany with all her faults, than with the cruelty, the godlessness, and the barbarism that exist in Soviet Russia."[109]

Roosevelt feared that Lindbergh's argument might be a persuasive one. Given the widespread desire to have both miscreants fight each other to extinction, the inclusion of Communist Russia in America's defense perimeter was likely to reduce support for the administration. Roosevelt abhorred the Soviet Union (contrary to the distorted vision through which his right-wing critics saw him), but like Churchill, arch-conservative and imperialist, he felt that Hitler was Satan incarnate and that any countervailing force, however odious, must be encouraged, praised, cosseted, and warmly welcomed as an ally. Convincing the American people to go along with him gave Roosevelt an additional headache—and further reason to discredit Lindbergh and the American First Committee.

From FBI informers Lindbergh learned that his phone was being tapped. The discovery—still unverified but entirely plausible—came as no surprise to him, but it did assuredly rub him the wrong way. One can even speculate wildly, it is nothing more, that he might purposely have been let in on the secret in hopes of baiting him to commit further indiscretions.[110]

On July 13, 1941, he took a blow that truly hurt. For on that day Interior Secretary Ickes, in a speech commemorating the Free French, had this to say: "No one has ever heard Lindbergh utter a word of horror at, or even aversion to, the bloody career the Nazis are following, nor a word of pity for the innocent men, women and children who have been murdered by the Nazis in practically every country in Europe." Nor had anyone "heard this Knight of the German Eagle denounce Hitler or Nazism or Mussolini or Fascism." Lindbergh's function, it seemed to Ickes, was "to knock down the will of his fellow citizens to resist Hitler and Nazism."[111] The reference to the "Knight of the German Eagle" was clever, for it reminded the public of the medal Lindbergh had gotten from the notorious Hermann Göring and never returned, even as he had returned his United States Army commission. It was also a reminder of what had become of that other eagle who had flown the Atlantic and had been the admiration of humanity.

The remarks had their intended affect. Lindbergh's letter to Roosevelt—via the press—betrayed the pain he felt. It was the worst letter he could have written because he dwelled at length and without apologies on his receipt and possession of the medal in question. He gave his word that "I have no connection with any foreign government. I have no connection, directly or indirectly, with anyone in Germany or Italy since I was last in Europe," and if any doubts of his loyalty remained he would open all his files to a formal investigation and appear before a presidential committee. In the absence of incriminating information, Lindbergh went on, he must insist on an apology from Ickes.

Roosevelt responded perfunctorily through his press secretary. Ickes never apologized, saying only, and obviously for public consumption, that he charged Lindbergh not with having foreign connections and communications but with supporting Hitler's cause, and Lindbergh still could redeem himself by denouncing "Hitler and his brutal aggressions."[112]

Ickes—and, it can be assumed, Roosevelt—was delighted with the exchange. Ickes's analysis of Lindbergh's mistake was brilliantly accurate. Until July 14, he wrote in his diary, he had thought "no one could get under his [Lindbergh's] skin enough to make him squeal." He "had always admired Lindbergh in one respect. No matter how vigorously he had been attacked personally he had never attempted to answer. . . . But

at last I had succeeded." Concerning the medal, Ickes was satisfied that
he had caught his quarry on the horns of a dilemma. "He is now in the
position where he is damned if he gives it back and damned if he doesn't."
Moreover, Lindbergh erred badly "by writing a querulous letter to
'teacher.' He should have slammed right back at me." Lindbergh "has
allowed himself to be put on the defensive and that is always a weak
position for anyone."[113] Lindbergh could have done worse than consult
Ickes before writing to Roosevelt.

Lindbergh's defensiveness arose from the German "connection"
imputed to him. The more he denied it or insisted on proof of its
existence the more damning was the imputation. His friends advised him
to mollify public opinion by including in his speeches sympathetic
references to embattled England and critical references to the Nazis—in
short, to meet some of Ickes's objections: had he done so earlier Ickes
would not have been able to make them.[114] But Lindbergh, as already
noted, tended to grow more stubborn and righteous under pressure.
Telling the public what it wanted to hear, playing on its credulity, its
false hopes, was the sort of thing politicians did; it was what Roosevelt
was best at, and he, Lindbergh, would not stoop to it. If he disappointed
his friends, causing some of them to turn away from him, so be it.

The exchange, at all events, had its intended effect. It provoked
Lindbergh, whose *amour-propre* was seriously wounded by now, into
becoming more combative, more politically engaged. This was precisely
what Roosevelt and Ickes wanted. They understood he was *not* a political
person and was therefore apt to make political mistakes. They had lured
him to a place where wiser angels would have feared to go.

In his public statements Lindbergh never discussed the "organized
minority," which, he contended, was trying to drag America into war.
He almost did so in an article that *Collier's* published on March 29, 1941.
One draft of it, according to Wayne S. Cole, singled out for special
obloquy capitalists, politicians, intellectuals, and Jews. Another draft
blamed "the Capitalists, the Politicians, and the Jew . . . for America's
trend toward war." Yet another again included intellectuals among the

"organized minority" whom he apostrophized in these words: "[You have] sacrificed our American destiny to your idol of money, to your academic idealism and selfish desire for power." All these references Lindbergh prudently struck from the final draft.[115]

Toward the end of the summer, his conflict with the Roosevelt administration having entered a much more embittered phase, he decided that he would name "the war agitators," come what may. In the handwritten draft of the speech he was scheduled to give at Des Moines on September 11 he stated that "tomorrow's headlines will say 'Lindbergh attacks Jews.' The ugly cry of anti-Semitism will be eagerly, joyfully pounded upon and waved about my name. It is so much simpler to brand someone with a bad label that to take the trouble to read what he says."[116] His wife pleaded with him to tone down the part mentioning the Jews. She feared "the anti-Semitic forces will rally to him, exultant." Lindbergh's answer was in character. What mattered, he held, was not how his speech would be interpreted but "whether or not what he said is *true* and whether it will help to keep us out of the war." She said that "the negative results will outweigh the positive." He did in the end tone down "the Jewish paragraph" "to avoid all traces of rancor or bitterness."[117] Lindbergh, then, was fully aware of what he was doing; he was aware of what consequences would flow from his exposure of the "organized minority."

Actually, Lindbergh said quite a bit about the Jews in his September 11 Des Moines speech.[118] Jews comprised one of the three main groups which, he claimed, were responsible for leading the American people by the nose, the others being the British, with their vast propaganda apparatus, and the Roosevelt administration, determined to usurp more and more power, even to establish a totalitarian state. He threw in several lesser groups as well: some capitalists, Anglophiles, intellectuals, and, with Russia's entry into the war, the Communists of course. But for these groups there would be peace. In his attacks on the British and at the administration he offered nothing new. What he said about the Jews, however, was not only new; it was extremely offensive. One can only wonder what Lindbergh had in mind before he toned it down. Here is the statement in question.

. . . It is not difficult to understand why Jewish people desire the overthrow of Nazi Germany. The persecution they suffered in Germany would be sufficient to make bitter enemies of any race. No person with a sense of the dignity of mankind can condone the persecution the Jewish race suffered in Germany. But no person of honesty and vision can look on their pro-war policy here today without seeing the dangers involved in such a policy, both for us and for them.

Instead of agitating for war the Jewish groups in this country should be opposing it in every possible way, for they will be among the first to feel the consequences. Tolerance is a virtue that depends upon peace and strength. History shows that it cannot survive war and devastation. A few farsighted Jewish people realize this and stand opposed to intervention. But the majority still do not. The greatest danger in this country lies in their large ownership and influence in our motion pictures, our press, our radio, and our government.

This last paragraph contains the standard anti-Semitic fare, the assumption that Jews, through their alleged control of the media and the movies, are telling the Gentiles what to think and how to act. Lindbergh makes no effort to support the assertion, cites no examples of how Jews use their presumed control of the media and the movies to get their way. The underlying message, it will be noticed, is that Jews are all-powerful, constitute an iron-clad and homogeneous bloc, deviously wield their tremendous influence, and seek to get others to do their dirty work. More offensive yet is the veiled warning to the Jews, provided by someone who has their well-being at heart. Lindbergh thus places himself in the position of knowing better than the Jews where their interests lie and what the limits of tolerance are. This also is standard anti-Semitic fare, whether Lindbergh realized it or not. Father Coughlin, it will be remembered, posed as a protector of the Jews and demanded, as the condition of his tolerance, that they comply with his orders. Lindbergh was guilty of the same kind of solicitude.

He dismissed the cries of outrage which he had anticipated, though their volume and intensity might have given him pause. He could not have anticipated the cries issuing from the throats of people closest to him—leaders of the America First Committee, elder statesmen like Herbert Hoover, publishers like Hearst and McCormick, isolationists of every hue and coloration (except downright Fascists). They were out of patience with him less for having said the wrong thing than for having said what he did wrongly, tactlessly. The wrong consisted in his having made himself, and by extension America First and the isolationist movement at large, the center of controversy, thereby deflecting attention away from Roosevelt and his policies. Lindbergh had brought about the opposite of what he had intended.[119]

His friends perceived what Roosevelt must have perceived earlier—that Lindbergh possessed the singular vices of his singular virtues. The obdurate self-reliance, inseparable from his fierce pride, which served him so well in technical work, in feats of daring and courage, he could not carry over to politics—the art of reconciling differences for the sake of attaining a common objective. Had he shown the speech to others besides his wife and listened to their suggestions he would have avoided the terrible afterclap that descended on him.[120]

The September 11 speech marks Lindbergh's defeat at Roosevelt's hands. Having ceased any longer to appear objective, detached, apolitical, he lost his effectiveness. He never admitted defeat, and was determined to soldier on, though more and more the pressure was wearing him down. To the chairman of America First he confessed on October 21 that he was intellectually drained, "written out," and would like to "withdraw gradually from participation in these rallies." He wanted instead to keep himself "in readiness to assist" those in Britain who would "demand" negotiations with Hitler after Russia's surrender, assuming Roosevelt by then had not pushed the United States into the war.[121]

Lindbergh's exhaustion and anger made him still more strident, to the point of recklessness, in his attacks on Roosevelt. He informed a Fort Wayne crowd on October 3 that "we are about to enter a dictatorship." On October 30, before a full house in Madison Square Garden, he repeated the charge and stated that the threat to the United States came from Roosevelt, not Hitler. "There is no danger to this nation from without. The only danger to us is from within."[122] Who but the most die-hard Roosevelt-hater or pro-Fascist believed such a thing? But the more hyperbolic Lindbergh's language, the more Roosevelt must have gloated, uttering not a word in reply. Here was young Lindbergh, once his formidable foe, repeating the same tactics that had brought down Al Smith, Father Coughlin, and John L. Lewis, and probably would have brought down Huey Long had he lived. The only difference between Lindbergh and them was that he had been harder to provoke.

For that matter America First was a declining if not a spent force. Fissures were opening wider and wider in the organization between the militant isolationists of the Lindbergh stamp and the moderates who detested Fascism as much as liberal interventionists did but felt there was nothing the United States could or should do about it. The very future of America First was in question.[123]

But this scarcely meant that isolationism was finished. Far from it. Aid to Britain, the Soviet Union, and China short of war—beyond that policy Roosevelt still dared not go because American public opinion still would not let him. In fact, Roosevelt had gone as far as he could. He had ordered the Navy to "shoot on sight" any ships that interfered with American sea lanes. And after German U-boats had sunk the American destroyers *Kearny* and *Reuben James* off Iceland, Congress had, at Roosevelt's instance, repealed the Neutrality Act, thereby permitting the government to send armed convoys to Britain and Russia.

Meanwhile, relations with Japan had been swiftly deteriorating. Roosevelt had practically cut off trade with Japan following her occupation of French Indo-China. He had named General Douglas MacArthur (living in retirement in the Philippines) commander-in-chief of American forces in the Far East. He made it clear to Japan that the United States would do what she must to protect American interests in the event of further Japanese expansion. These were tough moves, but they did not necessarily mean war, not unless Japan or Germany decided to start it. The choice was entirely theirs. The American people, however little they thought of the Axis powers, however much they empathized with the victims of aggression, were, as ever, in no mood for combat.

That was evident from the perilously close votes in Congress on renewing the Selective Service Act (by a single House vote) and repealing the Neutrality Act. Had Japan not bombed Pearl Harbor and Germany and Italy not declared war on the United States, Roosevelt would have been stymied. The status quo, tense as it was, would have prevailed. There would have been no need for an America First Committee because its cause would have been vindicated. Robert E. Sherwood speaks of Roosevelt's deepening frustration as late as a week before Pearl Harbor. "He had said everything 'short of war' that could be said. He had no more tricks left. The hats from which he had pulled so many rabbits was empty."[124]

Pearl Harbor brought the vexing issue to a thunderous conclusion. Isolationism died then and there. America First dissolved soon after. Everyone who had sympathized with the Axis cause now kept their own counsel while joining the populace in rallying around the flag.

FIVE

DENOUEMENT

AL SMITH

Al Smith's retirement from politics was poignant. The world which had nurtured him, the world not only of Tammany Hall but of the Irish Catholic big-city machine in general, was passing, yielding before the plenary power of the federal government and its multifarious agencies in public works, welfare, employment, housing, and the like. It was a development Smith may not have regretted all that much. His fellow Tammanyites had abandoned him in his quarrels with Roosevelt, and he pretty much abandoned them, though he would often return to the old and deteriorating Wigwam on ceremonial occasions. In everything but title Al Smith, greatest of Tammany politicians, was now a Republican.

Something of a reconciliation did take place between him and Roosevelt when in 1941 he spoke out strongly for the administration's effort to help Britain in her lonely, desperate resistance to Nazi Germany. Roosevelt greatly appreciated this, especially since his policy did not go over well with many Irish-Americans. Thereafter the two men kept in touch and managed to get together and reminisce about the people and events of olden days and share a hearty laugh.[1] If they had lived longer than they did—Smith died in October 1944, six months before Roosevelt did—they might even have become friends again.

FATHER COUGHLIN

Japan's attack on Pearl Harbor failed to daunt Father Coughlin. He was as defiant as ever. The American people were now solidly behind their President and commander-in-chief, whatever some of them might think of him personally and politically, and their fury at the Japanese and the other Axis powers (Germany and Italy having also declared war on the United States) knew no bounds. But *Social Justice* kept blaming the usual suspects, the Jews—the cabal of international bankers and Communists—for causing the conflict. Obviously, Coughlin was spoiling for a showdown with the Roosevelt administration, a showdown which would inevitably lead to Coughlin's suppression, a martyr to the truth. No other conclusion can be drawn from his behavior in the months immediately after Pearl Harbor—months of enemy triumphs on every front.

Eager to take up the challenge, Roosevelt asked his Attorney General, Francis Biddle, to do something, such as dust off Title I of the 1917 Espionage Act, which gave Biddle and the Postmaster General, Frank C. Walker, carte blanche to halt mail delivery of literature they deemed seditious to the armed forces. Biddle accordingly sent Walker excerpts from *Social Justice*,[2] in particular those from the March 16, 1942 number, in which Coughlin asserted, "If pro-Americanism consists in casting the entire civilized world into a seething cauldron of bloody war for the protection of 600,000 racialists or religionists [a distorted allusion to the German Jews] . . . then Americanism, under that interpretation, is not worth fighting for." In mid-April, Walker informed Coughlin he would hold hearings in two weeks on the fate of *Social Justice,* obviously a formality, the case having for all intents and purposes been decided.[3]

Meanwhile Biddle was pursuing a parallel course, one less likely to produce a martyr if successful. In his public discussion of the affair Biddle would have us believe he worked out the strategy himself.[4] In fact Roosevelt's fingerprints are all over it. Whatever Biddle's virtues, and he possessed many, political finesse was not one of them. He asked a prominent lay Catholic, who happened to be a friend of Roosevelt's and also a member of the administration, if he could take up the Coughlin matter with Coughlin's superior, Archbishop Mooney, who, it can be inferred, was waiting for just such a request. The order quickly came down: as of May 1 Coughlin must close down the magazine and cease publicly commenting on politics altogether.[5] And so it was that the Church and not the government, certainly not President Roosevelt, finally put the quietus on Father Coughlin.

For the rest of his career he continued, with his wonted vigor, to preside over the magniloquent Royal Oak church he had built and which stands today as a memorial to the epoch of his notoriety. In retirement and until death in 1979 at the grand age of 88 he would occasionally and without apologies talk about his ten year encounter with Franklin D. Roosevelt and "that small group of people who [still] run the world."

JOHN L. LEWIS

Lewis had been humbled and reduced by Roosevelt, but he was still the absolute boss of the largest and most important body of workers in the country, and at a time when their labor was more in demand than ever. Rare was the miner who thought ill of the great man who had brought the union so much. He was the same John L. Lewis, unchastened and unyielding in the pursuit of his one objective—to improve the lives of his 600,000 charges and their families.

He was in a position to inconvenience Roosevelt, and America too. Thanks to his fall, he no longer had to appease public opinion. If he was the least liked person in America—he laid good claim to this distinction—so much the worse for those who thought so. He was serving the miners, not them. As far as the miners were concerned, the unpopularity of their leader was the mark of his effectiveness in representing them. That the world at large could never appreciate, much less sympathize, with the men who went into the pits was an *idée fixe* in the minds of most of them. In his recent crises Lewis had the unflagging loyalty of the rank and file; they made whatever sacrifices he asked of them, and his legion of adversaries, from Roosevelt to the mine operators, knew it.

Late in 1941, with war looming on the horizon, Lewis took a portion of the miners out on strike because U.S. Steel, owner of the largest of the "captive mines" (those which produced coal exclusively for steel companies), refused to meet his terms for settlement; they never had for that matter. At one point, Roosevelt pleaded with him "to come to the aid of your country" and not strike. "If," Lewis replied, "you would use the power of the State to restrain me, as an agent of labor, then, Sir, I submit that you should use that power to restrain my adversary in this issue, who is an agent of capital. My adversary is a rich man named Morgan, who lives in New York." In the end, after much pulling and hauling, Roosevelt used "the power of the State" to give Lewis "a stunning victory," as Irving Bernstein describes it. Roosevelt was not about to use "the power of the State," power which he certainly now possessed, to force the miners to work at bayonet point. Lewis was keenly aware of that.[6]

He also was aware of that in his next and most serious contretemps with Roosevelt, which occurred in the middle of the war. Despite his "no-strike" pledge Lewis struck four times in 1943 because no satisfactory contract could be worked out with the coal operators. Roosevelt seized the mines, making the Interior Department the operators, and was sorely tempted to call out the troops, or ask for legislation that would have enabled the government to draft workers engaged in stoppages up to the age of 65 (Lewis was then 63). Such a law, the War Labor Disputes (Smith-Connally) Act, was in fact passed. So massive was the public's dislike of Lewis that Congress, in passing the act, had easily overridden Roosevelt's veto of it. Nothing like such a broadly repressive law had ever existed in America.[7]

The realization that Lewis's antics would call forth yet more repressive measures, and against all of labor, prompted his ex-comrade Philip Murray and the other CIO leaders to break completely with him. He then pulled the UMW out of the CIO after insisting, to no avail, that it repay the huge sums ($1,665,000, he claimed) he had lent it and its constituent unions in the 1930s. Lewis, his capacity to pull surprises undiminished, asked to rejoin the AFL. Rejoin his union did at last, bringing him back to the same table with Bill Green and the gerontocrats of the AFL executive council whom he had denounced and ridiculed and belittled without letup for so many years. Now as always he cultivated friends only because they were the enemies of his enemy.[8]

Lewis survived Roosevelt by 24 years. For that matter, he survived practically all his contemporaries, the few he got along well with and the many he fought against. He was 80 when, in 1960, he finally retired from the United Mine Workers. Longevity in his case may have been a mixed blessing. He had lived long enough to preside over the catastrophic decline of his once great union. The advance of technology, the change in fuel consumption, the paucity of a talented cadre,[*] had seen to that. Its golden age, and his, had been the age of Franklin D. Roosevelt.

CHARLES A. LINDBERGH

Had Lindbergh held on to his commission he certainly would have been called back to service following Pearl Harbor, for few Americans were, or would have been, more valuable to the war effort, especially then, when thousands of pilots had to be recruited and trained posthaste. He wanted desperately to serve; he was under 40 and in perfect health. Aside from thinning hair and the addition of a few more pounds he was the same youthful hero of old.

On December 20, 1941 he wrote his friend General H. H. (Hap) Arnold, the Army Air Corps chief of staff, asking to be called up.[9] Arnold told him to see Secretary of War Henry L. Stimson. The meeting took place in Washington on January 12, 1942. Speaking bluntly as was his custom, Stimson said he was not inclined to look favorably on Lindbergh's request because he believed that Lindbergh (to quote from Stimson's letter to the President), "took a very different view of our friends and enemies in the present war from not only that of ourselves but from that of a great

---

[*] His chosen successor went to jail for life because he had a rival and his rival's family murdered.

majority of our countrymen." One can imagine the pain Lindbergh must have felt when he heard the following (to again quote from the letter): "I should be personally unwilling to place in command any man who had such a lack of faith in our cause. . . ."[10] And Lindbergh was further humiliated, this time by Stimson's assistant, Robert A. Lovett, who also interviewed Lindbergh and quite as frankly doubted if he could perform his duties "loyally" under President Roosevelt. So unwanted was Lindbergh he was even prevented from giving indirect help to the Air Corps. His punishment could not have been severer.[11]

Roosevelt may not have pulled the strings of Lindbergh's destiny, but he knew exactly who would pull them. On December 30 Roosevelt had received an angry memo from Interior Secretary Ickes, who had just learned that Lindbergh was seeking readmission to the Army. Lindbergh is described as "a ruthless and conscious fascist" who had nefarious ambitions of his own. He is compared to other men who had compiled distinguished war records before becoming dictators, the likes of Hitler, Mussolini, Kemal of Turkey, Pilsudski of Poland, et al. This fantastic charge, this display of pseudo-knowledge, accompanies a recommendation that Lindbergh never be allowed "a chance to gain a military record" and "should be buried in merciful oblivion."[12] Roosevelt agreed "wholeheartedly" with Ickes's descent into hysteria. Equally exaggerated, and even sillier, were Navy Secretary Frank Knox's comments actually accusing Lindbergh of having had "no training as an officer" and suggesting that he "enlist as air cadet like anybody else."[13] Roosevelt agreed with this memo too and passed it on, with Ickes's, to Stimson before the latter's meeting with Lindbergh.

Most of Lindbergh's biographers, even those critical of him, fault Roosevelt for being so vindictive and, incidentally, for depriving the United States of Lindbergh's talents when she most needed them. But Roosevelt's vindictiveness was for cause. At no time between December 7 (Pearl Harbor) and December 30, when Lindbergh's letter to General Arnold became public knowledge, did Lindbergh make the slightest gesture of conciliation. He vehemently refused to issue a statement of support for Roosevelt and the war against Fascism, a statement admitting, at least tacitly, that perhaps he had miscalculated, had committed an honest error of judgment. His hatred of Roosevelt was obviously so profound he could not bring himself to pen any kind of letter that in any way might be construed as an apology or a plea of forgiveness. Lindbergh's journal gives us an idea of what he thought of Roosevelt. "I do not know a single man who knows Roosevelt . . . who trusts what he says from one week to the next."[14] Lindbergh was convinced that an apology would effect nothing anyway, that Roosevelt would exploit his self-abasement after taking him back into service and exiling him to some backwater air base where he would be forgotten.

Roosevelt was bringing out definite feelings of paranoia in him. This is hardly surprising, given his opinion, a good deal of it justified, of what Roosevelt had single-handedly wrought.

There is also the fact that Lindbergh's outlook, his conception of international affairs, remained what it had been since 1939 and earlier. On January 5, 1942, widely syndicated columnists Drew Pearson and Robert S. Allen reported that Lindbergh had on December 17 attended a dinner in New York City given by leading America First people at which he was heard to say that Britain, not Germany, was responsible for bringing on the war. New York newspapers elaborated on the story: Lindbergh, according to their account, had argued that Britain and Germany should form "a bloc against the yellow people and bolshevism." For anyone who followed his speeches over the years this was old hat. But to have asserted it now caused something of a sensation. Eleanor Roosevelt sent a copy of the news articles to her husband, who included them in the packet of incriminating material on Lindbergh that he gave Stimson. Lindbergh did not disavow the reports. He said nothing.[15]

In his journal, published decades later, he attempts to set the record straight concerning that dinner. His reasoning is curious. He denies absolutely that he called for Britain and Germany to get together or that he mentioned the "yellow race." But he then admits that he stated, in effect, that "it is a tragic error for the Western nations to turn their backs on Russia and Japan to carry on a prostrating war among themselves." And also: "England and the United States have managed to get into a war where *if they win, they lose.* If we win, we will have created worse conditions than those we went to war against." He goes on to admit that he privately may have said the things ascribed to him in the newspapers and columns, "and if so I have no apologies to make."[16]

Stimson, then, was correct when he told Lindbergh he "evidently had a lack of faith in our cause." The plain truth is that Lindbergh had made it impossible for his friends such as General Arnold to help him. The fault lay primarily with Lindbergh, not Roosevelt.

The war, paradoxically, was Lindbergh's deliverance. It saved him from the notoriety he had always hated and returned him to the sanctuary of a quiet, unobserved life, this time for good. Never again would he and his family dominate the headlines.

And he managed to serve the country despite the circumscriptions. Henry Ford, whose company was mass-producing bombers and airplane engines, hired him as a consultant. He also test flew Marine Corsair fighters for United Aircraft. Later, unbeknownst to the White House, he flew scores of missions, some in combat, with the Air Corps in the South Pacific. He paid back the favor—it was balm to his soul—manyfold by demonstrating how pilots could, by a simple procedure, save fuel and so stay longer in the air. One can only guess what Lindbergh might have contributed to the winning of the war had he been effectively utilized from the outset.[17]

About Roosevelt's conduct of the war Lindbergh said nothing publicly. Like many or most America Firsters Lindbergh was certainly dissatisfied with it. He thought the United States should have concentrated on fighting the Japanese rather than the Germans. Even in war he was the inveterate isolationist. The success of Soviet arms, aided and abetted by the Roosevelt administration, hardly astonished him. He had prophesied what would happen to Western civilization if Germany ceased to be the bulwark against the Communist-led multitudes pressing in relentlessly from the fleshpots of Asia. He was vindicated, at least in his own eyes, but it brought him no satisfaction.

After the war, Lindbergh and most other ex-isolationists did change their thinking. Now that the Soviet Union was America's adversary they became ardent interventionists. To Lindbergh it was a change of method, not principles; of means, not ends. As always, he equated civilization with the white race and barbarism with Soviet Communism.*

He welcomed the obscurity that closed over him for the rest of his life. He was of course unceasingly active, thanks to his splendid health and manifold interests, among them space exploration (whose significance he had appreciated before all but a few had), the preservation of wildlife and primitive cultures, and, surprisingly perhaps, the threat to mankind from the excesses of science and technology. He questioned the tenets he had once cherished and advanced as the hallmarks of civilization: progress, technical proficiency, the capacity to vanquish nature.[18]

When his name cropped up occasionally it did little more than awaken ancient memories. He was a figure from a distant epoch. In 1953 his book on the flight that made him famous, *The Spirit of St. Louis,* was published to uniformly excellent reviews, becoming a best-seller and the basis of a movie (with down-home Jimmy Stewart playing young Lindbergh). It is a first-rate memoir, something of a masterpiece in fact. The reader cannot help admiring the man who writes with, and is the subject of, such carefully understated prose, who permits the remarkable story to unfold so delicately of its own accord.

It is increasingly clear with the passage of time that Franklin D. Roosevelt's most formidable enemies lost because in opposing him they resisted historic forces which chose him as their instrument. Confronting one life-and-death crisis after another, he ushered in the modern American state, centralized and ever-expanding, as guarantor of social justice and national security. Judged by this imperative, this legacy, the enemies Roosevelt defeated seem to us—such disagreeable qualities as they possessed notwithstanding—quaint, old-fashioned, innocent, pathetic, the reliquiae of a bygone age.

---

* See his book, *Of Flight and Life* (New York: Scribner's, 1948), where the argument is tediously bodied forth.

NOTES

INTRODUCTION

1. Borne out by Roosevelt's speeches during the 1932 campaign. *The Papers and Addresses of Franklin D. Roosevelt,* edited by Samuel I. Rosenman (New York: Random House, 1938-50), I, 795ff.

2. Richard Hofstadter writes: "When Hoover bumbled that it was necessary only to restore confidence, the nation laughed bitterly. When Roosevelt said, 'The only thing we have to fear is fear itself,' essentially the same threadbare half-true idea, the nation was thrilled." *The American Political Tradition and the Men Who Made It* (New York: Knopf, 1948), 312.

3. In her series of interviews for the Columbia University Oral History Collection (COHC) Roosevelt's longtime Secretary of Labor, Frances F. Perkins, recalled the remarks by the head of the all-important National Recovery Administration (Hugh Johnson): "We're in a war. . . . The individual who has the power to apply and enforce those regulations is the President. There is nothing the President can't do if he wishes to!" III, 50-1. Also see William E. Leuchtenberg, "The New Deal and the Analogue of War," in *Change and Certainty in Twentieth Century America,* edited by John Braeman, Robert H. Brenner and Everett Walters (Columbus: Ohio University Press, 1964).

4. Richard M. Ketchum is on target when he writes from personal knowledge: "For all his [Roosevelt's] keen knowledge of the contemporary scene, his roots in a particular place and a particular class made him at heart a nineteenth century man. He was raised in a gentler day in the tradition of stability, raised to believe that man (upper class man at any rate) was perfectible and his world subject to improvement; . . . he was taught that the old standards of rectitude were the proper guides to conduct, no matter how the world may change." *The Borrowed Years, 1938-1941* (New York: Random House, 1989), 397.

5. The great economist Joseph A. Schumpeter makes this point in his classic *Business Cycles* (New York: McGraw-Hill, 1939), II, chapter 15.

6. Political psychologist James David Barber notes: "A major source of that warped judgment was no doubt Roosevelt himself." *The Pulse of Politics: Electing Presidents in the Media Age* (New York: Norton, 1980), 245.

7. *Fortune,* no friend of Roosevelt's, described him in August 1935 as "the best actor in talking pictures and the best voice in radio. Until Mr. Roosevelt taught the world how that titanic trombone of tubes and antennae could be played no one had any idea of the possible range of its virtuosity." XII, 103.

8. In Ketchum's words: "He was a born actor-producer, with the talent to play the impresario and the leading man simultaneously, and even the costumes and props he employed—the cape, the pince-nez, the long cigarette-holder—delighted his fans, infuriated his foes, and were meat and drink to cartoonists." *The Borrowed Years,* 398.

9. Roosevelt, writes Isaiah Berlin, "sensed the tendencies of his time and their projections into the future to a most uncommon degree. His sense, not only of the movement of public opinion but of the general direction in which the larger human society of his time was moving, was what is called uncanny. The inner currents, the tremors and complicated convolutions of this movement, seemed to register themselves within his nervous system with a kind of seismographic accuracy." *Personal Impressions* (London: Hogarth Press, 1980), 11.

CHAPTER ONE

1. On Roosevelt's 1910 election: Geoffrey C. Ward, *A First-Class Temperament: The Emergence of Franklin D. Roosevelt* (New York: Harper and Row, 1989), 103-23 and Kenneth S. Davis, *FDR: The Beckoning of Destiny, 1882-1928* (New York: Putnam's, 1972), 239-42.

2. Even though he left no paper trail we have a solid study of Boss Murphy, the theme of which is summed up in its subtitle: Nancy Joan Weiss, *Charles Francis Murphy, 1852-1924: Respectability and Responsibility in Tammany Politics* (Northampton, MA.: Smith College, 1968). See also John M. Allswany, *Bosses, Machines and Urban Voters* (Baltimore: Johns Hopkins, 1986), 60-90.

3. On January 22, 1911 The *New York Times* (hereafter *NYT*) was happy to quote Roosevelt: "There is nothing I love so much as a good fight. I never had so much fun in my life as I am having right now."

4. Sullivan, according to reporter Ernest K. Lindley, also told Boss Murphy: "The Roosevelts runs [sic] true to form and this kid is likely to do for us what the Colonel is going to do to the Republican party—split it wide open." *Franklin D. Roosevelt* (Indianapolis, IN: Bobbs-Merrill, 1931), 78.

5. So cousin Theodore wrote him: "we are really proud of the way you handled yourself." Theodore Roosevelt to Franklin D. Roosevelt, January 29, 1911 (Franklin D. Roosevelt Library [hereafter FDRL]).

6. The best accounts of Roosevelt's run-in with Tammany over Sheehan is Frank Freidel, *Franklin D. Roosevelt: The Apprenticeship* (Boston: Little Brown, 1952), chapter 6, and Ward, *First-Class,* chapter 4.

7. Many books detail Smith's early life. For example, the Josephsons, *Al Smith;* Norman Hapgood and Henry Moscowitz, *Up from the City Streets* (New York: Harcourt Brace, 1927); and Oscar Handlin, *Al Smith and His America* (Boston: Little Brown, 1958).

8. For an in-depth examination of Smith's assembly career: Daniel Silveri, "The Political Education of Alfred E. Smith: The Assembly Years, 1904-1914" (Ph.D. dissertation, St. John's University, 1964).

9. So it was, writes Geoffrey C. Ward, that Smith regarded Roosevelt as an "impractical 'damn fool,' a showy snob whose word could not be trusted, who talked too much and did too little and was unwilling to work enough for the success he so markedly craved." *First-Class,* 498.

10. It is worth noting that the man finally chosen, Joseph A. O'Gorman, was a state judge whose vacated office Boss Murphy's son-in-law would fill. Party professionals, according to an aide of Al Smith, tended "to laugh at Roosevelt. They would much rather have had nominated O'Gorman in the first place." Joseph M. Proskauer, COHC, 48.

11. On January 21, 1911, a *New York Times* reporter wrote: "no one would suspect behind that highly polished exterior the great force and determination that are now sending cold shivers down the spine of Tammany's striped mascot."

12. Roosevelt lost to his opponent three to one in the vote count and in 44 out of 66 counties. Ward, *First-Class,* 256-57.

13. No one was more surprised by Smith's victory than Roosevelt. He had expected Smith to lose, opening the way for him to run as governor in 1920. Alfred B. Rollins Jr., *Roosevelt and Howe* (New York: Knopf, 1962), 113, and Freidel, *The Apprenticeship,* 342.

14. Paula Eldot, *Governor Alfred E. Smith: The Politician as Reformer* (New York: Garland, 1983), 27-35, 311-28.

15. Smith's seconding speech was short and perfunctory. But Roosevelt's seconding speech for Smith, who had been nominated briefly for President, was effusive: "I love him as a friend; I look to him as a man. . . ." Ward, *First-Class,* 511, 509.

16. Rollins, *Roosevelt and Howe,* is the fullest account of their extraordinary relationship, which ended only with Howe's death in 1936, his life's hope fulfilled.

17. *NYT,* July 8, August 14, 1922; and Smith's warm thank you letter to Roosevelt, August 15, 1922 (FDRL).

18. With the South and West in mind Smith asked Roosevelt to be his campaign director. *NYT,* April 29, May 1, 6, 1924, and Edward J. Flynn, *You're the Boss* (New York: Viking, 1949), 41-42. How hard Roosevelt

labored for Smith is evident from the number of boxes on the campaign in the Hyde Park library.

19. Robert K. Murray, *The 103d Ballot: Democrats and the Disaster in Madison Square Garden* (New York: Harper and Row, 1976), is the definitive study of the subject.

20. Davis, *Beckoning,* 756-57.

21. The most detailed description of Smith's governorship is Eldot, *Governor Al Smith.* The quote is from H.L. Mencken, *A Carnival of Buncombe: Writings on Politics,* edited by Malcolm Moos (Chicago: University of Chicago, 1984), 142.

22. "I am not temperamentally fitted to serve in the United States Senate. I do not think I can endure the atmosphere of that verbose and eminently respectable club." Roosevelt to Charles C. Burlingham, July 17, 1928 (FDRL).

23. Moses called Howe "lousy Louie" and Roosevelt a "poor excuse for a man," among other epithets. Naturally, these remarks got back to Roosevelt. Robert A. Caro, *Power Broker: Robert Moses and the Fall of New York* (New York: Knopf, 1974), 287-96.

24. For a liberal Democrat's assessment of Smith's conservatism see Claude Bowers, *My Life: The Memoirs of Claude Bowers* (New York: Simon and Schuster, 1962), 225-26.

25. Roosevelt to Smith, September 17, 1926 (FDRL).

26. "I tried the definite experiment this year of writing and delivering my speech wholly for the benefit of the radio audience and press rather than for any forensic effect it might have on the delegates . . . ." Roosevelt to Walter Lippmann, August 6, 1928 (FDRL).

27. Roosevelt said he resented being treated by Raskob and others in the Smith camp "as though I was one of those pieces of window dressing that had to be borne with because of a certain political value in non-New York City areas." Ward, *First-Class,* 787.

28. Roosevelt instructed the bellboy at the Warm Springs Inn to tell callers, "I've gone on a picnic—you don't know where I am—and I won't be back all day." At night the bellboy was to tell them, "I am going to a meeting somewhere." Ward, *First-Class,* 791.

29. Howe advised Roosevelt to base his excuse on frail health. ("There is no answer to the health plea.") A few days later Roosevelt informed Smith he might be able to discard his braces by the winter of 1930 provided he continued his Warm Springs therapy without interruption. Howe to Roosevelt, September 25, 1928; Roosevelt to Smith, September 30, 1928 (FDRL).

30. Ward, *First-Class,* 791-94. In despair Howe wrote Roosevelt on October 2, "For once I have no advice to give" (FDRL).

31. *NYT,* November 7, 1928.

32. One of Roosevelt's biographers neatly summed up the formula for victory. "Some upstate Protestants probably did not vote for Ottinger [Roosevelt's opponent] because he was Jewish, Catholics voted for Roosevelt because he was behind Al Smith, Jews voted for him because Herbert Lehman would be his lieutenant governor, Protestants voted for him because he was prominent Episcopalian who headed a fundraising for the Cathedral of St. John the Divine." Ted Morgan, *FDR: A Biography* (New York: Simon and Schuster, 1985), 295.

33. "Written for the Record," *F.D.R.: His Personal Letters,* edited by Elliot Roosevelt (New York: Duell, Sloan and Pearce), 1947-50, III, 772-73.

34. Shortly after the election Eleanor warned him not to "let Mrs. M. get draped around you. It will always be one for you and two for Al." Eleanor Roosevelt to Franklin Roosevelt, November 16, 1928 (FDRL). Years later Roosevelt's Labor Secretary, Frances Perkins, recalled his account of Eleanor's warning: "If Mrs. Moscowitz is your secretary she will run you. She won't hurt you. . . . She will run you in such a way that you won't know you're being run. . . . Everything will be arranged so subtly . . . it will be natural to decide to do the things that Mrs. Moscowitz has already decided should be done. That's the way she works." (COHC, III, 14.) Frank Freidel even claims that Roosevelt might have hired Moscowitz if Eleanor had not warned him as forcefully as she did. *Franklin D. Roosevelt: The Triumph* (Boston: Little Brown, 1956), 15-22.

35. James A. Farley, *Behind the Ballots* (New York: Harcourt Brace, 1938), 54-55; Rollins, *Roosevelt and Howe,* 249-50; Bernard Bellush, *Apprenticeship for the Presidency: F.D.R. as Governor of New York* (Ann Arbor, MI: University Microfilm, 1950), 99-101.

36. Roosevelt had every right to take Smith at his word when, after his overwhelming defeat in 1928, he declared he would never run again. Farley, *Ballots,* 59-60.

37. On election day 1930 the Democratic National Committee sponsored a letter of support for President Hoover in this the nation's hour of need. Al Smith was of course one of the signers. *NYT,* November 5, 1930.

38. Farley gives an insider's view of how Roosevelt humbled Raskob on the Prohibition issue. *Ballots,* 74-76.

39. *NYT,* October 16, 17, 27, November 1, 1931; Freidel, *The Triumph,* 231-33.

40. The inimitable Mencken made this observation on May 2, 1932: "[Roosevelt's] chief strength at this moment does not lie among people of his own place and kind, but among the half-witted yokels of the cow and cotton States, and these hinds prefer him, not because they have any real confidence in him, but simply because they believe he can . . . beat Al Smith and the Pope." *A Carnival,* 254-55. From the "yokel" side,

however, see Cordell Hull, *Memoirs of Cordell Hull* (New York: Macmillan, 1948), I, 145.

41. Looking back, Eleanor wrote: "I think he [Smith] always felt that since he had risen up from modest beginnings, others would be expected to do the same thing." *This I Remember* (New York: Harper, 1949), 50-51

42. Hence Smith's prescription for the crisis: lower taxes, reduced tariffs, improved government efficiency. *New Outlook,* December 1932, 10.

43. Roosevelt, *Public Papers,* I, 624-27 for the full text.

44. *NYT,* April 14, 1932. As Smith wrote months later, "We should stop talking about the Forgotten Man and about class distinctions. . . . The Forgotten Man is a myth and the sooner he disappears from the campaign the better it will be for the country." *New Outlook,* October 1932, 3.

45. *A Carnival,* 277.

46. McAdoo claimed he wanted nothing from Roosevelt in return. Revenge was satisfaction enough. Daniel C. Roper, *Fifty Years of Public Life* (Westport, CT.: Greenwood Press, 1968), 258-60.

47. Farley, *Ballots,* 177.

48. Walter Lippmann, probably the most influential newspaper columnist of the era, repeatedly deprecated Roosevelt's qualifications. For example: Roosevelt "doesn't happen to have a very good mind, and he rarely comes to grips with a problem which has any large dimensions. . . ." He is, in a word, a "kind of amiable boy scout." Lippmann to Newton D. Baker, November 24, 1931. Quoted in Ronald Steel, *Walter Lippmann and the American Century* (Boston: Little Brown, 1980), 291.

49. Sidney Fine, *Frank Murphy: The Detroit Years* (Ann Arbor, MI: University of Michigan Press, 1975), chapter 16.

50. Roosevelt had known of Coughlin's interest in him at least since early May 1931. His brother-in-law G. Hall Roosevelt, comptroller in Murphy's administration, had informed him that Coughlin "would like to tender his services." But Hall Roosevelt also warned: "He would be difficult to handle and might be full of dynamite." Hall Roosevelt to Franklin D. Roosevelt, May 5, 1931 (FDRL).

51. "Father Coughlin (pronounced Kauglin)," *Fortune,* 9 (February 1934), 110.

52. His voice, Wallace Stegner writes, was "of such mellow richness, such manly, heartwarming, confidential intimacy, such emotional and ingratiating charm, that anyone turning past it almost had to hear it again." "The Radio Priest and His Flock," *The Aspirin Age, 1919-1941,* edited by Isabel Leighton (New York: Simon and Schuster, 1949), 232. And according to another writer, "His voice was musical; he ran arpeggios with it and trilled his rrrs; he could be high and plaintive in the style the Irish call keening, or he could be deep and solemn." "Father Coughlin (pronounced Kauglin)," *Fortune,* 36.

53. Charles E. Coughlin, *By the Sweat of Thy Brow* (Royal Oak, MI: Radio League of the Little Flower, 1931), 24; Coughlin, *The New Deal in Money* (Royal Oak, MI: Radio League of the Little Flower, 1933), 7-8.
54. Coughlin, *The New Deal*, 94-95.
55. Coughlin, *By the Sweat*, 35-36. He would routinely refer to Marx as "the German Hebrew" and would disclose the "real" names of Jews who had adopted other ones.
56. One form of anti-Semitism consists in decrying Jews who are not a credit to their race so to speak, the anti-Semite having decided what the "race" is or should be and how the Jews fail to measure up and what they should do about it. Thus Coughlin asserts in one of his broadcasts: "It is a notorious fact that the Rothschilds, clinging to the Egyptian heresy, disparaging the teachings of their forebears, despising the precepts of their great leader Moses, mocking the doctrines of the Talmud and the precepts of the Old Testament, these Rothschilds re-established in modern life the pagan principle of charging interest on non-productive or destructive debts. Under the flag of their leadership there assembled the international bankers of the world. . . ." Louis B. Ward, *Father Charles E. Coughlin, An Authorized Biography* (Detroit: Tower Publications, 1933), 155.
57. Ward's authorized biography gives Coughlin's view of the affair (83-85). A more objective view is Charles S. Tull, *Father Coughlin and the New Deal* (Syracuse, NY: Syracuse University Press, 1965), 6-7.
58. Three months later CBS refused to renew the contract. The National Broadcasting Company turned down his offer. He then formed his own network of independent stations, 26 in all, from Miami to Denver. His audience grew larger than ever, and so did the contributions to the "Radio League of the Little Flower." Ward, *Father Coughlin*, 85.
59. He described Hoover as "the banker's friend, the Holy Ghost of the rich, the protective angel of Wall Street." David H. Bennett, *Demagogues in the Depression* (New Brunswick, NJ: Rutgers University Press, 1969), 33-34.
60. Roosevelt, *Public Papers*, I, 775. This speech may well have "cemented the New Deal Catholic working alliance." Donald R. McCoy, *Angry Voices: Left of Center Politics in the New Deal Era* (Lawrence, Kan.: University of Kansas Press, 1958), 42
61. "It was," wrote Mencken, "a fight to the death between gorillas and baboons. The whole combat was typical of political science in the Hookworm Belt." "The Glory of Louisiana," *Nation*, May 3, 1933, 508.
62. *NYT,* March 27, 30, April 7, 12, May 15, 16, 17, 1929.
63. Of the many books on Long two stand out for their objectivity, thoroughness, and scholarship, especially in disclosing the details of his early life, his character and his political virtuosity: William Ivy Hair, *The Kingfish and His Realm* (Baton Rouge: Louisiana State University Press,

1991, chapters 1-9, and above all T. Harry Williams, *Huey Long* (New York: Knopf, 1969), chapters 1-8.

64. Williams, *Long,* chapters 4 and 5.

65. Matthew Josephson, *Infidel in the Temple* (New York: Knopf, 1967, 335), gives a vivid account of Long in action.

66. For Long's startling success his first year see Williams, *Long,* chapters 12-15, and Hair, *Kingfish,* chapter 10.

67. On the Cyr affair and Long's takeover of the state's political apparatus: *NYT,* October 14, 15, 16, 17, 1931; Williams, *Long,* chapters 16-19; Hair, *Kingfish,* chapters 11 and 12.

68. Williams, *Long,* 573-76

69. *NYT,* June 26, 28, 29, 1932.

70. Farley, *Ballots,* 117.

71. Farley, *Ballots,* 117.

72. *NYT,* June 24-28, 1932.

73. Samuel I. Rosenman, *Working with Roosevelt* (New York: Harper's, 1952), 69-70.

74. Thomas A. Stokes, *Chip Off My Shoulder* (Princeton, NJ: Princeton University Press, 1940), 321-22; Flynn, *You're the Boss,* 101.

75. Farley, *Ballots,* 170-71.

76. *Congressional Record,* 72nd Congress, 1st Session, 6451-53

77. Of Robinson T. Harry Williams writes: "The massive Arkansan was one of the most autocratic leaders in the Senate's history. Arrogant and imperious he held no caucuses and issued orders through his lieutenants, orders which were always obeyed. . . . Many Democrats resented him, but none had dared take him on." *Long,* 592.

78. *NYT,* April 17, 1932.

79. *Congressional Record,* 72d Congress, 1st Session, 9214-17, 10003.

80. *NYT,* August 2, 10, 1932; Williams, *Long,* 583-93.

81. Farley, *Ballots,* 171.

82. Versions of the incident differ slightly. See Williams, *Long,* 601-2; Farley, *Ballots,* 171; Grace Tully, *F.D.R. My Boss* (New York: Scribner's, 1949), 323-24.

83. Hair, *Kingfish,* 251.

CHAPTER TWO

1. In one such letter, following Roosevelt's receiving an honorary degree from Catholic University, he wrote: "You have done more than any other person in the history of America to break down the barriers of prejudice and to build up the bulwarks of solidarity and fraternity . . . a thousand such honors could

never manifest the gratitude which the American people owe you. . . ." Coughlin to Roosevelt, June 14, 1933 (FDRL).

2. Years later Coughlin claimed that Roosevelt had asked him to provide a draft of the speech and that parts of it were incorporated into the one Roosevelt delivered with such shattering effect. Others disputed Coughlin's claim and he offered no proof to back it up. Sheldon Marcus, *Father Coughlin: The Tumultuous Life of the Priest of the Little Flower* (Boston: Little Brown, 1973), 49.

3. "I am defending a principle," Coughlin declared. "I am defending Pope Leo XIII and Pope Pius XI. I am defending a Protestant President who has more courage than 90 percent of the Catholic priests in this country, a President who thinks right, who pleads for the common man, who knows patience and suffering, who knows that men come before bonds, and that human rights are more sacred than financial rights. . . . He is a President who wants to give Christian doctrine a chance to make good, who is willing to make Christian experiments." Marcus, *Coughlin*, 58.

4. Roosevelt to Marvin McIntyre, August 7, 1933, and McIntyre to Coughlin, August [?]1933 (FDRL).

5. *NYT,* March 7, May 8, 13, 1933; Van L. Perkins, *Crisis in Agriculture: The Agricultural Adjustment Administration and the New Deal, 1933* (Berkeley: University of California Press, 1969), 58-59.

6. Roosevelt was heard to tell members of his cabinet: "if we continued another week or so longer without my having made this move on Gold, we would have had an agrarian revolution. . . ." *From the Morgenthau Diaries,* edited by John Morton Blum (Boston: Houghton Mifflin, 1964), 72.

7. Coughlin, *The New Deal,* 34.

8. *NYT,* April 29, June 12, 19, 1934; Allan Seymour Everest, *Morgenthau, New Deal and Silver* (New York: King's Crown Press, 1950), 41-45.

9. Though many years later he had this to say about Roosevelt's role in publishing the list. "We were supposed to be partners. He said he would rely on me, that I would be an important advisor. But he was a liar. He never took my advice. He just used me and when he was through with me he doublecrossed me on that silver business." Marcus, *Coughlin,* 70.

10. *NYT,* November 22, 1933; Coughlin memo to Marvin McIntyre, November 23, 1933 (FDRL).

11. In his 1970 interview with Marcus, Coughlin said, "Listen, I was never stupid. I realized that the President now considered me burdensome, but he owed me things. After all, I helped make him President." Marcus, *Coughlin,* 70.

12. On December 9, 1934, Coughlin openly denounced Cardinal O'Connell. For 40 years, he claimed, "the Cardinal has been more notorious for his silence on social justice than for any contribution which he may have

given either in practice or in doctrine toward the decentralization of
wealth and toward the elimination of those glaring injustice which
permitted the plutocrats of this nation to wax fat at the expense of the
poor." *NYT,* December 10, 1934.

13. *NYT,* February 18, March 25, 1935; Charles E. Coughlin, *A Series of
     Lectures on Social Justice* (Royal Oak, MI: Radio League of the Little
     Flower, 1936), 130-31, 168.

14. *NYT,* July 27, 1935.

15. *NYT,* November 12, 1934.

16. The full text is in Bennett, *Demagogues,* 69. Theologian Reinhold
     Niebuhr gives an insightful analysis of Coughlin's middle-class appeal:
     "Pawns for Fascism—Our Lower Middle Class," *American Scholar,* 6
     (Spring 1937), 145-49.

17. Bennett, *Demagogues,* 71.

18. For a sample of the many speeches he delivered during that historic
     Congress see *NYT,* March 19, 1933, and *Congressional Record,* 73d
     Congress, 1st Session, 3319ff, 4258ff.

19. "In downtown New Orleans people would stand on the sidewalk,
     sometimes taking up a whole block, listening to Huey's voice blaring
     from a radio in a barroom until one o'clock in the morning." Williams,
     Long, 629-30.

20. Elmer Irey and William J. Slocum, *The Tax Dodgers* (New York:
     Greenberg Publishers,1948), 89-95.

21. *Ballots,* 241-42.

22. *Ballots,* 243.

23. *Morgenthau Diaries,* 97-99; Roosevelt to Edward M. House, February 16,
     1935, *Personal Letters,* I, 452-54.

24. The magnitude of the patronage and cash at Long's disposal is suggested
     in Williams, *Long,* 755-59.

25. *NYT,* October 8, 1933.

26. Long laid out his plan in *Congressional Record,* 73d Congress, 2nd
     Session, 1920-21.

27. Long wrote a ditty to celebrate the movement:
     Why weep or slumber, America?
         Land of brave and true,
     With castles, clothing, and food for all
         All belongs to you.
     Ev'ry man a kind, ev'ry man a king.
         For you can be a millionaire. . . .
     There's enough for all to share.
         When it's sunny June and September too,
     Or in the wintertime or spring,
         There'll be peace without end,

Ev'ry neighbor a friend,
With ev'ry man a king.

28. The best description of the Share Our Wealth structure is in Williams, *Long,* 692-93, 696-98.

29. *NYT,* February 24, 1934; *Congressional Record,* 73d Congress, 2nd Session, 3450-53.

30. Williams, *Long,* 700-1.

31. Long had a chance to defend himself from just such a charge in a debate he held with the Socialist Party leader Norman Thomas before a crowd at New York's Mecca Temple on March 2, 1934. "Resolved, that capitalism is doomed and cannot now be saved by redistribution of wealth" was the question before them. Long obviously had no intention of getting drawn into a discussion of Share Our Wealth or any other subject for that matter. He of course amused and entertained the audience of curiosity-seekers, keeping them and Thomas at bay. They were not his sort of folk and never would be and their criticisms or jeers meant nothing to him. He took seriously only those who might help or hurt him. *NYT,* March 3, 1934.

32. For a trenchant analysis of Long's appeal by all means see Alan Brinkley, *Voices of Protest: Huey Long, Father Coughlin and the Great Depression* (New York: Knopf, 1983), chapter 9.

33. Williams, *Long,* chapters 25-27.

34. A good summary of his total control of Louisiana is Allan P. Sindler, *Huey Long's Louisiana: State Politics, 1920-1952* (Baltimore: Johns Hopkins Press, 1956), 91-97.

35. Recounted in Williams, *Long,* 733-36.

36. Hodding Carter, "Huey Long, American Dictator," *Aspirin Age,* 363; Hamilton Basso, *Mainstream* (New York: Reynal and Hitchcock, 1943), 179; Josephson, *Infidel,* 327-28.

37. "He was completely without prejudice in his personal relations, and he had friends and associates in a spectrum of religious and ethnic groups in Louisiana and other places. He liked to say that some of his best friends . . . were Jews. He did not mean, as do so many who use this cliche, that he liked a few Jews who were different from the mass of their people. He meant that in choosing his friends he did not consider such matters as ethnic background." Williams, *Long,* 702.

38. In this view I concur entirely with Williams. *Long,* 762. Long's responsible critics, notably Alan Brinkley (*Voices of Protest*), do him a disservice by not comparing him and his achievements to other Southern demagogues—Tom Watson, Ben Tillman, Theodore Bilbo, et al.—who exploited the same issues he did, but as virulent racists.

39. *American Messiahs* (New York: Simon and Schuster, 1935), 41.

40. During his campaign for governor in 1928 Roosevelt claimed that the enemies of a workers' compensation bill he had supported as state senator had called him a "Red" and should he continue on the same path as governor they would call him "Bolshevik." Rosenman, *Working with Roosevelt*, 43; Roosevelt, *Public Papers*, I, 30-31.

41. Perkins, *The Roosevelt I Knew*, 325; Irving Bernstein points out that progressives generally trusted government, not unions, to raise workers' living standards. *Turbulent Years* (Boston: Houghton Mifflin, 1975), 3.

42. Irving Bernstein, *The Lean Years* (Baltimore: Penguin Books, 1966), 94-97.

43. Arthur M. Schlesinger Jr., *The Coming of the New Deal* (Boston: Houghton Mifflin, 1959), 92-102.

44. An excellent discussion of the NIRA's purpose and function is Ellis W. Hawley, *The New Deal and the Problem of Monopoly: A Study in Economic Ambivalence* (Princeton, NJ: Princeton University Press, 1966), chapters 1-3, see also Bernard Bellush, *The Failures of the NRA* (New York: Norton, 1975), chapter 1.

45. Bernstein, *Lean*, chapter 10; *Turbulent*, 41.

46. That Lewis in fact read little beyond newspapers and rarely wrote his own speeches, that he was a very skillful poseur in other words, is detailed by Melvyn Dubofsky and Warren Van Tine, *John L. Lewis: A Biography* (New York: Quadrangle Books, 1979), 207.

47. One major advantage he had over his legion of enemies: he had no personal vices. He neither drank nor womanized nor succumbed to avarice. One passion he did have: the trappings of status. He and his family had servants; he rode in a chauffeured limousine, wore expensively tailored clothes, ate in the best restaurants, and belonged to the better clubs. He was criticized for these extravagances, but the rank and file seemed not to mind them. Indeed, they were proud that the head of their union was the equal of any corporate executive or government official. A good portrait of Lewis is Louis Adamic, *My America, 1928-1938* (New York: Harper and Brothers, 1938), 388; see also Bernstein, *Lean*, 126, and Dubofsky and Van Tine, *Lewis*, 296-99.

48. Bernstein, *Lean*, 120-24; Dubofsky and Van Tine, *Lewis*, 112-13.

49. *NYT*, September 8, December 5, 1931.

50. Bernstein, *Turbulent*, 41-42.

51. John Kennedy Ohl, *Hugh S. Johnson and the New Deal* (De Kalb, IL: University of Illinois Press, 1985), 137.

52. Harold L. Ickes, *The Secret Diary: The First Thousand Days, 1933-1936* (New York: Simon and Schuster, 1953), 10, 25.

53. Howard Brubaker of the *New Yorker*, quoted in Bernstein, *Turbulent*, 45; on the agreement: *NYT*, September 17, 19, 22, 1933.

54. Saul Alinsky, *John L. Lewis* (New York: Putnam's, 1949), 67-69.

55. Bernstein, *Turbulent*, 352-54.

56. Bernstein, *Turbulent*, 393.

57. *NYT*, March 26, 1934; Sidney Fine, "President Roosevelt and the Automobile Codes," *Mississippi Valley Historical Review*, 45 (June 1958), 23-50.

58. The whole issue of representation, as it unfolded in 1934, is nicely summed up in Bernstein, *Turbulent*, 172-205.

59. *NYT*, October 8, 12, 13, 1934; Bernstein, *Turbulent*, 352-68.

60. Notably the Josephsons, *Al Smith*, chapter 16, and Handlin, *Al Smith*, chapter 8.

61. A persuasive argument for the continuity between Smith's administration and the New Deal is given by Eldot, *Governor*, 396-402.

62. *The Citizen and His Government* (New York: Harper's, 1935), 146.

63. *NYT*, October 24, 1933.

64. Emily Smith Warner, with Hawthorne Daniel, *The Happy Warrior* (Garden City. NY: Doubleday, 1956), 264. On November 30, 1933 Secretary of the Interior Ickes stated publicly that disappointed ambition best explained Smith's criticisms of the New Deal. *NYT*, December 1, 1933.

65. *NYT*, November 25, 1933; Smith, "Sound Money," *New Outlook* (December 1933), 10.

66. The whole episode was played out before an eager press. *NYT*, November 28, 29, December 2, 14, 17, 1933.

67. Which is why a number of highly placed administration officials—fiscal conservatives who had supported Roosevelt—resigned in a huff, Undersecretary of the Treasury Dean Acheson, economic consultant James P. Warburg, and Budget Director Lewis W. Douglas, among others. *NYT*, August 23, 1934; Schlesinger, *Coming of New Deal*, 241-44, 292-93.

68. *F. D. R.: Personal Letters*, I, 417.

69. *NYT*, January 10, February 15, 1934.

70. *NYT*, February 10, 1934; Roosevelt, *Public Papers*, III, 93.

71. *NYT*, February 11, 1934.

72. *NYT*, January 11, February 18, 1934.

73. *NYT*, March 14, 15, 1934; Roosevelt, *Public Papers*, III, 141.

74. *Coming of New Deal*, 455.

75. Charles A. Lindbergh, *Autobiography of Values* (New York: Harcourt Brace Jovanovich, 1977), 122.

76. The only biography of the elder Lindbergh has a brief, laudatory introduction by his son. Bruce L. Larson, *Lindbergh of Minnesota* (New York: Harcourt Brace Jovanovich, 1973).

77. *NYT*, June 14, 1927. Lindbergh's extraordinary reception, from his landing in Paris to the parade up Broadway, is amply set forth in A. Scott

Berg's definitive biography, *Lindbergh* (New York: Putnam's, 1998), chapter 7.

78. *NYT,* October 4, 1928

79. Leonard Mosley, *Lindbergh: A Biography* (Garden City, NY: Doubleday, 1976), 51.

80. See Lindbergh's wonderful account of the flight many years later: *Spirit of St. Louis* (New York: Scribner's, 1953).

81. On Carrel: Walter Ross, *The Last Hero: Charles A. Lindbergh* (New York: Harper and Row, 1969), 229-42; Mosley, *Lindbergh,* 218-21; Berg, *Lindbergh,* 234-36.

82. Pages 17, 133-34. A. Scott Berg writes: "Nobody in Charles Lindbergh's adulthood affected his thinking more deeply than Alexis Carrel." *Lindbergh,* 230.

83. In a book published after his death Carrel returned to the same argument: "Instead of encouraging the survival of the unfit and the defective, we must help the strong; only the elite makes the progress of the masses possible." *Reflections on Life* (New York: Hawthorne Books, 1952), 17.

84. (New York: Halcyon House, 1935), 292-319 and the introduction to the 1939 edition.

85. Lindbergh, *Autobiography,* 139-42. She refers to his buoyancy after presenting a bitter and harrowing description of how the murder affected them. Anne Morrow Lindbergh, *Hour of Gold, Hour of Lead* (New York: Harcourt Brace Jovanovich, 1973), 211-30.

86. *NYT,* August 17, 1934.

87. Like most papers, the *New York Times* gave the kidnapping, the inquiry, and the capture of the putative culprit, Bruno Hauptmann, page one coverage from March 2, 1934 on.

CHAPTER THREE

1. Williams, *Long,* 797-98.

2. Williams, *Long,* 811-12, 833-35, 841-43.

3. *Congressional Record,* 74th Congress, 1st session, 1114-32.

4. Ickes, *First Thousand,* 294-300; Farley, *Ballots,* 243-49.

5. *NYT,* March 5, 1935.

6. He did, however, get off a typically Longian barrage: "What is the trouble with this administration of Mr. Roosevelt, Mr. Johnson, Mr. Farley, Mr. Astor and all their spoilers and spellbinders? They go gunning for me. It reminds us of old Davy Crockett, that kept firing and firing one night at a possum in a tree—but found out it was no possum at all, only a louse in his own eyebrow. . . . While millions have starved and naked gone, while babies have cried and died for milk, while people have begged for

meat and bread, Mr. Roosevelt's administration sails merrily along, plowing under and destroying the things to eat and wear. . . ." *NYT,* March 8, 1935.

7. The Unofficial Observer, *Messiahs,* 22-23. The Unofficial Observer went on to explain why Roosevelt had cause for concern: Long "is, for the first time since Jackson's day giving a voice to the economic untouchables of the Baptist Belt. He is uniting the poor white farmers, the tenants, the croppers—and even the Negroes—behind his program and bids fair to make himself the master of a rejuvenated social system in the Lower Mississippi Valley" (29).

8. Farley, *Ballots,* 249-51. The Democratic National Committee's recent poll estimated that 3.36 million voters would go for Long. Emil Hurja's Papers, (FDRL).

9. On Roosevelt's worries about the prospect of class warfare see Rexford Guy Tugwell, *The Democratic Roosevelt* (Garden City, N.Y.: Doubleday, 1957), 348-51.

10. *F.D.R.: Personal Letters,* II, 452-53.

11. Tugwell also points out that Long's "extremism" provoked "actions that otherwise could not have been undertaken." *Democratic,* 345.

12. *Congressional Record,* 74th Congress, 1st Session, 9906-7.

13. *Long,* 818.

14. Biting portraits of Smith can be found in Josephson, *Infidel,* 33; Williams, *Long,* 698-700; and *Time,* April 18, 1935, 15-17.

15. Williams describes Smith in action. He would ask the crowd how many of them owned four suits. None of course. How many owned three? None. Two? None. "Then, with a sob catching in his throat, he revealed that J. P. Morgan owned hundreds of suits." Smith, echoing Long, would promise his listeners "a real job, not a little old sow-belly, black-eyed pea job, but a real spending money, beefsteak and gravy, Chevrolet, Ford in the garage, new suit, Thomas Jefferson, Jesus Christ, red, white and blue job for every man!" He would close out the speech with a prayer: "Lift us out of this wretchedness, O Lord, out of this poverty, lift us who stand here in slavery tonight. Rally us under this young man who came out of the woods of north Louisiana, who leads us like Moses out of the land of bondage into the land of milk and honey where every man is a king but no man wears a crown. Amen." *Long,* 700

16. *NYT,* September 13, 1935. Thomas Martin gives us a sample of Smith's eulogy: "He fell in the line of duty. He died for us. This tragedy fires the breast of every comrade. His untimely death makes restless the souls of us who adored him. Oh God, why did we have to lose him. . . . To use the figure, he was the Stradivarius. He was the Unfinished Symphony," etc., etc. *Dynasty: The Longs of Louisiana* (New York: Putnam's, 1960), 146.

17. Alan A. Michie and Frank Ryhlick, *Dixie Demagogues* (New York: Vanguard Press, 1939), 118-19.

18. *NYT,* December 10, 1935; Farley, *Ballots,* 251-52.

19. An example of Coughlin hyperbole: "The League of Nations and its perverted brain, the World Court, is nothing more than a Frankenstein, raised by the international bankers and the plutocrats of the world [that is, Jews] for preserving by force of arms that plutocratic system against the onslaught of communism." *NYT,* January 28, 1935. According to historian Robert Dallek, that vote was especially significant because it demonstrated the extent to which isolationism "now dominated national thinking about world affairs." *Franklin D. Roosevelt and American Foreign Policy, 1932-1945* (New York: Oxford University Press, 1979), 97.

20. Benjamin Stolberg, "Dr. Huey and Mr. Long," *Nation,* 141 (September 25, 1935); *NYT,* March 5, 1935.

21. Kenneth S. Davis, *FDR: The New Deal Years, 1933-1937* (New York: Random House, 1986), 576.

22. *NYT,* March 12, 1935.

23. *NYT,* March 13, 1935

24. *NYT,* April 23, 1935.

25. *NYT,* April 24, 1935

26. Roosevelt to Baker, March 29, 1935 (FDRL).

27. *NYT,* May 23, 1935.

28. Coughlin claimed it was he who first informed Roosevelt of Long's death. Roosevelt "blanched white [*sic*]. It was a shock to him" Marcus, *Coughlin,* 99.

29. *NYT,* September 12, 1935; the Hyde Park meeting is described at length in Michael Beschloss, *Kennedy and Roosevelt: The Uneasy Alliance* (New York: Norton, 1980), 118-20.

30. Sidney Fine, *Frank Murphy: The New Deal Years* (Chicago: University of Chicago Press, 1979), 222.

31. *NYT,* January 9, 1936; Marcus, *Coughlin,* 106.

32. *NYT,* February 17, 18, 24, 27, 1936.

33. Coughlin, *A Series of Lectures,* 41.

34. *NYT,* January 6, 1936; Bennett, *Demagogues,* 71-73.

35. "Father Coughlin," *Fortune,* 110,112.

36. Forrest Davis, "Father Coughlin," *The Atlantic Monthly,* 165 (December 1965), 659, 663.

37. Marcus, *Coughlin,* 11; *NYT,* May 14, 1936.

38. *NYT,* August 18, 1936.

39. *NYT,* July 17, 24, November 1, 1936.

40. *NYT,* October 18, 1936.

41. *NYT,* October 14, 18, 1936

42. *NYT,* July 17, 1936.

43. *NYT,* July 21, 1936

44. *Social Justice,* July 6, 1936, 13.

45. *NYT,* July 17, November 8, 1936.

46. It put out a 10-point program which amounted to a wish list for the restoration of the pre-1929 status quo, the best of all possible worlds. An additional 12-point program followed a year later. *NYT,* January 10, December 26, 1935.

47. Smith and Roosevelt did stay in touch on a more or less friendly or cordial basis. See, for example, Smith to Roosevelt, March 21, 1934, and Roosevelt to Smith, March 27, 1934, and May 22, 1935 (FDRL).

48. *NYT,* January 4, 1936

49. "Surely the Al of gaudy legend, with such a speech in him, would never have got himself up in long tails and white tie and gone to a dinner of Palm Beach crocodiles and boa constrictors to make it. He would have worn his old brown derby and loosed it before an audience of his ancient lieges—horrible, hairy, human. . . . But the Al of today wears a boiled shirt, prefers champagne to schooners, and plays golf instead of pinochle." Mencken, *A Carnival,* 300-1.

50. Two of his advisors of yore, Proskauer and Moses, both notably contemptuous of Roosevelt, helped him write the speech. *NYT,* January 24, 1936.

51. *NYT,* January 26, 1936.

52. He left to the accompaniment of "The Sidewalks of New York." *NYT,* June 24, 1936.

53. Jim Farley was explicit on Roosevelt's strategy. The Liberty League, he wrote, was "one of the most vulnerable ever to appear in politics and our campaign was developed on that theory." In a word, "to ignore the Republican Party and to concentrate fire on the Liberty League." *Ballots,* 294.

54. *Public Papers,* V, 364.

55. *Public Papers,* V, 488.

56. *Public Papers,* V, 557-58.

57. "In his political and economic views Landon was considerably less conservative than the majority of his own party and far less so than the Liberty League. . . ." Davis, *New Deal Years,* 625. See also Donald R. McCoy, *Landon of Kansas* (Lincoln: University of Nebraska Press, 1966), 260-61, 331.

58. *NYT,* November 1, 1936.

59. *NYT,* May 28, 1935.

60. *NYT,* August 31, 1935; Davis, *New Deal Years,* 548-50. But Raymond Moley writes that Roosevelt sent the bill to the House knowing the Court would find it unconstitutional. *After Seven Years* (Lincoln: University of Nebraska Press, 1971), 304.

61. Dubofsky and Van Tine, *Lewis,* 216-17.

62. *NYT,* October 17-20, 1935; Dubofsky and Van Tine, *Lewis,* 217-21.

63. Waxing poetic, Irving Bernstein writes: "The future was uncertain, and the future that Lewis painted was one that was lit by lightning and torn by upheaval. It was a future in the skies. If ever anyone had his eyes lifted to the stars it was Lewis. . . . His words dissolved the fears, doubts and rationalizations of his companions. They were ready for the crusade." *Turbulent,* 398.

64. Dubofsky and Van Tine, *Lewis,* 227.

65. The fascinating story of how the CIO organized the rubber industry is told splendidly by Bernstein, *Turbulent,* 589-602.

66. When AFL president Green announced that he would expel any union that joined the CIO Lewis sent him an open letter which said: "Perchance you were agitated and distraught. . . . It is inconceivable that you intend doing what your statement implies, i.e., to sit with the women under an awning on the hilltop while the steel workers in the valley struggle in the dust and agony of industrial warfare." A day later Lewis added, "Your lament is that I will not join you in a policy of anxious inertia. Candidly, I am temperamentally incapable of sitting with you in sackcloth and ashes, endlessly intoning, 'O tempera, O mores!'" Bernstein, *Turbulent,* 416

67. For detailed account of the subcommittee's findings: Jerrold S. Auerbach, *Labor and Liberty: The La Follette Committee and the New Deal* (Indianapolis, IN: Bobbs-Merrill, 1966).

68. Harry A. Levenstein, *Communism, Anticommunism and the CIO* (Westport, CT: Greenwood, 1981), chapter 2, provides a thorough understanding of the relations between Lewis and the Communists. See also Bert Cochran, *Labor and Communism: The Conflict that Changed American Labor* (Princeton, NJ: Princeton University Press, 1977), chapter 4, and Alinsky, *Lewis,* 152-53.

69. *NYT,* April 15, 27, 1937.

70. *NYT,* April 2, May 12, 1936. About a third of the amount went to the Democratic Party, about a hundred thousand went for radio broadcasts, and the rest went for the presidential campaign and miscellaneous purposes. Dubofsky and Van Tine, *Lewis,* 252.

71. The strike receives a good deal of attention in Bernstein, *Turbulent,* 499-554. Enormously valuable too are Sidney Fine, *Sit-Down: The General Motors Strike of 1936-1937* (Ann Arbor, MI: University of Michigan Press, 1969); Roger Kieran, *The Communist Party and the Auto Workers Union* (Bloomington, IN: Indiana University Press, 1980), chapter 7; and Cochran, *Labor,* 108-21.

72. Perkins, *The Roosevelt I Knew,* 158-59.

73. *NYT,* January 22, 23, 1937.

74. At her own press conference Secretary Perkins suggested that the sit-down was not necessarily illegal and that GM, and Sloan in particular, should

negotiate in good faith. Newspapers criticized her. So did Vice President Garner. *NYT,* January 27, 1937; Perkins, COHC, III, 136; James A. Farley, *Jim Farley's Story: The Roosevelt Years* (New York: Wittlesey House, 1949), 85-86.

75. *NYT,* January 28, 1937.
76. That Lewis at his January 21 press conference rubbed Roosevelt the wrong way is also true. Ickes, *Inside Struggle,* 56. Meanwhile, dyed-in-the-wool conservative Vice President Garner sided with GM. When Roosevelt told Garner, "I couldn't get those strikers out without bloodshed," Garner replied, "Then John L. Lewis is a bigger man than you. . . ." Bascom N. Timmons, *Garner of Texas* (New York: Harper's, 1948), 216. Looking back three and a half years later, Roosevelt had this to say: "Little do people realize how I had to take abuse and criticism for inaction at the time. . . . I believed, and I was right, that the country, including labor, would learn the lesson of their own volition without having it forced upon them by marching troops." Roosevelt to Samuel L. Rosenman, November 13, 1940 (FDRL). And Madame Perkins remembered Roosevelt saying at the time: "'Well, it is illegal, but what law are they breaking? The law of trespass. . . . And what do you do when a man trespasses on your property? Sure, you order him off. . . . But shooting it out and killing a lot of people because they had violated the law of trespass somehow offends me. I just don't see that as an answer. The punishment doesn't fit the crime.'" *The Roosevelt I Knew,* 321-22.
77. "Memorandum for President Roosevelt," "Proposal for Agreement," February 3, 1937 (FDRL).
78. The journalist's name was Heber Blankenhorn. Dubofsky and Van Tine, *Lewis,* 269.
79. *Lewis,* 145.
80. *NYT,* March 3, 1937; *Fortune,* 15 (May 1937), 90-94; Bernstein, *Turbulent,* 470-71.
81. Lee Pressman, COHC, 185.
82. Bernstein, *Turbulent,* 569-71, 478-98.
83. *NYT,* June 30, 1937.
84. *NYT,* September 7, 1937.
85. Dubofsky and Van Tine, *Lewis,* 228.
86. Bernstein, *Turbulent,* 684-85.

CHAPTER FOUR

1. A flood of mail pleaded with him to return to the air. *NYT,* November 15, 1936; Marcus, *Coughlin,* 139.
2. *NYT,* March 16, August 3, 1936.

3. Tull, *Coughlin and the New Deal,* 180.

4. *NYT,* December 12, 1937.

5. Marcus, *Coughlin,* 146.

6. David J. O'Brien, *American Catholics and Social Reform* (New York: Oxford University Press, 1968), 84-88.

7. *Social Wellsprings,* edited by Joseph Husslein (Milwaukee: Bruce Publishing Co., 1942), II, 59.

8. Boston's Cardinal O'Connell called Franco "a fighter for Christian civilization," this soon after the Rebel bombing of Barcelona on March 18, 1938, in which a thousand civilians perished. John F. Stack Jr., *International Conflict in an American City* (Westport, CT: Greenwood Press, 1979), 60.

9. *NYT,* October 6, 1937.

10. So Father Francis Talbot, once so favorably disposed toward Roosevelt, could write in the Jesuit magazine *America* that the New Deal "plunges directly toward Leftist Liberalism. . . ." (September 1939), 78.

11. In the June 21 *Social Justice* Coughlin outlined the "Christian" character of the National Union for Social Justice. "[We] believe that the Christian scheme of economics is better than either the Brahmin or the Buddhist or the Jewish scheme of economics" (4-6). Given the paucity of Brahmins or Buddhists in America he could only have meant the "Jewish scheme," a sinister combination of Bolshevism and predatory capitalism. See on this *Social Justice,* March 28, 1938, 6; April 4, 1938, 2, 14; January 30, 1939, 7.

12. O'Brien, *Americans Catholics,* 179.

13. *Social Justice,* July 25, 1938, 3.

14. *Social Justice,* July 25, 1938, 5.

15. *Social Justice,* November 21, 1938, 4.

16. Donald S. Strong, in his book, *Organized Anti-Semitism in America* (Washington: American Council on Foreign Affairs, 1941), 61-63, cleverly placed Goebbels's remarks about "Jew Bolsheviks" alongside Coughlin's. One example will suffice. Goebbels had said, by way of justifying Nazi repression: "The Social Democratic 'League of Free Thinkers' alone had a membership of 600,000. The Communist 'League of Proletarian Free Thinkers" had close to 64,000 members. Almost without exception the intellectual leaders of Marxist atheism were Jews." The December 5, 1938, *Social Justice* repeated the canard word for word. See also Stegner, *Aspirin Age,* 251.

17. His list is a potpourri of distortions and falsehood drawn bodily from Nazi sources. Except for Lenin, it informs us, the 25 members of the first Bolshevik cabinet, Josef Stalin included, were all "atheistic Jews"! Charles E. Coughlin, *"Am I an Anti-Semite"?* (Detroit, MI: Social Justice, 1939), 37-38, 41.

18. Coughlin, *"Am I?"*, 44-46.
19. Coughlin, *"Am I?"*, 38.
20. Coughlin, *"Am I?"*, 64.
21. Coughlin, *"Am I?"*, 85.
22. Coughlin, *"Am I?"*, 104.
23. Soon after Hitler seized the remainder of Czechoslovakia the March 27, 1939, *Social Justice* featured him as its "Man of the Week."
24. "We stand unalterably opposed, as Americans who are Catholic, to the psuedo-democrats, the soured liberals, the concealed Communistic forces that are applying such unholy pressure on the President and Congress to plant American guns in Spain, to fill the Spanish air with American planes and to riddle the men of Spain with American bullets." From *America*, the Jesuit publication, quoted in David Valaik, "Catholics, Neutrality and the Spanish Embargo, 1937-1939," *The Journal of American History*, 54 (June 1967), 77. For some reason *America* offered no objection to the presence in Spain of German and Italian planes, guns and bullets—and military personnel.
25. Charles E. Coughlin, *Why Leave Our Own?* (Royal Oak, MI: Radio League of the Little Flower, 1939), 73.
26. *NYT*, September 26, 1939. The fights would often start when *provocateurs* hawked *Social Justice* in the neighborhood and shouted out the headlines. Harold Lavine, *Fifth Column in America* (New York: Doubleday, Doran, 1940), 97-99.
27. Strong, *Organized Anti-Semitism*, 66.
28. *NYT*, January 14, 1940, and extensively from April 4 to June 26, 1940. A good account of the whole episode is Dale Kramer, "The American Fascists," *Harper's*, 181 (September 1940).
29. *Social Justice*, September 22, 1941, 4.
30. *NYT*, November 16-19, 1938.
31. Philip Taft, *The A. F. of L. from the Death of Gompers to the Merger* (New York: Harper's, 1959), 200-2.
32. According to Farley, most Democratic leaders attributed the heavy losses in that election to the CIO in general and Lewis in particular. *Jim Farley's Story*, 153-54.
33. *NYT*, August 14, 16, 18, October 16, 21, 28, December 2, 11, 1938.
34. *NYT*, April 25, 26, July 1, August 2, December 12-26, 1939.
35. *Turbulent*, 714.
36. *Lewis*, 330-31, 346.
37. *NYT*, September 4, 1939.
38. Dubofsky and Van Tine, *Lewis*, 332
39. *Lewis*, 347; *NYT*, January 25, February 11, April 2, June 19, 1940.
40. *Communism in America*, edited by Albert Fried (New York: Columbia University Press, 1997), 240-41.

41. *NYT,* February 12, 1940.

42. *Eleanor and Franklin: The Story of Their Relationship* (New York: Norton, 1972), 604-5; Michael Straight, *After Long Silence* (New York: Norton, 1983), 149.

43. Steven Fraser, *Labor Will Rule: Sidney Hillman and the Rise of American Labor* (New York: Free Press, 1991), 447, 452-53.

44. Dubofky and Van Tine, *Lewis,* 360.

45. *The Roosevelt I Knew,* 125-27.

46. *Lewis,* 340-41

47. Bernstein, a cautious historian, accepts Perkins's story. *Turbulent,* 714, 717. Lee Pressman, the CIO's chief counsel, doubted the story, but he goes on to repeat another and certainly less probable version, which he heard from Lewis's confidant Philip Murray. According to Murray (as Pressman relates it) Lewis told Roosevelt he would lose the election "'unless you have a representative of labor on the ticket, and unless that representative is myself.'" Roosevelt's perfect riposte was, "'That's very interesting John, but which place on the ticket are you reserving for me?'" Pressman, COHC, 196.

48. *NYT,* June 19, 1940.

49. *NYT,* October 18, 1940.

50. So Alinsky asserts on the basis of interviews with Lewis. *Lewis,* 186-87.

51. See, for example, Ladislas Farago, *The Game of Foxes* (New York: D. McKay Co., 1971), 47.

52. Alton Frye, *Nazi Germany and the American Hemisphere, 1933-1940* (New Haven, CT: Yale University Press, 1967), 142 ff. That Hoover denied shadowing Lewis goes without saying. (Hoover to Stephen T. Early, October 31, 1940 [FDRL]). But the question remains unanswered to this day.

53. Bernstein, *Turbulent,* 719.

54. Len DeCaux, *Labor Radical* (Boston: Beacon Press, 1970), 66-71. In any case the threat astonished—and presumably delighted—Roosevelt. Perkins, *The Roosevelt I Knew,* 312.

55. *NYT,* October 26, 1940.

56. *Roosevelt and Hopkins* (New York: Harper's, 1948), 192.

57. *NYT,* November 19, 1940.

58. Gardner Jackson to Roosevelt, November 8, 13, 1940 (FDRL); Fraser, *Labor Will Rule,* 450-51.

59. *NYT,* December 23, 24, 1935.

60. On Smith: Anne Morrow Lindbergh, *The Flower and the Nettle:* (New York: Harcourt Brace Jovanovich, 1976), 435; Bella Fromm, *Blood and Banquets* (New York: Harper's, 1942), 223-24.

61. Harold Nicolson, *Diaries and Letters, 1931-1964* (London: Collins, 1980), 102; William L. Shirer, *Berlin Diary* (New York: Knopf, 1941), 63; Berg, *Lindbergh,* 377-81.

62. "The German government had vowed that they would show him everything he asked to see, and since he did not ask to see concentration camps, political prisoners, Jews, Communists, Socialists, Social Democrats, or other opponents of the regime, his picture of the Nazi Reich was a decidedly favorable one." Mosley, *Lindbergh,* 218. This is borne out in the letters he wrote at the time. For example: Hitler "is undoubtedly a great man, and I believe he has done much for the German people. He is a fanatic in many ways. . . . It is less than I expected, but it is there. On the other hand, Hitler has accomplished results (good in addition to bad), which could hardly have been accomplished without some fanaticism." Berg, *Lindbergh,* 382.

63. *The Flower and the Nettle,* 100.

64. His racial views he candidly set forth in a *Reader's Digest* article, "Aviation, Geography and Race," published in November 1939.

65. Wayne S. Cole, *Charles A. Lindbergh and the Battle against Intervention in World War II* (New York: Harcourt Brace Jovanovich, 1974), 81-82.

66. Cole, *Lindbergh and the Battle,* 37-38.

67. Truman Smith, *Berlin Alert* (Stanford, CA: Hoover Institute Press, 1984), 114-18; Mosley, *Lindbergh,* 229.

68. Mosley, *Lindbergh,* 225.

69. This was the view of the dominant wing of the British Tory establishment. It had already reconciled itself to the necessity of sacrificing democratic Czechoslovakia. On November 22, 1937, Lord Halifax, who was close to Prime Minister Neville Chamberlain, spoke at length with the Führer. Here is the official account of Halifax's remarks. "Halifax admitted of his own accord that certain changes in the European system could probably not be avoided in the long run. The British did not believe that the status quo had to be maintained in all circumstances. Among the questions in which changes would probably be made sooner or later was Danzig, Austria and Czechoslovakia [all to be gobbled up by Hitler]. England was interested in seeing that such changes were brought about by peaceful means. . . . In his introductory remarks [Halifax] described Germany as the bulwark of the West against Bolshevism." Anthony Eden, *Facing the Dictators* (Boston: Houghton Mifflin, 1962), 578; Telford Taylor, *Munich: The Price of Peace* (New York, Vintage Books, 1980), 312.

70. Mosley, *Lindbergh,* 261-62; Beschloss, *Kennedy and Roosevelt,* 178; Anne Lindbergh, *The Flower and the Nettle,* 411-15.

71. Truman Smith, *Berlin Alert,* 154-55.

72. Telford Taylor writes: "What England needed at that moment was the capacity for calm and informed appraisal of the many factors in the crisis. Instead, Lindbergh came crying doom and destruction, and counseling only the hopelessness of anything other than surrender to the German juggernaut." *Munich,* 852.

73. Taylor, *Munich,* 764-65, 849-52.

74. Lindbergh, *Autobiography,* 155-56; Mosley, *Lindbergh,* 236. Later, in one of his speeches, Lindbergh said: "From 1936 to 1939, as I traveled through European countries, I saw the phenomenal military strength of Germany growing like a giant at the side of an aged and complacent England. France was awake to her danger, but far too occupied with personal ambitions, industrial troubles and internal politics to make more than a feeble effort to rearm. In England there was organization without spirit; in France there was spirit without organization; in Germany there was both." *Vital Speeches* (New York: City News Co., 1940), VI, 645.

75. Lindbergh, *Autobiography,* 175-76, 182-85.

76. *NYT,* October 7, 1938; Berg, *Lindbergh,* 400. Anne Morrow Lindbergh apologetically describes it as "an unforeseen incident that took place in the course of his duties while carrying out a planned mission for U.S. intelligence." (*The Flower and the Nettle,* xxii.) She does not explain why he kept the medal after his "intelligence" duties ended.

77. *NYT,* November 16, 1938.

78. *NYT,* December 18, 1938; Ickes, *Diary: Inside Struggles,* 532-34.

79. *The Wartime Journals of Charles A. Lindbergh* (New York: Harcourt Brace Jovanovich, 1970), 115.

80. *Journals,* 131.

81. *Journals,* 127-30, 139-40.

82. *Autobiography,* 187.

83. *NYT,* April 15, 1939; Berg, *Lindbergh,* 410.

84. Lindbergh, *Autobiography,* 189-191; Kenneth S. Davis, *The Hero: Charles A. Lindbergh and the American Dream* (Garden City, NY: Doubleday, 1958), 384-85; Berg, *Lindbergh,* 410-12.

85. Mosley is convincing in his acidulous description of this little group (*Lindbergh,* 252-53). For Hugh Wilson's views see his memoir, *Diplomat Between the Wars* (New York: Longman, 1940), 115, and especially his March 3, 1938, letter to Roosevelt (FDRL).

86. From "the moment Hitler came into power, Roosevelt regarded him with a strong, almost religious dislike, and considered him a serious threat." Frank Freidel, *Launching the New Deal,* 123-24.

87. *NYT,* September 4, 1939.

88. *Autobiography,* 191; *Journals,* 257-58.

89. Lindbergh for his part knew, or thought he knew, Roosevelt's motive in leading the anti-Hitler crusade, and of course it was sordid. "I feel sure he would, consciously or unconsciously, like to take the center of the world stage away from Adolf Hitler." *Journals,* 437.

90. "What Substitute for War?" (March 1940), 306.

91. "Aviation, Geography and Race," 65.

92. "Aviation, Geography and Race," 67. Aviation, Lindbergh wrote in a draft of this piece, is "a gift of heaven to those Western nations who were already the leaders of their era, . . . a tool specially shaped for Western hands, a scientific art which others only copy in a mediocre fashion, another barrier between the teeming millions of Asia and the Grecian inhabitants of Europe—one of those priceless possessions which permit the White race to live at all in a pressing sea of Yellow, Black and Brown." Berg, *Lindbergh,* 418.

93. *NYT,* November 4, 1939.

94. Cole, *Lindbergh and the Battle,* chapters 13 and 14.

95. *America First: the Battle Against Intervention, 1940-1941* (Madison, WI: University of Wisconsin Press, 1953), chapter 2.

96. Brought out as a book by the same title (New York: Harcourt Brace, 1940), 40. Roosevelt, according to his chief speechwriter, Samuel I. Rosenman, had Anne Morrow Lindbergh in mind when, in his third inaugural address (January 20, 1941), he said, "There are men who believe democracy as a form of government and a frame of life is limited or measured by a kind of mystical and artificial fate—that, for some unexplained reason, tyranny and slavery have become the surging wave of the future and freedom is an ebbing tide." *Working with Roosevelt,* 270.

97. *War Within and Without* (New York: Harcourt Brace Javonovich, 1983), 97, 138, 147.

98. Roosevelt to Henry L. Stimson, May 21, 1940 (FDRL).

99. *NYT,* May 20, 1940.

100. Stephen P. Early to Edwin M. Watson, May 27, 1940 (FDRL); *Journals,* 352.

101. *Hearings Before the Committee on Foreign Affairs,* House of Representatives, on H.R. 1776, January 23, 1941, 77th Congress, 1st Session, 191-435; *Hearings Before the Committee on Foreign Relations,* U.S. Senate, on S. 275, February 6, 1941, 77th Congress, 1st Session, 491-550.

102. Roosevelt to Attorney General Biddle, November 1, 1941 (FDRL); Cole, *America First,* 117-18.

103. *NYT,* April 14, 1941.

104. John F. Carter, "Memorandum on the 'Copperhead Movement,' April 22d" (FDRL); *NYT,* April 27, 1941.

105. *NYT,* April 29, 1941; Mosley, *Lindbergh,* 293.

106. *Journals,* 479.

107. And further: "Charles is life itself—pure life, force, like sunlight—and it is for this that I married him and this that holds me to him—caring desperately what happens to him and whatever he happens to be involved with." *War Within and Without,* 178, 182.
108. *NYT,* May 24, 1941.
109. *NYT,* July 2, 1941; Berg, *Lindbergh,* 447.
110. J. Edgar Hoover to Steve Early, March 1, 1941 (FDRL); Mosley, *Lindbergh,* 288.
111. *NYT,* July 14, 1941.
112. *NYT,* July 16, 1941. The press secretary pointed out to Lindbergh that Roosevelt got Lindbergh's letter a day after reading it in the papers, the second time Lindbergh had done this, and concluded with a nicely aimed barb: "In keeping with time honored tradition the text of this letter will not be given to the Press, at least until you have received it. Since it is not written primarily for the Press, it is possible it may never be given to the newspapermen." Cole, *Lindbergh and the Battle,* 133.
113. Harold L. Ickes, *The Secret Diary: The Lowering Clouds, 1939-1941* (New York: Simon and Schuster, 1954), 581-82.
114. Cole, *Lindbergh and the Battle,* 146.
115. Cole, *Lindbergh and the Battle,* 159.
116. Cole, *Lindbergh and the Battle,* 173.
117. *War Within and Without,* 221.
118. *NYT,* September 12, 1941, for full text.
119. Lindbergh, *Journals,* 541-42; Cole, *Lindbergh and the Battle,* 177-78.
120. Anne Morrow Lindbergh was shaken by the experience. She thought her husband had committed a dreadful blunder. He had "lit a match near a pile of excelsior," and she told him so, going so far as to say flatly she would "prefer to see the country at war than shaken by violent anti-Semitism" because "the kind of person the human being is turned into when the instinct of Jew-baiting is let loose is worse than the kind of person he becomes on the battlefield." Her diary omits his response. *War Within and Without,* 223-24.
121. Cole, *Lindbergh and the Battle,* 200-2.
122. *NYT,* October 4, 31, 1941.
123. Cole, *America First,* 152-54.
124. *Roosevelt and Hopkins,* 383.

CHAPTER 5

1. *NYT,* March 17, 1943; Tully, *F.D.R. My Boss,* 58-59.
2. "Memo" from Edwin M. Watson to Roosevelt, March 30, 1942 (FDRL), which included incriminating passages from *Social Justice* that Frank

Murphy, now a Supreme Court justice, had gathered and sent to Watson. Four days later Roosevelt sent the material on to Biddle.
3. *NYT,* April 15, 1942.
4. *In Brief Authority* (Garden City, NY: Doubleday, 1962), 242-48.
5. *NYT,* May 5, 1942.
6. *NYT,* September 16, October 28, November 23, 1941; Bernstein, *Turbulent,* 752-67.
7. *NYT,* June 16, 23, 24, 26, 1943.
8. Dubofsky and Van Tine, *Lewis,* 409-13, 430.
9. *NYT,* December 31, 1941.
10. Stimson to Roosevelt, January 12, 1942 (FDRL).
11. Lindbergh, *Journals,* 579-84.
12. Ickes to Roosevelt, December 30, 1941 (FDRL).
13. Knox to Roosevelt, January 2, 1942 (FDRL).
14. *Journals,* 584.
15. *New York Post,* January 9, 1942; Cole, *Lindbergh and the Battle,* 213-17; Berg, *Lindbergh,* 461.
16. *Journals,* 598-99.
17. Cole, *Lindbergh and the Battle,* 216-17; Berg, *Lindbergh,* 472-483; Lauren D. Lyman, "The Lindbergh I Knew," *Saturday Evening Post,* (April 4, 1953), 22-24.
18. The point is made by Cole, *Lindbergh and the Battle,* 231-38.

BIBLIOGRAPHY

Adamic, Louis. *My America.* New York: Harper's, 1938.

Alinsky, Saul. *John L. Lewis.* New York: Putnam's, 1949.

Allswany, John M. *Bosses, Machines and Urban Voters.* Baltimore: Johns Hopkins, 1986.

Auerbach, Jerrold S. *Labor and Liberty: The La Follette Committee and the New Deal.* Indianapolis: Bobbs-Merrill, 1966.

Barber, James David. *The Pulse of Politics: Electing Presidents in the Media Age.* New York: Norton, 1981.

Basso, Hamilton. *Mainstream.* New York: Reynard and Hitchcock, 1943.

Bellush, Bernard. *Apprenticeship for the Presidency: F.D.R. as Governor of New York.* Ann Arbor, MI: University Microfilms, 1950.

———. *The Failure of the NRA.* New York: Norton, 1975.

Berlin, Isaiah. *Personal Impressions.* London: Hogarth Press, 1980.

Berg, A. Scott. *Lindbergh.* New York: Putnam's, 1998.

Bernstein, Irving. *The Lean Years.* Baltimore: Penguin Books, 1966.

———. *Turbulent Years.* Boston: Houghton Mifflin, 1975.

Beschloss, Michael. *Kennedy and Roosevelt: The Uneasy Alliance.* New York: Norton, 1980.

Biddle, Francis. *In Brief Authority.* Garden City, NY: Doubleday, 1962.

Bowers, Claude. *My Life.* New York: Simon and Schuster, 1962.

Brinkley, Alan. *Voices of Protest: Huey Long, Father Coughlin and the Great Depression.* New York, Knopf: 1983.

Caro, Robert A. *Power Broker: Robert Moses and the Fall of New York.* New York: Knopf, 1974.

Carrel, Alexis. *Man, the Unknown.* New York: Halcyon House, 1938.

———. *Reflections on Life.* New York: Hawthorne Books, 1952.

Carter, Hodding. "Huey Long, American Dictator." In *The Aspirin Age, 1919-1941,* Edited by Isabel Leighton. New York: Simon and Schuster, 1949.

Cochran, Bert. *Labor and Communism: The Conflict That Shaped American Labor.* Princeton, NJ: Princeton University Press, 1977.

Cole, Wayne S. *America First: The Battle against Intervention, 1940-1941.* Madison, WI: University of Wisconsin Press, 1953.

————. *Charles A. Lindbergh and the Battle Against Intervention in World War II*. New York: Harcourt Brace Jovanovich, 1974.

Communism in America: A Documented History. Edited by Albert Fried. New York: Columbia University Press, 1997.

Congressional Record. 1931-1941.

Coughlin, Charles E. *Am I an Anti-Semite?* Detroit, MI: Social Justice, 1939.

————. *By the Sweat of Thy Brow*. Royal Oak, MI: Radio League of the Little Flower, 1931.

————. *The New Deal in Money*. Royal Oak, MI: Radio League of the Little Flower, 1933.

————. *A Series of Lectures on Social Justice*. Royal Oak, MI: Radio League of the Little Flower, 1936.

————. *Why Leave Our Own?* Royal Oak, MI: Radio League of the Little Flower, 1939.

Dallek, Robert F. *Franklin D. Roosevelt and American Foreign Policy 1932-1945*. New York: Oxford University Press, 1979.

Davis, Forrest. "Father Coughlin," *Atlantic Monthly*. December 1965.

Davis, Kenneth S. *FDR: The Beckoning of Destiny, 1882-1928*. New York: Putnam's, 1972.

————. *The Hero: Charles A. Lindbergh and the American Dream*. Garden City, NY: Doubleday, 1959.

————. *The New Deal Years, 1933-1937*. New York: Random House, 1986.

DeCaux, Len. *Labor Radical*. Boston: Beacon Press, 1970.

Dubofsky, Melvyn and Warren Van Tine. *John L. Lewis, a Biography*. New York: Quadrangle Books, 1979.

Eden, Anthony. *Facing the Dictators*. Boston: Houghton Mifflin, 1962.

Eidot, Paula. *Governor Alfred E. Smith: The Politician as Reformer*. New York: Garland, 1983.

Everett, Allan Seymour. *Morgenthau, New Deal and Silver*. New York: King's Crown Press, 1950.

Farago, Ladislas. *The Game of Foxes*. New York: Mckay, 1971.

Farley, James A. *Behind the Ballots: The Personal History of a Politician*. New York: Harcourt Brace, 1938.

————. *Jim Farley's Story: The Roosevelt Years*. New York: Wittlesey House, 1949.

Fine, Sidney. *Frank Murphy: The Detroit Years*. Ann Arbor, MI: University of Michigan Press, 1975)

————. *Frank Murphy: The New Deal Years*. Chicago: University of Chicago Press, 1979.

————. "President Roosevelt and the Automobile Code," *Mississippi Valley Historical Review.* June 1958.

————. *Sit-Down, the General Motors Strike of 1936-1937.* Ann Arbor, MI: University of Michigan Press, 1969

Flynn, Edward J. *You're the Boss.* New York: Viking, 1947.

Fortune, vols. 1-16. New York: Time Inc, 1930-1937.

Fraser, Steven *Labor will Rule, Sidney Hillman and the Rise of American Labor.* New York: Free Press, 1991.

Freidel, Frank. *Franklin D. Roosevelt: The Apprenticeship.* Boston: Little Brown, 1952.

————. *Franklin D. Roosevelt: Launching the New Deal.* Boston: Little Brown, 1973)

————. *Franklin D. Roosevelt: The Triumph.* Boston: Little Brown, 1956.

Fromm, Bella. *Blood and Banquets.* New York: Harper's, 1942.

Frye, Alton. *Nazi Germany and the American Hemisphere, 1933-1940.* New Haven, CT: Yale University Press, 1967.

Hair, William Ivy. *The Kingfish and His Realm.* Baton Rouge, LA: Louisiana State University Press, 1991.

Handlin, Oscar. *Al Smith and His America.* Boston: Little Brown, 1958.

Hapgood, Norman and Henry Moscowitz. *Up from the City Streets.* New York: Harcourt Brace, 1927.

Hawley, Ellis W. *The New Deal and the Problem of Monopoly: A Study in Economic Ambivalence.* Princeton, NJ: Princeton University Press, 1966.

Hofstadter, Richard. *The American Political Tradition and the Men Who Made It.* New York: Knopf, 1948.

Hull, Cordell. *Memoirs of Cordell Hull.* New York: Macmillan, 1948.

Ickes, Harold L. *The Secret Diary: The First Thousand Days, 1933-1936.* New York: Simon and Schuster, 1953.

————. *The Secret Diary: The Inside Struggle, 1936-1939.* New York: Simon and Schuster, 1954.

————. *The Secret Diary: The Lowering Clouds, 1939-1941.* New York: Simon and Schuster, 1954.

Irey, Elmer and William J. Slocum. *The Dodgers.* New York: Greenberg, 1948.

Josephson, Matthew. *Infidel in the Temple.* New York: Knopf, 1967.

————. and Hannah Josephson. *Al Smith: Hero of the Cities.* Boston: Houghton Mifflin, 1969.

Ketchum, Richard M. *The Borrowed Years, 1938-1941.* New York: Random House, 1989.

Kieran, Roger. *The Communist Party and the Auto Workers Union*. Bloomington, IN: University of Indiana Press, 1980.

Kramer, Dale. "The American Fascists," *Harper's*. September 1940.

Larson, Bruce L. *Lindbergh of Minnesota*. New York: Harcourt Brace Jovanovich, 1973.

Lash, Joseph. *Eleanor and Franklin: The Story of a Relationship*. New York: Norton, 1972.

Lavine, Harold. *Fifth Column in America*. New York: Doubleday Doran, 1940.

Levenstein, Harry A. *Communism, Anticommunism and the CIO*. Westport, CT: Greenwood Press, 1981.

Leuchtenberg, William E. "The New Deal and the Analogue of War." In *Change and Certainty in Twentieth-Century America*. Edited by John Braeman, Robert H. Brenner, and Everett Walters. Columbus, OH: Ohio University Press, 1964.

Lindbergh, Anne Morrow. *The Flower and the Nettle*. New York: Harcourt Brace Jovanovich, 1976.

———. *Hour of Gold, Hour of Lead*. New York: Harcourt Brace Jovanovich, 1973.

———. *War Within and Without*. New York: Harcourt Brace Jovanovich, 1980.

Lindbergh, Charles A. *Autobiography of Values*. New York: Harcourt Brace Jovanovich, 1973.

———. "Aviation, Geography and Race." *Reader's Digest*. November 1939)

———. *Of Flight and Life*. New York: Scribner's, 1948.

———. *Spirit of St. Louis*. New York: Scribner's, 1953.

———. *Wartime Journals*. New York: Harcourt Brace Jovanovich, 1970.

———. "What Substitute for War?" *Atlantic Monthly*. March 1940.

Lindley, Ernest K. *Franklin D. Roosevelt*. Indianapolis, IN: Bobbs-Merrill, 1931.

Long, Huey Pierce. *Every Man A King: The Autobiography of Huey P. Long*. New Orleans: National Book Company, 1933.

———. *My First Days in the White House*. Harrisburg, PA: Telegraph Press, 1935.

Lyman, Lauren. "The Lindbergh I Knew," *Saturday Evening Post*. April 4, 1953.

McCloy, Donald R. *Angry Voices*. Lawrence, KS: University of Kansas Press, 1958.

———. *Landon of Kansas*. Lincoln, NE: University of Nebraska Press, 1966.

Marcus, Sheldon. *Father Coughlin: The Tumultuous Life of the Priest of the Little Flower*. Boston: Little Brown, 1973.

Martin, Thomas. *Dynasty: The Longs of Louisiana*. New York: Putnam's, 1960.

Mencken, H.L. *A Carnival of Buncombe, Writings on Politics*. Edited by Malcolm Moos. Chicago: University of Chicago Press, 1984.

———. "The Glory of Louisiana," *Nation*. May 3, 1933.

Michie, Allan A. and Frank Ryhlick. *Dixie Demagogues*. New York: Vanguard Press, 1939.

Moley, Raymond. *After Seven Years*. Lincoln, NE: University of Nebraska Press, 1970.

Morgan, Ted. *FDR: A Biography*. New York: Simon and Schuster, 1985.

Morgenthau, Henry Jr. *From the Morgenthau Diaries*. Edited by John Morton Blum. Boston: Houghton Mifflin, 1964.

Mosley, Leonard. *Lindbergh: A Biography*. Garden City, NY: Doubleday, 1976.

Murray, Robert K. *The 103d Ballot: Democrats and Disasters in Madison Square Garden*. New York: Harper and Row, 1976.

New York Times. 1910-1942.

Nicolson, Harold. *Diaries and Letters, 1930-1964*. London: Collins, 1980.

Niebuhr, Reinhold. "Pawns for Fascism—Our Lower Middle Class." *American Scholar*. Spring 1937.

O'Brien, David J. *American Catholics and Social Reform: The New Deal Years*. New York: Oxford University Press, 1968.

Ohl, John Kennedy. *Hugh S. Johnson and the New Deal*. De Kalb, IL: University of Illinois Press, 1985.

Perkins, Frances F. Columbia University Oral History Collection.

———. *The Roosevelt I Knew*. New York: Viking, 1946.

Perkins, Van L. *Crisis in Agriculture: The AAA and the New Deal, 1933*. Berkeley, CA: University of California Press, 1969.

Pressman, Lee. Columbia University Oral History Collection.

Proskauer, Joseph M. Columbia University Oral History Collection.

Rollins, Alfred B. Jr. *Roosevelt and Howe*. New York: Knopf, 1962.

Roosevelt, Eleanor. *This I Remember*. New York: Harper's, 1949.

F.D.R.: His Personal Letters. Edited by Elliot Roosevelt. 4 vols. New York: Duell, Sloan and Pearce, 1947-1950.

Roosevelt, Franklin D. *Public Papers and Addresses*. Edited by Samuel I. Rosenman. 13 vols. New York: Random House, 1938-1950.

Roper, Daniel C. *Fifty Years of Public Life*. Westport, CT.: Greenwood Press, 1968.

Rosenman, Samuel I. *Working With Roosevelt*. New York: Harper's, 1952.

Ross, Walter. *The Last Hero: Charles A. Lindbergh*. New York: Harper and Row, 1969.

Schlesinger, Arthur M. Jr. *The Coming of the New Deal*. Boston: Houghton Mifflin, 1959.

Schumpeter, Joseph A. *Business Cycles*. 2 vols. New York: McGraw Hill, 1939.

Sherwood, Robert E. *Roosevelt and Hopkins.* New York: Harper's, 1948.

Shirer, William L. *Berlin Diary.* New York: Knopf, 1941.

Silveri, Daniel. *The Political Education of Alfred E. Smith: The Assembly Years, 1904-1914.* Ph.D. dissertation. St. John's University, 1964.

Sindler, Allan P. *Huey Long's Louisiana: State Politics, 1920-1952.* Baltimore: Johns Hopkins, 1956.

Smith, Alfred E. *The Citizen and His Government.* New York: Harper's, 1935.

————. "Sound Money," *New Outlook.* December 1933.

Smith, Truman. *Berlin Alert.* Stanford, CA: Hoover Institution Press, 1984.

Social Wellsprings. Edited by Joseph Husslein. 2 vols. Milwaukee, WI: Bruce Publishers, 1942.

Stack, John F. Jr. *International Conflict in an American City: Boston's Irish, Italians and Jews, 1935-1944.* Westport, CT: Greenwood Press, 1979.

Stegner, Wallace "The Radio Priest and His Flock," In *The Aspirin Age, 1919-1941.* Edited by Isabel Leighton. New York: Simon and Schuster, 1949.

Steel, Ronald. *Walter Lippmann and the American Century.* Boston: Little Brown, 1980.

Stokes, Thomas A. *Chip Off My Shoulder.* Princeton, NJ: Princeton University Press, 1940.

Stolberg, Benjamin. "Dr. Huey and Mr. Long." *Nation.* September 25, 1935.

Straight, Michael. *After Long Silence.* New York: Norton, 1983.

Strong, Donald S. *Organized Anti-Semitism in America.* Washington: American Council On Foreign Affairs, 1941.

Taft, Philip. *The A. F. of L. from the Death of Gompers to the Merger.* New York: Harper's, 1959.

Taylor, Telford. *Munich: The Price of Peace.* New York: Vintage, 1980.

Timmons, Bascom N. *Garner of Texas.* New York: Harper's, 1948.

Tugwell, Rexford Guy. *The Democratic Roosevelt.* Garden City, NY: Doubleday, 1957.

Tull, Charles S. *Father Coughlin and the New Deal.* Syracuse, NY: Syracuse University Press, 1965.

Tully, Grace. *F.D.R. My Boss.* New York: Scribner's, 1948.

"Unofficial Observer." *American Messiahs.* New York: Simon and Schuster, 1935.

Valaik, David. "Catholicism, Neutrality and the Spanish Embargo, 1937-1939." *Journal of American History.* June 1967.

Ward, Geoffrey C. *A First-Class Temperament: The Emergence of Franklin D. Roosevelt.* New York: Harper and Row, 1989.

Ward, Louis B. *Father Charles E. Coughlin: An Authorized Biography.* Detroit, MI: Tower Publications, 1933.

Warner, Emily Smith with Daniel Hawthorne. *The Happy Warrior.* Garden City, NY: Doubleday, 1956.

Weiss, Nancy Joan. *Charles Francis Murphy, 1852-1924: Respectability and Responsibility in Tammany Politics.* Northampton, MA: Smith College, 1968.

Williams, T. Harry. *Huey Long.* New York: Knopf, 1969.

Wilson, Hugh. *Diplomat Between the Wars.* New York: Longman's, 1940.

INDEX

Albania, 10, 155, 183
Alinsky, Saul, 83-84, 138
Amalgamated Clothing Workers of
America, 85, 128
America First Committee
See Charles A. Lindbergh
American Federation of Labor (AFL),
78-79, 81, 83, 84, 85-86, 101, 127-
28, 158-59, 212, 213
American Liberty League, 101, 106,
118, 120-21, 122-25, 135
See Smith and Roosevelt
American Youth Congress, 164
Anti-Comintern (Axis) bloc, 10, 11,
155, 196, 206, 207, 210
Arnold, General H. H. (Hap), 213,
214, 216
Austria, 10, 153, 178

Baruch, Bernard M., 111-12
Bernstein, Irving, 160, 172, 212
Biddle, Attorney General Francis, 210
Black-Connery-Perkins Bill, 79
Black Shirts, 2, 153, 193

Carrel, Alexis, 96-98, 176
Catholics, Catholic Church, Vatican,
146-48, 153, 154-55
And Spanish Civil War, 146-47,
239n24
Chamberlain, Prime Minister Neville,
180
Chicago Convention of 1932, 37-38,
43, 48-50
China, 10, 155, 196, 206

Christian Front
See Coughlin
Churchill, Prime Minister Winston S.,
190, 191, 200
Cole, Wayne S., 176, 192, 202
Comintern (Communist International), 147
Committee (later Congress) of Industrial Organizations (CIO), 11, 83,
128-29, 130-32, 140, 143, 145-46,
158-60, 166, 170, 171-72, 212
Communism, Communists, 63, 101,
145, 146, 147, 148, 149, 151, 152,
153, 154, 156, 159-60, 163, 165,
172, 175, 179, 188, 191, 196, 200,
203, 216, 241n62
As an integral part of the CIO, 131,
132-33, 136
Coolidge, President Calvin, 25, 26, 94
Coughlin, Father Charles E., 5, 11, 12,
39, 42, 58, 59, 70, 87, 89, 106,
112, 114, 116-17, 133, 145, 146
Making of a "radio priest," 39-40,
41-42, 206
Early anti-Semitism, 40-41, 61
Adulation of Roosevelt, 42-43, 57
Advocate of easy money, 59-60
Proponent of new banking system,
62-63
Disenchantment with Roosevelt,
62
Launching the National Union for
Social Justice, 63-65
Struggle against Roosevelt

Morgenthau, Henry Jr., 57, 61, 69,
101, 102, 111
Moscowitz, Belle, 31, 223n34
Mosely, Leonard, 178, 198, 242n85
Moses, Robert, 25, 27, 31, 222n23
Munich agreement, 180, 181, 183
Lindbergh's involvement with,
178-81
Murphy, (Tammany boss) Charles F.,
16-17, 18, 19, 20, 22, 23, 221n10
Murphy, Mayor, Governor, Frank, 39,
42, 114
During General Motors strike,
133, 134, 136, 137-8, 145
Mussolini, Benito (Il Duce), 2, 11, 76,
77, 147, 165, 183, 201

National Industrial Recovery Act,
Administration (NIRA), 70, 79-
80, 83, 86, 126, 130, 219n3
National Labor Board, 86
National Labor Relations [Wagner]
Act, 126, 130, 141, 160, 214, 238
National Labor Relations Board
(NLRB), 160
National Union for Social Justice
(NUSJ)
See Coughlin
New Deal, New Dealers, 6, 7, 8, 9, 65,
66, 70, 71, 79, 81, 86, 86, 87, 88,
89, 90, 99, 101, 103, 105, 106,
115, 117, 120-21, 125, 130, 132,
140, 148, 161, 168, 169

O'Connell, Cardinal William H., 62,
154, 227n12, 238n8

Perkins, Secretary of Labor Frances F.,
78, 134, 135, 219n3, 236n74,
237n76
Poland, 10, 155, 162, 183, 185
Pope Pius XI, 43, 147-47, 148
Popular Front, 146, 148, 149, 154, 155
Prohibition, 33-34

Rakob, John J., 27, 28, 30, 32, 33-34,
40, 88, 90, 123, 135, 222n27
Republican party, 4, 15, 32, 117, 125,
161, 168 220n4
Robinson, Senator Joseph, 52-53, 66,
226n77
Roosevelt, Eleanor, 6, 26, 29, 164-65,
215, 223n34
Roosevelt, Franklin D., 1, 4, 5, 20, 21,
22, 38, 39, 40, 41, 43, 44, 65, 66,
71, 72, 74, 76, 78, 82, 83, 88, 93,
94, 101, 110, 121, 122, 126, 127,
148, 154, 156, 158, 159, 172, 174,
179, 182, 193, 205, 209, 212, 213,
216
His enemies in general, an over-
view, 7-9, 10-13
Albany years: Tammany's vociferous foe, 15-20
1920 vice presidential candidate—
with Tammany support, 21-
22
Al Smith's faithful associate, 23-30
Reluctant gubernatorial candidate,
28-30
Governor contra Smith
Discards Smith's advice, 30-32
As presidential candidate, 33-
38
Coughlin his cheerleader, 43, 57-
59
Conflict with Coughlin, however,
over monetary and banking
policies, 59-63
Conflict with Long over investiga-
tion and patronage, 67, 69-70
Oval Office showdown, 67-69
Criticized by Smith for fiscal irre-
sponsibility, 88-89, 90
Opposed by Smith and reactionary
American Liberty League, 90-
91
Incurs Lindbergh's wrath over air-
mail policy, 92-93
Long as his gadfly, 102-103